Never Say Die

Never Say Die

Chris O'Brien

HarperCollins*Publishers*

From 'Stopping by Woods on a Snowy Evening' from *The Poetry of Robert Frost* edited by Edward Connery Lathem, published by Jonathan Cape. Reprinted by permission of the Random House Group Ltd.

'if there are any heavens my mother will(all by herself)have' is reprinted from *Complete Poems 1904–1962*, by E.E. Cummings, edited by George J. Firmage, by permission of W.W. Norton & Company. Copyright © 1991 by the Trustees for the E.E. Cummings Trust and George James Firmage.

HarperCollins*Publishers*

First published in Australia in 2008
by HarperCollins*Publishers* Australia Pty Limited
ABN 36 009 913 517
www.harpercollins.com.au

Copyright © Christopher J. O'Brien Pty Limited 2008

The right of Christopher J. O'Brien to be identified as the author
of this work has been asserted by him under the *Copyright Amendment
(Moral Rights) Act 2000*.

HarperCollins*Publishers*
25 Ryde Road, Pymble, Sydney, NSW 2073, Australia
31 View Road, Glenfield, Auckland 10, New Zealand
1–A, Hamilton House, Connaught Place, New Delhi – 110 001, India
77–85 Fulham Palace Road, London, W6 8JB, United Kingdom
2 Bloor Street East, 20th floor, Toronto, Ontario M4W 1A8, Canada
10 East 53rd Street, New York NY 10022, USA

National Library of Australia Cataloguing-in-Publication data:

O'Brien, Chris, 1952–
  Never say die / Chris O'Brien
  ISBN: 978 0 7322 8809 9 (pbk.)
  O'Brien, Chris, 1952–
  Surgeons – Australia – Biography.
  Cancer – Patients – Australia – Biography.
  Cancer – Treatment.
617.092

Cover design by Darren Holt, HarperCollins Design Studio
Front cover photograph courtesy of timbauerphoto.com
Back cover photograph of author by Mark Mawson; author and family by
  Jacky Ghossein/Fairfaxphotos
Typeset in 11/18 Garamond LT by Kirby Jones
Printed and bound in Australia by Griffin Press
70gsm Classic White used by HarperCollins*Publishers* is a natural, recyclable product
made from wood grown in sustainable forests. The manufacturing processes conform
to the environmental regulations in the country of origin, Finland.

10 9 8 7   08 09 10 11

For Gail, Adam, Juliette and James

AUTHOR'S NOTE

The contents of this book are entirely original except for four items. There are quotations from Joseph Conrad's short novel *Heart of Darkness* and e e cummings' poem 'if there are any heavens', and these are italicised. In addition I have borrowed two phrases when describing Gail — 'a tender-faced beauty' and 'graceful femininity'. These phrases were used by Elaine Feinstein in her foreword to a recent edition of Alexander Pushkin's novel *The Captain's Daughter* and both were so apt that I decided that I could not improve upon them.

But I have promises to keep,
And miles to go before I sleep,
And miles to go before I sleep.

From 'Stopping by Woods on a Snowy Evening'
by Robert Frost (1923)

Contents

Prologue

LIFE-CHANGING EXPERIENCES, whether driven by fate or by chance, can take on myriad forms. They may exert their influence on our lives as a gentle coercive force or a dominating, even catastrophic, burst of energy. Whether it is the birth of triplets, a huge lottery win, an accident resulting in critical injury, or a journey that leads to an intellectual or spiritual awakening, things are never the same afterwards.

I have had several experiences of this kind, but the most recent and profound came on the afternoon of Saturday, 25 November 2006, when it was found that I had a highly malignant brain tumour.

The first warning that a mass of mutant brain cells was proliferating in my head like a spider's web came three days earlier, on Wednesday morning. I awoke with a headache in the right frontal region and although it was moderately intense, I gave little thought to its possible cause, took a couple of paracetamol tablets and readied myself for the drive to Royal Prince Alfred Hospital for morning rounds.

On the previous day I had operated all day at RPA, as I had done on Tuesdays for nearly twenty years, but the operating list had been comfortably light — mainly benign thyroid tumours. Over the past three years or so, particularly since I had been appointed director of the Sydney Cancer Centre, I had increasingly needed to divide my Tuesdays between the operating theatre and my office in the Centre (also based at RPA), relying on the team to keep the list moving forward efficiently and safely when I was occupied with administrative matters. At one point on that particular Tuesday I had scrubbed and entered the operating room. One of the clinical fellows, a very competent English ear, nose and throat surgeon, was removing a large thyroid gland but I was confused about exactly what was being done and why. This uncertainty caused me no special alarm at the time, but I did leave the operating room and admonish myself that I was overtired and needed to rest. I made my way back to the Cancer Centre to finish more paperwork and then returned to the operating theatre floor at around six o'clock for our customary team gathering.

This little ritual had been established about sixteen years earlier with my friend and colleague Ian Douglas, our anaesthetist and a model of understated competence and quiet equanimity. The gathering involved sharing a couple of bottles of red wine, sometimes with cheese or other food, for an hour or more at the end of the day with the anaesthetics team and the residents, registrars and fellows as well as the medical students who were attached to the head and neck surgery service for periods ranging from ten weeks to one year.

During this time we would talk as equals about the day's events or about books, films, wine and anything else non-medical that presented itself. People may sniff cynically at the word 'equals' but I had worked hard over the years to develop a culture of mutual respect and harmony in the unit, based on the principle that we were all simply at different stages of our medical careers (a critically important concept I learned from a wise heart specialist at RPA named Phil Harris) and therefore had different roles and responsibilities. These little bonding sessions created an opportunity for us to become better acquainted with the junior members of the team and to learn about their lives and ambitions, and allowed the older ones to dispel the frustrations that may have developed during our ten hours together. Sometimes, for example, they were not able to do the operations they had hoped to carry out, or perhaps I needed to interrupt or take over from one of them to deal with a technical difficulty or push things along.

When we adjourned for home, everyone was cheerful and felt they'd had a good day. Because of this inclusive policy, or so I believed, the head and neck term was very popular among students and junior staff. The two fellowship positions we offered were also keenly sought after by young overseas surgeons. The program gave individuals hoping to carve out a career in head and neck surgery the opportunity to work in a busy, productive unit, learn new skills and carry out research, while earning a reasonable salary and living in one of the best cities in the world.

By the time I got to Prince Alfred on Wednesday morning my headache had subsided. I did, however, show some confusion as we reviewed Tuesday's patients and stopped at their bedsides to check their post-operative status. I couldn't recall who was who or what procedure each had had. The team noticed it too and we joked briefly about this uncharacteristic absentmindedness before I went off to consult for the rest of the day in my rooms at St George Private Hospital. I felt profoundly fatigued all afternoon but managed to get through this consulting session without any difficulties.

The next day I woke again with a bad frontal headache, but it settled after a couple of tablets and I was at St George Private by 7.30 a.m. to carry out my private operating list, which usually finished around 8 or 9 p.m. Things went smoothly, without confusion and without technical difficulties, but I continued to have the same feeling of overwhelming tiredness. My good friend Donn Ledwidge had acted as anaesthetist for this list for many years, mixing clinical skill with cheerful buffoonery. Fortunately Donn's efficiency and humour carried us through the session to an early finish.

By Friday, when I usually spent a very long day in the Cancer Centre attending, and mostly chairing, back-to-back meetings, making calls and talking to anyone from the Area CEO to one of the cleaners, a student looking for a research project or one of our fundraisers, the headache was persistent and more intense. Jenny, my personal assistant, found herself dispensing repeated doses of pain tablets and I was dreading the thought of attending the Cancer Institute's Clinical Services Advisory Committee meeting, scheduled for four o'clock that afternoon. These meetings tended to be frustratingly unproductive and this one, poorly attended as if to emphasise the point, was no different. Beset with increasing lethargy and a constant background thud in my head, I struggled through the meeting, drove home and went to bed early.

Things deteriorated on Saturday morning. Again, I awoke with the same headache but now it was more severe. I managed to do my rounds at St George Private, reviewing and discharging Thursday's patients, but the drive home afterwards proved an unexpected and almost insurmountable challenge when I was overcome by escalating exhaustion and nausea and had to stop by the roadside a couple of times to vomit. By the time I reached home the combination of headache, nausea and exhaustion had provoked a sense of painful desperation as the gravity of my situation started to become apparent. Clearly something was dreadfully wrong, but it still did not occur to me that the cause of this massive change in my usually robust health was a brain tumour, least of all a malignant glioma, a cancer with a reputation for rapid, relentless and almost inevitable lethality.

When Gail greeted me she very quickly saw that I was much worse than when I had left the house earlier in the morning. We talked briefly about whether or not I might have meningococcal meningitis, a horrible illness which had killed a young cardiac surgeon at RPA some years earlier. Importantly, we agreed that there was no time for speculation, so she loaded me into the car and we headed for the hospital.

Twenty minutes later, with what must have been a terrifying sense of dread and foreboding for her, Gail drove me into the grounds of RPA, the institution which had been the focal point of my professional life and where our love affair, friendship and life together had started over thirty years before.

I arrived at the emergency department, so debilitated by this time that I would have apathetically submitted to any test or intervention. A canula was inserted into a vein in my arm, blood was taken for analysis and people fussed around me. I was now on a treadmill of investigations, treatment and monitoring, and I would stay there for the rest of the year.

An urgent CT scan was carried out and soon after, as I lay on a trolley in an unusually quiet emergency department, two young female doctors approached us. One, the emergency physician, was clearly saddened by the information she had to share and the strain of this burden showed on her young face.

'Professor, I'm sorry but the scan shows something,' she said.

'Is it a neoplasm?' I asked, calm, unmoved, ready for whatever would come next, ready for the worst.

'Yes,' she replied in a soft voice that was really saying, 'I wish I didn't have to tell you this.'

'What's a neoplasm?' Gail asked. 'A tumour,' I responded. 'Can it be treated?' she asked, her face pale, sad, questioning.

The other doctor was the neurosurgery registrar, a pretty young woman with Indian features who had apparently just passed her final exams. She spoke briefly to Gail as I measured the implications of what I had been told.

'Yes, it can be treated, but it's incurable,' came her reply.

Gail strained to take in this information, make sense of it, maintain her composure and find strength in a whirlpool of cascading emotions. I took her hand and held it tight, feeling calm, not at all fearful, relieved if anything that we now knew what had been happening.

'Don't worry, darling. I'll be alright,' I reassured her, a mountaineer tumbling into a bottomless crevasse and calling back with unfounded confidence to his lifelong climbing partner.

That my situation represented the ultimate of role reversals was not lost on me for a moment. By a totally unexpected twist of fate, viewed by my family, friends, colleagues and people I didn't even know as the cruellest of ironies, I was now on the receiving end of devastating news, without any time for preparation, and with the prognosis delivered like a hammer blow. I had experienced this scenario a hundred times before but I had been the deliverer of the news, not the recipient. To be told my prognosis so bluntly, with no hope offered, brought home to me as nothing else could the importance of delivering such news well.

Breaking bad news is never easy and I had always felt very strongly that it must be done with gentleness, kindness and a sense of hope — that all was not lost and that much could, and would, be done. There are training courses and written guidelines available which are aimed at teaching clinicians of all kinds how to break bad news. Most importantly, people in this, the most vulnerable of predicaments, should not have their hope taken away. They need to be embraced by a sympathetic, supportive doctor or team who can demonstrate their willingness and ability to put into action a plan of investigations and treatment to get matters sorted out and, if a cure is at all possible, to pursue it with unremitting energy. Patients with poor-prognosis diseases will never do well if they are treated by individuals or teams who nihilistically believe they have no chance of success.

'Would you like me to get in touch with anyone?' the emergency doctor inquired.

'Yes,' I responded, 'if Michael Besser is around, I'd like you to give him a call.'

I had known Besser for about twenty years as a friend and colleague and I respected him enormously. His reputation as a neurosurgeon was outstanding. We had done quite a lot of running together with other friends some years back, competing in a couple of half marathons, but we were not especially close.

Michael arrived within about twenty minutes, compact, dapper, professional. Reluctantly, quietly and with obvious regret in his tone he said, 'It's not good, Chris. It's probably a glioblastoma. The survival time is six to twelve months, but we'll get you into hospital now and start you on steroids. That will make you feel a lot better — there's a massive amount of cerebral oedema.'

He was referring to the build-up of fluid in and around my brain as a result of the tumour: the same reactive outpouring of tissue fluid that accompanies any injury or infection, whether it is a sprained ankle or appendicitis or pneumonia. It was this slow accumulation of fluid and the build-up of pressure inside my skull that had caused the lethargy, headache and nausea, climaxing in the state of near collapse I had reached by the time we arrived at the emergency room. Besser commented that I probably would have been unconscious in another forty-eight hours.

Gail and I stayed there in the emergency department as preparations were made for my admission to hospital. She phoned home to let our three children know what was happening and I took a few moments to fathom my plight.

The scope of my world had suddenly contracted but instead of it becoming more keenly focused than ever before, it had turned blurry and soft in the centre. I was fifty-four years old, recognised as one of the leaders in my field of work, with a wonderful family, a dozen other jobs and endless unfinished business, now lying with a death sentence over my head in a hospital only a few kilometres from where I had grown up. Had I really not come very far? Would the circle close prematurely? I was not afraid, but I did not feel ready.

CHAPTER 1

Teachers and farmers

I GREW UP HAPPILY IN SYDNEY, in the small sleepy western suburb of Regents Park, a little place of monumental ordinariness and one of several small villages located inconspicuously on the railway line between Lidcombe and Bankstown. Our modest Housing Commission house, built of fibro and tile and my parents' first home, was comfortably ensconced in a quiet street which still had a few vacant blocks of land and only a few trees and which epitomised the safe, inward-looking complacency of lower middle-class suburbia in the 1950s. Over a period of years new houses were built on the nearby vacant lots and number fifteen Berry Street underwent progressive enhancements, including the erection of a carport (remarkably upright and professional looking given that it was built by Dad, my brother and me) in the front, a large garden shed, and eventually a first floor addition, comprising extra bedrooms, a bathroom and living space, which was completed around the time that my brother, sister and I left home.

My mother was pregnant with my older brother Michael when she married my father. She was the second of four children born to Richard and Lurline Healey, who were both primary school teachers. The Healeys met at teacher's college in Sydney and had their first posting in Broken Hill. Mum was born in Armidale and her young parents carried on a peripatetic existence, making their way in stepwise fashion to the city, as my grandfather occupied successive headmaster positions at primary schools in Cobar, Trangie, St Marys and finally Ashfield. Mum was bright, outgoing, very good at sport and her studies, and when she was about sixteen was made school captain of Our Lady of Mercy College, Parramatta, situated on the other side of Victoria Road from the Marist Brothers school that Michael and I would later attend. Good at singing, tennis and French and a voracious reader, she matriculated ahead of her age group and went to Sydney University to study arts.

My father was born in Gunnedah, the youngest of four and, by all accounts, a robust and cheerfully undisciplined farm boy who loved riding and rugby league and who was invited to leave most of the schools he attended because of repeated truancy. His parents — Frank, a soldier and farmer, and Dorothy, a prim schoolteacher — were, like the Healeys, the very definition of Democratic Labor Party voters: devoutly Catholic, upright and conservative. They lived modestly on a succession of farms between Tamworth and Cessnock.

Dad's formal education finished when he was fifteen years old. A year later he joined the navy with the singular intention of killing Japanese to avenge the death of his hero, his beloved older brother Leo, who was killed in Singapore. Dad's hatred of the

Japanese remained strong and barely beneath the surface until its eventual abatement when he was well over seventy.

After the war he joined the merchant navy but then went on to a succession of other jobs and attempts at establishing a career. One of these enterprises involved starting up a little building company, Colbourn, Crossley and O'Brien, with two larrikin friends who were apparently equally undisciplined and similarly blessed with a talent for creative incompetence. From all reports, the trio specialised in constructing fences that fell over the day after their erection, extensions that took forever to complete, and lengthy lunches in Paddington pubs. One such break from their muddled and shonky productivity followed a morning spent taking the roof off a nearby house with the plan of putting on a temporary cover late in the afternoon and then returning the next day to start the retiling job. As the three settled in for a liquid lunch, the weather took a dramatic turn for the worse and rain began to bucket down. The roofless house started to fill up like a swimming pool.

The chaos and destruction that followed the thunderstorm was enough to drive Colbourn, Crossley and O'Brien out of the building business. Dad joined the army, still without a skill, but he was optimistic, handsome, imaginative and prepared to work hard. In due course he was promoted to the rank of warrant officer, in command of a tank. Proud of his achievements in the armed forces, he would subsequently anchor all descriptions of his working history around this period.

Where my parents met is unclear, but Dad used to call on Mum when she was still living with her parents in a grand Victorian residence reserved for the headmaster of Ashfield Public School on Liverpool Road, Ashfield. By this time she had left university without finishing her arts degree and started at teachers college. I have at home a beautiful black and white photograph, taken by a street photographer near the GPO in Sydney early in Mum and Dad's courtship, showing the young couple confidently striding up Martin Place — a pretty young Maureen Healey with her strapping beau, Kevin.

Mum's pregnancy and Dad's modest background did not impress her parents, who remained resentful of and barely civil to my father for as long as I can remember. They were married in a side chapel of St Mary's Cathedral in Sydney without parents or family in attendance and immediately moved into a broom cupboard under the stairs in Juniper Hall, an elegant colonial building that still stands in Oxford Street, Paddington. The space must have been larger than a simple cupboard since the single room provided enough space for sleeping, dining and, according to my mother's proud descriptions, the preparation of a three-course meal on a small stove which burned methylated spirits.

Their Paddington sojourn was mercifully brief and was followed by a year or so in temporary housing in St Marys. By the time I was born, a war service loan had allowed them to establish themselves in Regents Park and I was brought home from the Paddington Women's Hospital to the bedroom I would share with my brother for the next twenty years.

Berry Street was populated by an odd assortment of families that seemed mostly older and weirder than ours. Across the road lived the Smiths, whose only son Billy had an abnormally large head, thick glasses that magnified his impossibly crossed eyes and a maniacal grin which showed off a mouth full of big green and yellow teeth separated by large irregular gaps. In addition it was generally agreed that Billy was a bit mental. A couple of doors up lived the Piggotts, a mean and unfriendly couple whose fastidiously kept fibro house represented a definite 'no go' zone. Mr Piggott was a bad-tempered and obsessive crank who wore his trousers pulled over a developing paunch nearly up to his nipples (in truth, I don't want to think about Piggott's nipples). He would spend hours manicuring his lawn and garden, probably trimming the edges with the same scissors he used on his toenails (I want to think about his toenails even less) and dusting and polishing the brass handles and fittings on his front-yard tap, his absurdly ornate letterbox and other bits of decorative paraphernalia he had hanging on his front porch.

During street cricket, baseball, tennis and other games we played on the road, any ball that was hit, kicked or thrown into the Piggott's front yard was confiscated and never returned. When occasionally we found courage enough to jump the front fence to retrieve a ball or any other possession that found its way onto Mr Piggott's property, we risked a barrage of abuse accompanied by furious window banging from their front room and a noisy and potentially painful attack from Treasure, a spoilt and savage little fox terrier that patrolled the premises.

With these and a few other bewildering but otherwise benign exceptions, Berry Street and the surrounding quiet roads were safe and friendly and the O'Brien kids — Mike, Chris and younger sister Carmel — were known, liked and welcome in most homes. Our neighbours kept mostly to themselves though and, despite a general sense of goodwill and cooperation, the thought of initiating or participating in a communal activity such as a street party would have been as foreign as flying to Mars.

I weighed an emphatic, even embarrassing, twelve pounds when I was born. How my mother survived my delivery boggles the mind. Apparently as a baby I proved to be a contented, cooperative bundle of flesh and fat, ate every bit of food offered to me, slept soundly, smiled continuously, performed all bodily functions on command and comfortably achieved all developmental and growth milestones. Michael, also a big baby though not at the gargantuan end of the scale, was by comparison an unstoppable livewire who ran Mum ragged from morning till night — swinging from the clothesline, disappearing down the road on his tricycle, attacking me, a relatively large and immobile target, with a range of heavy and sharp objects and generally causing mayhem. There was no medical diagnosis for his behaviour at that time and none was thought necessary. Gifted and talented children had not yet been invented either, so Michael was regarded as being either a very busy boy or a very naughty boy or something in between, depending on the phase of the moon and the outlandishness of his antics. Carmel, two years younger than me and with a similarly calm disposition, seemed to be able to participate in all our high jinks with impunity, rarely flouting the rules, causing problems or attracting much in the way of punishment. She was generally far better behaved anyway; but Mum and Dad were clearly averse to including her in 'beltings' and any other physical punishment regularly dished out to Michael and me.

When we were a little older, on a couple of occasions during school holidays Michael and I were sent to visit our great aunt Molly, Grandma O'Brien's sister-in-law, who was the matron and domestic supervisor at a Catholic boarding school and agricultural college for boys in Goulburn called Inveralochy. This was a large and rambling farming property run by Christian Brothers, and we were thrilled to be visiting a real farm. We were absolutely enthralled by every bit of it — the animals, the tractors and other equipment, the various outbuildings, the great open paddocks, and especially being free to roam virtually wherever we wished because the brothers and boys were all away on winter holidays, leaving only a skeleton religious contingent behind. A kindly old brother or one of the farm hands would drive us around the property on an old tractor and dear old Molly would spoil us with wonderful meals and delicious cakes for afternoon tea.

As it turned out we only had two holidays at Inveralochy, the second of which was cut short when Michael, presumably in an attempt to raise the tempo (and temperature) of the otherwise sleepy pace of life on the farm, set fire to a haystack that was being stored in a small brick side building. After the fire brigade had extinguished the blaze the two young O'Briens were bundled back to Sydney in disgrace and not invited back. Michael demonstrated no other tendencies towards pyromania subsequently but our names were well and truly mud in Goulburn for a while.

Michael and I also spent endless hours together exploring and wreaking havoc through our own quiet neighbourhood: raiding building sites, constructing cubby houses and elaborate fortresses, engaging in battles with friends and neighbours using every conceivable type of ammunition — rocks, mud and clay balls, penny and tuppenny bungers, rolled up newspapers (sometimes containing a hidden piece of wood), bamboo bows, arrows and spears and decomposing fruit of every variety. Injuries were uncommon and minor because we all wore old army helmets, bought or stolen from one of the war surplus stores that seemed to abound at that time, and because of our preference for wars of attrition rather than those demanding heroic charges which might lead to frantic confrontations, lost tempers and inevitable tears. I loved dressing up in army surplus gear and Mum was forever sewing stripes and patches onto my shirts and jackets as I regularly promoted myself and entertained fantasies of great battles and acts of audacious heroism which were never realised.

Transport around the streets was rudimentary. Mostly we walked but occasionally billycarts or the family bicycle, an ancient and ugly piece of rusting metal without lights or brakes, were called into service, particularly when contraband needed to be transported or when a quick getaway might be necessary. Berry Street sloped gently and the best way to slow the bike down was to jam a foot (a shoe really) between the rear frame and the tyre. Generally this was a reliable manoeuvre, although I was involved in a couple of disasters when one of my rubber thongs — our preferred summer footwear — became tangled between tyre and bike frame, causing a spectacular and noisy crash, a foot caught among deformed spokes and nearly every inch of unprotected skin grazed raw by bitumen and gravel.

I was a chubby boy until I was ten or eleven and although I was bright enough I was initially overshadowed by my older brother, who could read fluently by the age of six or seven, attracting much praise from parents and grandparents. I was an unconfident, stammery reader at first and this caused me embarrassment and feelings of inferiority in my first couple of years at school. Yet I loved drawing, colouring and reading and spent hours deeply and happily immersed in these endeavours; I also slowly found that I was strong and well coordinated and that skills like throwing, catching and kicking came quickly and naturally. My confidence grew progressively and my parents, teachers and other adults viewed me as being sensible, trustworthy and responsible.

During this time Mum worked as a schoolteacher at a variety of western suburbs primary schools. She was immensely popular at each of her postings, being a nurturing disciplinarian and a natural educator, methodical and utterly clear in her message. Dad, who would announce his homecoming each night with a cheery whistle as he passed the kitchen window, left the army and then had a number of jobs interspersed with periods of retraining, during which he studied a range of subjects including dress designing, real estate and accountancy. He was genuinely artistic and particularly skilful at drawing. Later he taught me how to draw, explaining patiently and demonstrating how to create pictures that were in proper proportion and in which the perspective was correct. I really enjoyed art and Dad seemed happiest when he was able to teach his children how to do things. This must have given his sense of purpose and self-esteem a lift, since we tended to rely almost exclusively on Mum for teaching and assistance with homework. Maybe he would have been more contented if he had stayed on the family farm and could have showed us how to care for horses or cows, or grow wheat or kill a snake. There seemed to be so few life skills that needed to be taught in suburbia, other than how to negotiate public transport and how to recognise and avoid potentially dangerous individuals among the various strange and eccentric people we might encounter. Finding a job was sometimes difficult but he was rarely unemployed and, until my teenage years, life at home was generally happy and we seemed to want for very little.

Summer holidays were usually spent camping at beachside caravan parks along the north or south coast of New South Wales. These vacations were carefree, fun and often included school friends and their families. We all seemed to have older, second-hand cars and the drive to our holiday destination was inevitably punctuated by breakdowns, which led to lengthy delays and a number of fathers spending hours under the bonnet of the recalcitrant vehicle. A cricket game, football match or some other entertainment would readily get under way to pass the time while we waited, sometimes for half a day, before the collective fatherhood managed to repair whatever problem had caused the breakdown and then we were off again.

Sunburn was accepted as being an inevitable part of our summer vacations at the beach. Mum would prepare for this by bringing along a big jar of thick cold cream which she would apply to roasted shoulders, necks and backs so that we could sleep a little more comfortably after a full day in the surf or on the beach. Apart from a smear of zinc cream on our noses, almost no attempt was made to prevent burning; rather, the provision of a messy and inadequate treatment for the associated pain was given high priority.

Over a period of years my father slowly grew depressed and tended to drink too much at family gatherings and social functions. His inability to advance in the world and earn a decent income contrasted dramatically with my mother's confidence and competence as a teacher; her promotions and successes contributed to his increasing feelings of inadequacy. Although Mum mostly handled this with diplomacy, humility and loving support, furious arguments would regularly erupt. My father's wartime experiences contributed to his episodic withdrawal into black depressions and there followed a succession of admissions to one or other of the psychiatric wards at Concord Hospital, where he spent weeks at a time having medication and psychotherapy.

We always visited Dad regularly when he was in hospital but I remained baffled about what really happened in there. Nonetheless, each time he returned home he seemed to have recovered his equanimity and was quieter and less edgy. The break from drinking probably contributed most to these periods of improvement. He would maintain his abstinence for a month or so but inevitably return to drinking as the old pressures again built up.

At the same time he suffered from the incapacitating effects of a savage and unrelenting duodenal ulcer, living for what seemed weeks at a time on blancmange, tripe and antacids and so crippled with pain that he would creep around the house doubled over in the middle. In Dad's early army days he experienced a major haemorrhage from this ulcer but he was so terrified of having surgery because he might be found to have cancer that he sat up all night in hospital sucking ice in the desperate hope that the bleeding would stop. The manoeuvre worked and so he avoided a gastrectomy and was able to live on with periods of relative comfort interrupted by bouts of agony. It would be more than forty years before two Australian medical researchers discovered that peptic ulcers were caused by a bacterial infection and not an imbalance of acid and pepsin secretion or overwork. Most peptic ulcers are now successfully treated with a program of drugs, not the gastrectomy that my father so feared.

Apart from the sad and sometimes explosive crises that erupted from time to time, life at home was happy and generally full of frivolity and laughter. We lived comfortably with almost none of the comforts, conveniences and appliances that are found in even the most modest houses in contemporary Australia. We didn't have a TV for a long time; when we could finally afford to buy one, it was second-hand and there seemed to be endless problems with the vertical hold or the horizontal hold or the rabbit ears antenna. Sometimes we would sit for long periods watching a snowstorm of interference in the hope that something recognisable might appear on the screen for a few seconds.

Luckily, a little further up the street from the Smiths lived Mr and Mrs Haig, an easy-going, childless, middle-aged couple who were happy for the O'Brien kids to stop by at 5 p.m. each weekday to watch *The Mickey Mouse Club*. We were mesmerised by the shining faces, big white teeth and sheer uninhibited confidence of the Mouseketeers. Occasionally we would stay on for an extra half hour to watch Chuck Faulkner read the six o'clock news and then scurry off home, delighted with our evening's entertainment. Mr Haig would always express his dislike for Chuck, opining nightly that he had a face like a hatful of monkeys' bottoms. Mrs Haig would castigate him gently every time and we looked forward to this little exchange.

The absence of a television set in our home was a positive in many ways as most evenings were spent around the wireless listening to serials. I loved these even more than television, as my imagination was encouraged to run wild, conjuring images of heroes, villains, cowboys riding noble and intelligent horses, and a wonderful array of other characters brought to life through the valves inside an art deco Bakelite box perched on the sideboard.

When a good film was showing at the Chullora Twin Drive-in, Mum and Dad would take us along, snug in pyjamas and dressing gowns and slippers, the back seat of our car filled with pillows and an army of soft toys. These were marvellous nights and we would always hope for the additional entertainment of seeing one or two cars drive off after the movie with the speaker still hanging inside the car window.

For some years we had no refrigerator and instead an ice chest stationed on the back verandah was our sole means of keeping perishable food and drink fresh and edible. Similarly, for a very long time Mum did the weekend washing using a wringer washing machine, building up considerable strength and stamina as she wound clothes through the wringer, shattering the odd button and squeezing the water out of sheets, shirts, jeans and every other article down to socks and handkerchiefs. When eventually she and Dad bought a second-hand washer with a spin dryer she was elated. We all were, as any small token of prosperity that brought our standard of living closer to that of friends or neighbours was welcomed with delight. Now, instead of having to spend hours cranking the wringer, occasionally with the assistance of a willing child, she could use her time more fruitfully unravelling the knot of twisted clothing and linen which had been woven by the action of the spin dryer. Still, it represented progress and we were proud to feel that we were becoming a little more modern and affluent.

CHAPTER 2

Fortior ito

I COMMENCED MY SCHOOLING at the St Peter Chanel convent in nearby Berala. Our early years seemed to involve endlessly reciting the contents of the Green Catechism, from which we learned parrot-fashion the fundamental tenets of the Catholic faith. A succession of brown-habited Josephite nuns, Sisters Jude, Vinian and Ligouri, liberally used the hard, unfurry end of a feather duster around the legs of their five-, six- and seven-year-old pupils to encourage a healthy work ethic and, presumably, to make being a little Catholic all the more fun. Michael was sent off to the Marist Brothers at Parramatta when he was in fourth grade while I stayed on with the nuns in second grade, charged with the daily responsibility of taking my little sister Carmel, aged five, to and from school on the bus and buying her lunch.

We were a devoutly Catholic family and I would kneel by my bed every night to say my prayers before going to sleep. 'God bless mummy and daddy, God bless Michael and Carmel, God bless (a litany of relatives, friends and teachers) and God bless me and make me a good boy.' This nightly ritual was followed by many minutes sorting through the names of those I'd missed and trying to comprehend the meaning of eternity and what it felt like.

When I was nine and due to start fourth grade, I joined Michael at Marist Brothers for the next phase of my schooling and an altogether new level of discipline and corporal punishment. We would walk down the hill to Regents Park station, about twenty minutes away, catch the train to Parramatta and then walk again from Parramatta station to the school, which sat shoulder to shoulder with The Kings School at the western end of Victoria Road. There was plenty of company on the train, including about ten boys named Fitzpatrick who came from a big local family and a number of kids from the neighbourhood who attended various other schools at Lidcombe, Auburn and Strathfield and places further afield. Among these was a good-natured delinquent named Bob Fittler who lived at Berala and travelled to Parramatta High School. Bob did us the great service of blowing the Piggott letterbox to smithereens one cracker night by wrenching off the lid and stuffing it full of bungers. We were having dinner at the time and suddenly there was an almighty boom! We raced as a family out the front door to the gate to see that Mr Piggott's pride and joy had been reduced to a smoking ruin as Fittler hurtled down Berry Street on his pushbike, hair and shirt flying, shoulders hunched, as if to duck a retaliatory spray of bullets, and legs pumping furiously. It was a beautiful sight. My parents just looked at one another quizzically, shrugged and returned to the dinner table.

There seemed to be a state of constant mutual hostility between several of the high schools in the Parramatta region, and acute episodes of aggression were often played out at or near the railway station where large numbers of students came and went and tended to congregate in the afternoons. Parramatta High boys in particular had a longstanding feud with their James Ruse counterparts. One afternoon we encountered Bob Fittler furiously slurping oranges on Parramatta station. As our train pulled in, we asked him what was going on.

'I'm gonna golly on the James Ruse kids,' came his perfectly reasonable reply.

Our small contingent of Marist Brothers boys that travelled as a group each day piled into the open area of the last carriage with the Parramatta High boys to watch the action. When our train stopped at Clyde station the enemy train was already there, stopped on the adjacent line. The opposing doors of the two trains — which were all manually operated in those days and barely half a metre apart — were thrown open, allowing the warring tribes to see each other and commence their daily exchange of insults and abuse, along with a barrage of missiles of every kind, hurled across the gap into the enemy throng.

All the while Fittler, who now had a river of orange juice pouring down his chin, hands and wrists, was slurping away and coughing and hawking up a disgusting coagulum of mucus and phlegm from the deeper recesses of his nose and throat. With a crazed look and shouting something like 'Lemme at 'em!' he suddenly charged forward. As his own troops parted to give him space, he unleashed a gigantic, orange-coloured, mucoid mass of spit which, like an enormous slimy amoeba, seemed to take minutes to traverse the short distance into the carriage opposite and completely engulfed the dozen or more stunned boys from James Ruse High.

A mighty cheer went up, the doors were slammed shut and the trains pulled out.

Parramatta Marist Brothers was by no means an elite private school. It was a big regional boys school of close to a thousand pupils, drawing its students from a wide geographical area and socioeconomic spectrum. Fights in the playground were relatively uncommon but inevitably attracted large crowds of barrackers.

The Marist Brothers who taught there were a mixture of inexperienced fuzzy-cheeked young men, barely out of school themselves, and grizzled, moody veterans with a casual and taciturn readiness to administer firm discipline — and what mostly seemed like rough justice — with the cane, rulers, an open hand, blackboard dusters or any other weapon or missile that might be at hand. It was almost impossible to avoid getting hit. Unpredictable, contradictory behaviour was all pervading and was no doubt an important component of a curriculum that was carefully designed to prepare us for the real world.

The class sizes were enormous: we had sixty boys in our fifth-grade class. I still have a school photo from that year, each face there to be counted. Our teacher, Brother Linus, was a sweaty, red-faced, red-headed man who could switch from patient, avuncular kindness to intemperate madness in a blink. He taught us to play chess, encouraged stamp collecting and, at his own cost, developed a private little library in the classroom to assist our reading. One day, after we came in from play lunch, our mid-morning break, he announced that because we had been so well behaved during the earlier part of the day, he would take us back into the playground while the rest of the school was back in class, so that we could have hopping races. But we had to do it *quietly*.

Needless to say, when sixty ten- and eleven-year-old boys found themselves the sole occupants of the playground and then started racing each other in teams across forty or fifty metres of asphalt on one or other leg, the scene very quickly turned into something Hieronymus Bosch might have painted. For some reason Linus had not anticipated this, apparently expecting that, by some miracle, a mass hopping race involving sixty fifth-graders would be a quiet and incident-free enterprise, the only noise perhaps coming from squeaking shoe soles, a little puffing and panting and the odd grunt as skin was torn from hands and knees during the inevitable spills and falls.

In any event, Linus went berserk as common or garden-variety schoolboy exuberance spiralled into screeching pandemonium. In an eye-bulging frenzy he herded us back upstairs into our classroom and proceeded to give every boy four thunderous and excruciating blows on the hand with his favourite weapon, a thick multi-layered strap made of a flexible rubberised flooring material, hidden in the sleeve of his soutane. How he fashioned or even dreamed up this device is beyond comprehension, but it was cruelly effective and seemed to give him a good workout. This mass execution took him the rest of the period and left Linus exhausted, sweating, tomato-red and, one would guess, seriously at risk of keeling over.

Opportunities for revenge were virtually non-existent in primary school, but when we moved into the secondary years, the collective cunning and wit of the class occasionally squeezed out from under the heavy rock of discipline. In first form we were given the responsibility, or so we presumed, of initiating and breaking in a new young brother, so obviously innocent and inexperienced in teaching and life that you could almost see the seventy boys in the year licking their lips and rubbing their sweaty paws in anticipation and relish. Brother Noel was very tall, awkward, slightly effeminate and gently spoken. He was given the nickname 'Lurch' after the *Addams Family* character on television.

Poor Noel was busier than a one-armed paperhanger trying to keep the class occupied and under control during the day. His tribulations were taken to a new level when he (or perhaps a sadistic superior) made the suicidal decision to introduce a question box into the classroom. It might have more appropriately been called Pandora's question box, because the aim of this little time bomb was to allow boys to ask sensitive and potentially embarrassing questions anonymously and to give the teacher the opportunity to talk about some of the more intimate and adult aspects of life and relationships in a mature setting and to, perhaps, share his experiences. The only ingredients missing were an experienced teacher and a mature setting.

Within two days of its introduction, the question box was absolutely jammed with pieces of paper bearing literally hundreds of questions that concerned one topic only — sex.

On the first day that the question box was to be opened and its contents included in our religion lesson, Noel arrived late to class looking terrible. He must have been awake all night worrying about what manner of torture our collective adolescent prurience would inflict upon him.

Young Brother Noel opened the box and felt inside like a man reaching into a bag full of snakes. As he withdrew a crumpled half page, beads of sweat now glistening on his forehead and top lip, the room was electric with anticipation.

With no way out, his voice a hoarse and tremulous whimper, Noel stammered bravely, 'The first question is … this.' He licked his lips and continued, concentration and effort furrowing his brow. 'What, what is, what is a … frenchie?' Explosive sniggers spilled through hands masking seventy grinning mouths and billowed through the room.

It could have been much worse of course and Noel knew it. He stammered his way through a fair attempt at an answer while suppressed laughs got the better of their owners here and there around the room for the next two or three minutes.

After one more question, this time about oral sex, Noel was, literally, saved by the bell as the period ended and he retreated, shaking and flushed crimson, to the playground.

The question box disappeared soon afterwards and did not make another appearance that year, despite occasional inquiries along the lines of: 'Brother Noel, do you think we'll get the question box back? We really liked it.'

The dominating authority during my early years at Parramatta Marist Brothers was the Principal, Brother Alman, known as 'Doc'. Doc was a big man with a severe short back and sides haircut and the thick glasses and misdirected, squinting, grimacing gaze of a severe myope. He established and maintained a policy of stern discipline, but at the same time engendered universal participation in and a love of sport along with fervent and genuine school spirit. We competed very successfully against the other big Catholic colleges of Sydney and the annual inter-school swimming and athletic carnivals were preceded by a day or two of war cry practice, which gave welcome relief from afternoon classes. With the house captains and prefects leading our chants from an elevated landing, Doc would exhort us to louder and more passionate efforts, encouraging us to rattle the windows of Kings next door.

Fortior ito is our cry, V-I-C-T-O-R-Y.
Who are who are who are we? We are the boys from the MBP.
Green and gold don't know defeat. Parramatta Parramatta can't
*   be beat.*
P-A-R-R-A-M-A-T-T-A ... Parramatta!!

It was a wonderful thing to be part of this powerful tribe. *Fortior ito* means 'Go forward strongly' but these days 'Go hard!' would be a very satisfactory shorthand.

Every day at lunchtime the entire school assembled into ranks and lines according to class and marched down Victoria Road to Parramatta Park, led by the school band. As drums and bugles rang out, a thousand boys swung their arms high, each with eyes fixed on the head of the boy in front and lips sealed in a display of might and discipline that was as much for the benefit of the neighbouring schools and passersby as it was for us.

At the park we would disperse into classes and, depending upon the season, either play cricket or kick footballs for three-quarters of an hour. When a fusillade of whistles sounded that time was up, we reformed our ranks and marched back. Prefects and teachers patrolled the flanks to castigate talkers, dawdlers and anyone irreverent enough to smile or laugh. More serious breaches were punishable by caning when we reached the school.

I was given responsibility for provisioning and helping to coordinate this large-scale recreation period when, in first form, I was given the key to the sports room and put in charge of the school's entire stock of sporting equipment. With four colleagues, it was my task to distribute bats, balls and stumps or footballs to a nominated boy from each class and then take delivery of returned equipment. We also had to prepare cricket kits and other gear for teams travelling away to compete, and inflate and lace the dozens of footballs that were used daily and for weekend games. This minor position of authority carried with it some risks because gear that was returned late or not at all needed to be recovered and accounted for each day before I could close and lock the sports room and get to class. We were at the mercy of the slowest and least organised of our fellow students and this chronic no-win scenario saw us (particularly me) repeatedly late for the first period after lunch and caned for it more often than not.

From time to time, and certainly regularly enough to sustain an atmosphere of apprehension and concern that Big Brother was definitely watching, Doc would stage unscheduled classroom inspections. The door would suddenly open and the room would darken as, unannounced and unexpected, his large frame filled the doorway; a shudder would ripple through the room as if an arctic breeze had just blown in.

The ritual was always the same. The teacher in the class at the time retired politely to a seat in the corner to watch the action and even cower a little himself.

'Good morning boys,' Doc would challenge.

'Morning Brother,' would come fifty, sixty or seventy voices, depending on the class.

'Stand up now please and take out your combs and comb your hair,' came the first command. Greasy combs were removed from back pockets and dragged across a forest of heads, sometimes with blatantly exaggerated and extravagant arm actions, particularly among those without combs.

'Now take out your handkerchiefs and blow your noses,' Doc continued, polite as a wolf asking a flock of sheep to relax and not make any special effort to entertain him. There followed a cacophony of honking and snuffling that went on longer and more loudly than was necessary, accompanied by a rising tide of sniggering and stifled laughter. All the while he waited patiently, squintingly surveying the room with his head tilted as we stood meekly at our desks, aware that things were only warming up.

'Now, polish your shoes on your socks,' rang Doc's final request.

Next, a boy was selected at random to write on the blackboard all the homework that had been given the night before. Doc would run through the list of subjects one by one and demand that we display the exercise book containing the relevant work on our chests for his inspection. In truth, his eyesight was so poor that he probably had trouble seeing the books, much less what was written on the pages, but no one dared test him. Boys who had not done their homework inevitably confessed and made their way to a line that slowly formed at the front of the class. Books were then put away and those who had not completed that particular subject were caned, usually four cuts.

We would then move onto the next subject and the process was repeated. A line of miscreants and idlers would again form out the front and Doc would dispense his punishment with lethal and indifferent efficiency. This would go on until the homework from five or six subjects had been accounted for, with some poor wretches finding themselves in the punishment line every time.

Homework inspections were only carried out in the secondary classes so the boys subjected to these mass canings were aged between twelve and eighteen. Tears were rare except among the youngest boys; certainly no self-respecting pupil in his teens would dare be seen with wet eyes, no matter how much caning he copped.

The other activity conducted on a mass scale was confession. This exercise was a logistical tour de force that took place every few weeks and necessitated the bussing in of priests from surrounding parishes, some of them so ancient that they must have almost been exhumed from nursing homes or worse. Nearly a thousand boys filled the old St Patrick's Cathedral, which was subsequently destroyed by fire and has since been rebuilt in a beautifully innovative modern style.

Confession, of course, affords Catholics the opportunity to be absolved of their sins; to re-establish good relations with God — known as a state of grace — and hence qualify for the privilege of receiving communion at mass; and finally (and most importantly in the minds of children in my early days), to avoid the eternal fires of Hell should death come unexpectedly when mortal sins had been committed and not yet forgiven.

The issue of mortal sin, transgressions that carry an automatic sentence to Hell for eternity, troubled me immensely. I tried and tried to fathom eternity and what that experience might be like, searching my conscience to exhaustion and increasingly feeling the almost intolerable weight of my unworthiness and inexorable doom. Eventually, as I matured and slowly recognised the importance of having my own 'too hard basket', I was happy to consign this and other mysteries to it and move forward.

School confession days no doubt provided a few hours of welcome entertainment for the visiting priests as they listened to the litany of crimes, misdemeanours, sins of omission, acts of self-abuse (a favourite term of religious authorities at that time) and other transgressions perpetrated by this horde of sweaty, pimple-infested schoolboys. They also represented a near-lethal form of Russian roulette for the boys, since lurking behind one of the numerous confessional doors or temporary screens would be the much-feared Monsignor McGovern, a bad-tempered and occasionally violent Irishman. His exact location would be uncertain until suddenly the atmosphere of strained and artificial reverence would be shattered by a bellow of 'You dirty little mongrel!', sometimes accompanied by a couple of loud thumps and the cries of shock and protestation of the unfortunate victim as he was dragged by the scruff of the neck out of the church and cast onto the footpath by the 'Mons'. Apprehensive glances were then exchanged across the crowded pews and long lines of waiting penitents, each boy reconsidering just what he might be prepared to divulge to the priest. 'A couple of simple little venial sins might be best now,' you could see everyone thinking.

As I went through the various grades I did well academically and had a reputation for being a reliable and cooperative pupil. Eager to please, I liked my teachers, worked hard, enjoyed everything and generally prospered. I fell from grace badly, however, in first form when I was about twelve. I attached myself to a group of boys of mixed ages who met each morning in the Capitol Milk Bar at the top of Church Street, stopping on the walk from the station to talk to a group of girls from nearby schools and to enjoy an early morning soft drink and a smoke. This activity was anything but covert and we were readily noticed by the school prefects. They, in hindsight, did me a service by giving my name, along with a number of others, to Doc and to the school's feared and hated master of discipline, a card-carrying sadist and potential serial killer with what looked like a self-administered crew cut, small close-set eyes and tight, thin lips twisted in a permanent snarl. Luckily he was only equipped with a cane and not a chainsaw!

To the great disappointment of my parents, who saw me as a model child and praised my achievements with pride, I was ignominiously suspended for the last three months of first form. Embarrassed and remorseful, I spent the time at home productively and did well in the end-of-year exams. I terminated my short-lived dalliance with smoking and decided to keep better company from then on.

CHAPTER 3

Cicero and charity

SENIOR BOYS WERE EXPECTED to wear a green blazer with the school crest and gold trim on the breast pocket and more trim on the cuffs and side pockets. These were relatively expensive and I was concerned about my parents' ability to afford one, so I decided to try out for one of the football teams since premiership-winning sides were awarded a blazer decorated with a pocket acknowledging the successful season. After the first couple of blazers had been won, further successes were marked by the award of additional pockets, which were sewn onto the blazers. By the time I finished school I had achieved much more than I had initially planned, accumulating a number of blazers, each with several pockets, along with numerous pennants and other trophies. Among the trophies is one that I have kept now for forty years and still value. It is a small angled plaque that sits on a stand and simply says, 'Fourth Form Oratory 1967 — Christopher O'Brien'. I enjoyed public speaking and particularly liked constructing and presenting persuasive and entertaining talks to my teachers and classmates.

Brought up on a diet of the Goons and other radio comedy that was later supplemented by American television comedy, I was a good mimic and joke teller, able to reproduce a range of accents, voices and silly noises. I wanted to believe that Cicero, one of my heroes, would have been proud.

So with a free blazer in mind, I started to play sport in earnest around the age of thirteen, when I was relatively big and fast for my age. I joined a group of boys in a school football team that, over the next four years, was remarkably successful. We played other schools on Thursdays and club teams throughout the sprawling Parramatta district on Saturdays and won both competitions undefeated for some years. Some of us were also selected to play in representative teams. Despite our different backgrounds, temperaments and academic levels, the boys who comprised this team became as close as brothers and, along with a number of the parents, we would often holiday together in one combination or another.

This period of my life was really dominated by rugby league. I was a competent centre, fairly fast and known as a strong tackler, and over time developed formidable rivalries with several other players who were, in general, quicker or more talented than I. My memories of playing these boys is vivid, especially Mina Mikalauskas from Patrician Brothers' Fairfield; he was huge, had legs like tree trunks and could run one hundred metres in around eleven seconds when he was fifteen. We beat these teams each time we played them so I suppose I held my own well enough.

By sixth form, in 1969, my position at the school was strong and I looked forward to every day. I was elected school captain, was president of the St Vincent de Paul Society and a member of the senior athletics and swimming teams; later that year I was named best back in the premiership-winning first-grade rugby league team as well as the school's outstanding sportsman-student.

Membership of the St Vincent de Paul Society and participation in its activities was very popular. The charitable ethos of the organisation was appealing, as were the opportunities and possibilities created by direct contact fieldwork. Sometimes we would visit elderly single men at what was then known as the Lidcombe Old Men's Home, distributing cigarettes, bags of jelly beans and *Pix* and *Post* magazines. The latter were full of black and white pictures of near-naked girls alongside various lightweight articles, crossword puzzles and advertisements. Patients at the Parramatta Psychiatric Centre were also fortunate recipients of our visitations and this largesse. At both institutions we were made to feel welcome and we happily distributed our merchandise with generosity and respect. But our favourite place to visit was the Matthew Talbot Hostel in the inner city, where homeless men would gather in the adjacent laneway hoping to be given shelter for the night. Anyone drunk or disorderly was turned away. Our role was to dish up the evening meal, talk with the evening's residents and then clean up the dining and kitchen area. Three or four of us would go along every couple of weeks and after the evening meal, we would head upstairs with the men to assist in the dispensary or talk further with the residents.

Those assigned to the dispensary gave out, in small plastic medicine cups, 10–15 ml doses of a sleeping draught or a cough draught from two big plastic containers that held several litres of a pink (sleeping) or brown (cough) solution. I have no idea what was in these liquids but the process took a long time, since the sleeping and cough draughts were popular nightcaps. Most of the men took both and then rejoined the back of the line, which started at the dispensary window and seemed to wind around the dormitory forever.

Everyone called each other 'brother' and there is no doubt that, as callow schoolboys, we learned a lot by witnessing the poverty, loneliness and mental distress of these fellow human beings. Our experiences with the school's St Vincent de Paul Society, undertaking these few and relatively insignificant charitable acts, provided me with important lessons about the benefits of simple human kindness.

These years at Parramatta were magical for me and for many others; we were very fortunate to have had some brilliant teachers. One in particular was a charismatic, pedantic, theatrical bachelor named Bill Sheil, who taught us Latin and economics. I was really devoted to these subjects and studied them at first level (along with maths, at which I was weak). Bill developed and encouraged a cult following among his favourites and some of these would be invited for extra lessons late in the afternoon and for weekend trips to the beach. 'Aim for the stars and you might reach the moon,' he would regularly admonish, exhorting us to try our very best and daring us to be outstanding.

Bill's failings included a robust liking for alcohol, but it never seemed to blunt his attendance record, his fastidious grooming or his ability to teach with energy, clarity and provocative humour. He also had a predilection for groping the smaller boys but, very much like the portrayal of the teacher with similar habits in the play *The History Boys*, these advances provoked neither surprise nor resentment, were easily repelled and did not diminish Bill's popularity as a teacher and mentor. He later moved to a large private school and died alone of alcohol-induced liver failure.

Fortunately my own self-satisfied world had its complacency pricked when a softly spoken, long-haired journalist named Malcolm Harrison arrived as a relief English teacher in the latter half of sixth form. From time to time he would bring along his guitar and sing Bob Dylan songs; he introduced us to the poetry of Dylan Thomas and e e cummings, the latter remaining my favourite poet to this day, and managed to bring *King Lear* to life as a meaningful and absorbing play. I owe much of my deep love of literature to Malcolm's influence. In the space of a few months he opened our minds and dispelled the torpor, incoherence and total lack of appreciation that had previously characterised our (or at least my) reading of the likes of Dickens and Shakespeare and instilled in the class a willingness to use our imaginations, to recognise and value the beauty of language, and not to prejudge.

By now my sister Carmel was attending Our Lady of Mercy College, Parramatta, while Michael had left Marist Brothers after the Intermediate (the public examination at the end of third form). Although he was quick and bright he found it difficult to adapt and conform to the iron discipline and academic rigour demanded of him. Brother Linus, in particular, victimised Mike, who enjoyed his greatest success at school in the cadets as a very proficient drummer in the school band.

Despite my boyhood fantasies of heroic soldiering, the cadets never appealed to me; in fact, I was the first school captain for a long time who was not a cadet leader. War worried me deeply and the whole idea of encouraging schoolboys to dress like soldiers and carry guns seemed inappropriate and bizarre, especially as I witnessed on an almost daily basis the damage my father had suffered during his time in the navy.

Through these years, the atmosphere and sense of hope or despondency at home was governed entirely by my father's state of mind. Overall, things were relatively stable and happy but my parents had their moments: periods of peace were regularly shattered by abrupt and noisy arguments that would be followed by days of cold war-like silence. In the end, however, they were devoted to each other and despite my father's personal torments and continued heavy drinking, there was never really a genuine risk that there would be a total disintegration of their relationship.

During hot summer nights as we lay awake, restless and sweltering in our small rooms with every window open, Mum and Dad would sit in cheap banana chairs in the back yard talking quietly, smoking and waiting for the southerly.

Music seemed to play almost continuously at home and my parents were never really happier than when they were listening and dancing to the great tunes of the Big Band era. They danced together with smooth precision and grace, and this unity of understanding and movement made everyone who watched them smile and feel warm inside. Years later, at my wedding reception, Mum and Dad stole the show during the bridal waltz as they swept around the floor in magnificent unison. Their fundamental compatibility was so great that the episodes of conflict that increased in frequency in my teenage years seem so aberrant now that I wonder if I imagined them.

Cicero and charity

Around this time Dad was working for Telecom in a clerical position while Mum was deputy headmistress at a large primary school. She had always been a wonderful singer with a warm alto voice and enjoyed being a member of choirs at church and with her teaching colleagues. Her involvement with school choirs reached its peak when she conducted a massed primary school choir at the Sydney Opera House during Education Week one year. Dad was ever supportive but at home provided almost intentional comical contrast to Mum's productivity by regularly rearranging the furniture in the belief that this was as good as, or even better than, saving up and moving to a better house. Despite his penchant for repeatedly rearranging the lounge and dining-room furniture, he was happy enough for heavy articles like refrigerators and washing machines to stay put for decades. In fact, when Dad was painting the laundry one time, he painted around these particular items rather than drag them out so that he could get at the wall behind. As time went on and Dad turned his decorating instincts to the garden we acquired an eclectic clutter of garden gnomes, birdbaths and all manner of useless kitsch accessories, which turned our small back yard into a crowded, chaotic menagerie.

Michael, Carmel and I were occasional but not particularly willing participants in our parents' gardening endeavours, although Michael and I happily joined Dad one day when he decided to chop down a large dead wattle tree which needed to be removed. I had spent a long time in the Scouts and I enjoyed the hiking, camping and general bushcraft immensely, only giving it up when my weekend sporting commitments progressively took precedence. So chopping down a tree would pose little challenge.

Dad, Michael and I decided that between the three of us we could predict the likely line along which the tree would fall, and further, that we could place the cuts of the axe in a way that would guarantee this result. About twenty minutes later, after a furious bout of tag-team chopping, the wattle tree crashed to earth exactly ninety degrees to the predicted line of its falling and demolished the Hills hoist, which until that time had occupied a position of prominence in the centre of the yard.

During my early years of high school I would occasionally stay for the weekend with my dad's parents. I would invariably awaken to cooking smells on Saturday morning because Grandma would already have vegetables simmering on the stove and meat of some kind slowly roasting in the oven in preparation for the arrival of my parents on Sunday afternoon, when they would bring Michael and Carmel, have lunch and then take me home. This habit of cooking food for thirty-six hours before serving it was puzzling and unique to my grandmother who, not surprisingly, served everything well done or mashed. In my view she effectively cancelled out her culinary limitations by keeping her house well stocked with chocolate biscuits, a more than adequate alternative to a tasteless baked dinner.

Books were plentiful in our home over the years of my growing up. Mum always seemed to have two or three hardcover novels on the go. Books also figured prominently in the loot that filled the pillowcases pinned to the end of our beds at Christmas time. I learned at an early age the joy of immersing myself in a novel during downtime from fishing, swimming and ball games when we were on holidays. For a long time my favourite book was *The Wind in the Willows* and I was also enthralled by and jealous of the adventures of Hal and Roger, two brothers who were the heroic young protagonists in Willard Price's exciting novels *Amazon Adventure* and *Volcano Adventure*. Similarly, *Treasure Island* and *Gulliver's Travels* provided me with endless pleasure.

In secondary school I read avidly but I was a slow reader and struggled to maintain enough interest in the novels set for study to complete them. I filled in gaps by devoting myself to study notes and cribs and still managed to write acceptable essays even when I knew little about the plot and even less about matters like characterisation, the dramatic impact of certain events and the cultural and social implications of a particular book. Perhaps I was preoccupied with Caesar's Gallic Wars or the writings of Cicero and Ovid, which I truly enjoyed. I will go back to Latin one day.

Throughout my schooling and, in fact, until my very last year of high school, my only career goal was to study architecture. As a youngster I would spend hours at home drawing houses and buildings, fiddling with the arrangement of bedrooms and designing grand homes and A-frame holiday cottages. Our local newsagency kept a range of interesting magazines and periodicals from America and I particularly enjoyed flicking through any magazine that contained house designs and plans.

Even more mesmerising were the copies of the *Saturday Evening Post*, which Mum and Dad regularly brought home. I was especially consumed by the glorious colour pictures of American football players, rendered preposterously muscular with their extravagant padding and wearing helmets that gave them a superhuman dimension. Baseball also fascinated me; I borrowed every book on the sport I possibly could and then played baseball for a local team called the Cumberland Redsox for a number of years, when the weekend games did not clash with my football responsibilities.

As sixth form continued I worked hard, still planning to go into architecture at the end of the year. Then a slow change took place. There was no road to Damascus conversion or any other event that could be called an epiphany but for some reason, it dawned on me that if I was going to make a difference in the world and any type of meaningful contribution I would need to study medicine and be a doctor. There were no doctors at all in my family and the only benchmark for this vocation that I had was my close friend Mark Malouf, who had started at Marist Brothers with me in fourth grade and who, with our other friend Chris Nash, claimed the top academic prizes year after year, and whose father and uncles ran a very large and well-known general practice in Parramatta. Mark was destined to be a doctor from the time of his conception

I was motivated by deep and earnest idealism — underpinned by a strong sense of responsibility — that if something needed to be done, then I should do it. Part of my desire to do good and to see justice done was a deep-seated (and difficult to explain) need to be thought well of.

Having decided to do medicine, I gave no other profession a thought and, along with Mark, applied to do medicine at the University of Sydney the following year.

Soon after I finished high school I grew my hair long and cultivated a messy beard, freed of the obligation and necessity of having short-cropped hair to meet both sport requirements and school regulations.

After the HSC I travelled with a close mate, Richard Oakes, in the back of his father Jack's Toyota ute with a heap of building equipment, to the north coast retreat of Crescent Head where we spent the summer holidays working at $1.00 per hour as builder's labourers and novice carpenters. The subsequent weeks were spent building a pair of substantial holiday cottages, one of which belonged to the Oakes family and served as our home while we were there.

Jack was a weathered, compact and wiry type, thoroughly tactless and ruthlessly bigoted. His conversation was ribald, often abusive and peppered with a litany of expletives joined by ands and buts, but he also had what seemed to be an endless repertoire of humorous aphorisms, anecdotes and filthy jokes. He proved an entertaining if choleric overseer and teacher. This working holiday taught me a great deal, and from both Jack and Richard I learned new skills and many of the fundamentals of building.

We finished work at 4 p.m. each day and Richard and I would surf Crescent's perfect right-hand break with the locals till dark, fill up on Jack's simple but plentiful cooking and then play guitars and sing until we were overtaken by weariness from the day's activities. It was a simple, beautiful, happy time.

I had worked diligently in preparation for the HSC and did well enough to gain a Commonwealth scholarship and a place in medicine at the University of Sydney. Almost anomalously my strongest subjects were Latin and economics; science was a weakness. When I started at uni, Richard went to teachers college to study physical education, which was later poetically renamed

45

human movement or something similar, aiming to teach high-school students. We stayed in touch for the first few years but lost contact as his personal life became increasingly complex and then, on the back of a series of failed relationships and misadventures on the part of his children, progressively unravelled. Our paths intersected only a year ago when I learned that he was living alone in a caravan park near the Tweed River, unable to work and debilitated by Parkinson's disease. His predicament might be expected to induce regret, self-pity and depression, yet when we caught up I found the same garrulous, irreverent, funny and affectionate person who had been one of my closest friends from the age of twelve.

This and other unexpected reunions have led me to the belief that life is not a linear experience but rather a circular process, as if it all began when countless pebbles were cast upon a vast pool, each creating its own expanding circle of existence. A million circles intersect, sometimes creating little eddies of turbulence or occasionally coalescing with others to form larger circles which are strengthened and enriched in their course by their partners and then often looping back to close an old unfinished circle or to re-establish an old contact. Or perhaps the growth and progression of the life force is multidimensional like a sphere, a balloon or indeed, like the expanding universe itself. A linear existence would leave behind too much and accommodate too narrow a path of experience, even if it was happily circuitous and meandering. If it is this way, our lives can touch and affect many individuals whom we may never even meet, and continue to be influential long after consciousness, respiration and the pumping of blood have ceased.

CHAPTER 4

Conscientious objector
seeks mentor

I STARTED FIRST-YEAR MEDICINE in 1970 with my close friend
Mark Malouf, ready for the next part of my life: new adventures,
new friends and having my beliefs and values challenged.

I was an eighteen-year-old product of the working-class
western suburbs, happily living at home and travelling to Redfern
each day by train. I walked with the throng of student commuters
from the station to the university each morning, feeling I was part
of a great adventure. Very quickly I found myself talking to people
who came from the affluent north shore, the eastern suburbs and
other areas that were still quite unfamiliar to me. Most of my peers
had long hair and some form of facial hair and were comfortable
enough in jeans, but medicine did attract a sprinkling of students
whose clothes suggested that they were impatient for middle age.
A couple inexplicably wore cravats and a handful of young
women in first year from Pymble or somewhere similar pitched up
each day in tweed skirts and twin sets, occupied the front row of
the lecture theatre and industriously knitted their way through the

first three years of the course. This went on week after week and month after month but did not prove detrimental to their studies since they did exceptionally well academically, certainly much better than I.

Then there were the legions of attractive girls who seemed to populate every table at Manning House, every inch of the Front Lawn and every desk in Fisher Library. Although I had gone out with a number of pretty girls while I was at school I was still sexually inexperienced. Coming from a boys-only world that ran on a blend of testosterone and holy water, this new co-educational environment proved, initially at least, an enormous distraction.

Despite the success I had enjoyed in every facet of my schooling, my humble domestic background and lack of social sophistication made me self-conscious and diffident. What I didn't appreciate was that hundreds of other new students carried this same burden of insecurity also.

My football career at school had been a bright one by any measure and I was keen to prove myself at the next level. I decided that I wanted to play rugby union for the university, so I joined the Sydney University Rugby Club. In those days rugby union was truly an amateur sport, unlike rugby league, its professional cousin. My grounding in rugby league was not only looked down on by some of the established players and young men who came to university with big reputations and high hopes from the GPS (Greater Public Schools) elite; I also had to present myself to the rugby authorities for so-called reinstatement, as if I was being returned to the one true church and path of righteousness after a period of thoughtless and wilful alienation, stooping so low as to fraternise with people who took money to play sport and who went to inferior schools, held inferior jobs and presumably had inferior values and morals.

After the absolution of my sins and the relegation to history of my life of crime as a junior rugby league player, I was delighted to settle into my new sport and particularly, to meet great new comrades, a number of whom are still my closest and dearest friends.

One of these was Bruce Purdue, a very good centre who was studying arts/law and who, because he lived in Panania and was a product of Picnic Point High, became my 'wrong-side-of-the-tracks' soul brother. We were both graded in fourth grade and spent the next few years bouncing between thirds and fourths with the occasional game in seconds or demotion to fifths, playing in the centres together and developing a close bond and understanding. Bruce's parents came to most games and his mother would bring a thermos of deliciously sweet milk coffee. It was a treat I looked forward to each week even if we were in different teams.

Bruce was constantly re-examining his decision to do law and came from time to time to the anatomy dissection room to marvel at the interesting things we were able to do in medicine. He was also jealously entranced by the prospect we had of working with pretty nurses wearing starched white uniforms and black stockings. Bruce married early and honoured me by asking me to be godfather to his first child, a daughter. Regrettably I played this role poorly and really did not rise to the occasion as I should have when he became estranged from his wife and later divorced.

I played rugby at uni competently enough but I really did not reach great heights, and I never played first grade. As the years have passed, I have met so many people who recall playing first grade for Sydney University that I have now concluded that I must have been almost the only person never to make it.

Sydney Uni was a very strong club at that time, boasting the Australian front row of Jim Roxburgh, Paul Darveniza and Jake Howard, as well as a number of other international players. The first-grade coach was Dave Brockhoff, a legendary tactician and motivator, who spoke to me only twice during my years playing at uni.

The first occasion was during second-year medicine when pre-season trial matches were being played on the St Johns College oval, adjacent to RPA. I had spent the summer holidays at the end of first year surfing in Queensland with my rugby friends, Bruce Purdue and Tony Freestone, and had sprayed my hair with a peroxide product called 'Sun In' believing that it would turn my hair blond. Instead, and not surprisingly, it turned a hideous pumpkin orange — much to the horror and disapproval of my parents, who refused to believe that the bizarre change was entirely natural and due only to the sun and surf.

As I ran onto the field at the start of one of the trial games I heard Brockhoff comment, 'Jesus, look at that bloke's hair!' I played well in the trial and he must have asked someone my name because as I came off, he made his way across to me and grunted in his abrupt baritone, 'Well trialled, Chris!' I was elated at this recognition and rare compliment but remained in the lower grades and had to wait three more years before he spoke to me again.

On that occasion we were playing Randwick at Coogee Oval. I was standing on the sideline as second grade were finishing their match when suddenly a University player emerged from a maul without shorts. A number of players turned to me calling, 'Chris! Chris! Quick! Get some more shorts, mate.' I danced around unproductively for a moment before further instructions were forthcoming: 'The dressing sheds!' someone cried. I raced off furiously to carry out my task so that the game could go on.

At this time Brockhoff had the first-grade team in the final stages of his carefully orchestrated and exquisitely delivered pre-game exhortation, moving from player to player and using all his powers of persuasion and oratory to detail with crystal clarity the scope and importance of each player's role — their duty even — and how that duty would be fulfilled.

This scene of concentration and profound gravity was suddenly shattered as the door burst open. I fell into the room like a creature possessed and shrieked, 'Anyone got any shorts?' All eyes turned to me as I stood there like the village idiot, ignorant of my faux pas, yet sensing I had interrupted an important ritual of a secret society. In fact, that is exactly what I had done. In a flash Brockhoff turned his attention to me; almost foaming at the mouth, he bellowed, 'Piss off, you!' I retreated in a cloud of startled embarrassment and returned to the sideline of the second-grade match to learn that multiple pairs of shorts had been found and that play had gone on with barely an interruption.

My early years in medical school were not characterised by great academic achievement. I went about my studies with a desultory sense of obligation but nothing like the enthusiasm or commitment I had been able to bring to my schoolwork. First year had a reputation for being a difficult year of high attrition and it was easy to see why. We concentrated on the basic sciences and although I liked biology, university-level physics and chemistry were difficult and dry, so I scraped and bounced along the bottom of this new academic seascape, passing relatively comfortably but doing not much more. I was more preoccupied in these preclinical years with playing rugby, experiencing a range of other new outdoor activities like sailing, caving and abseiling, developing new friendships and pursuing my first serious relationship with a girl.

Jill was an attractive blonde, a good two inches or more taller than I was. Far from petite, she made a lot of her own clothes and liked to wear very high heels when we went out. My average height had never been a concern to me but I was frequently dwarfed by this statuesque young woman during our four-year relationship. I didn't like that.

When we commenced our study of the medical sciences like anatomy, physiology and biochemistry, my level of interest rose significantly but I still struggled to keep pace with others in the year. Almost everyone else seemed brighter and quicker to grasp new facts and theories, so my grades continued to be mediocre even though my work rate had picked up. I had not, at that stage, developed the burning ambition and desire to reach the top that would eventually drive me to achieve all that I possibly could later in my professional life. I was still largely motivated by a constant and genuine sense of responsibility and an obscure, but equally real, need to be thought well of, both traits I had carried with me since childhood, but these did not quite generate the hunger to excel or the dedication needed to improve my ranking in the class.

Conscientious objector seeks mentor

After four years of playing rugby at university I decided that it was time to stop. I had been training two nights a week since I was thirteen years old and, with little prospect of reaching the top level in rugby and no real desire to do so, I decided without any qualms or regrets that I would reclaim my weekends and broaden my interests.

In retrospect, I do have some regrets about my lack of achievement while playing rugby. As a schoolboy playing rugby league I had been a key player in some outstandingly successful teams but, when success did not come easily playing rugby union at uni, instead of gritting my teeth and working doubly hard to improve, I lost confidence and began to feel I was out of my depth. It was an error that probably reflected a combination of immaturity and waning desire.

Those early years of medical school in the 1970s saw the continuation and escalation of the social and political upheaval that had begun in the 1960s, in the last few years of my schooling, and which was now an unstoppable global movement. I needed to break through my conservative carapace and develop my own response to critically important issues like Australia's involvement in Vietnam and our apparent complicity with apartheid, which was evidenced by a government-sanctioned tour of Australia by the South African rugby team. I felt it was my responsibility to join the Moratorium marches and to be among the phalanx of demonstrators at the Sydney Cricket Ground Rugby Test who chanted 'go home racists' at the Springbok players, at the same time feeling some ambivalence because University player John Taylor (and maybe others whom I cannot recall) was out there playing for Australia.

My contribution to these causes was as a participant only, involving nothing more than turning up. Certainly there was no personal risk but I felt obligated to stand on one side of the fence or the other and be counted. By the time I was in third-year medicine I would be twenty and eligible for conscription, so I needed to register my name in order to avail myself of the opportunity and privilege of being selected at random to go to Vietnam and possibly get killed there. At that time, for reasons which totally escaped me and which perhaps had as their basis some archaic and discriminatory rules about class or social status, university students could defer their National Service while ordinary young workers could not, so there was really no likelihood that I would be sent to Vietnam, even if my birth date was drawn in the ballot.

I could not say that I really understood the politics of the war and that I had an informed view of the true extent of the communist threat in Southeast Asia. I just could not accept with anything but bewildered sadness and evolving anger the senseless deaths of so many young soldiers — five hundred Australians and fifty thousand Americans ultimately — in what appeared to be a chaotic war with an unpredictable outcome. My views had taken a big shift to the left and, one way or another, would stay there.

I was confronted now by the biggest dilemma I had yet faced. I didn't want to register for National Service and this act of public defiance would certainly place me at odds with the law. Even more importantly, when I estimated the implications of such an action, it would amount to a dereliction of duty and an act of treachery in the eyes of my father. His mental state around this period was fragile and not assisted by my long hair, generally unkempt appearance and my liberal social and political views. 'If I hadn't fought for you, you'd be pulling a rickshaw now!' he would fume all too frequently, angered and frustrated by the growing anti-war sentiment and feeling bitterly insulted that his own military contribution, and that of other Australians who fought in previous wars, was being negated, diminished and even retrospectively criminalised.

Some years later I suggested he read Michael Herr's brilliant book *Dispatches*, which gut-wrenchingly portrays the experiences of American grunts in Vietnam, boys whose adventure went tragically wrong while their nation's optimism turned to bitter disillusionment.

He didn't read it. Why would anyone who had lived through a war?

I was desperate for advice and assistance at this time but really did not have a mentor or other trusted person outside the family to whom I could turn.

One of my patients, Arthur Fitzgerald, eventually became my trusted mentor and friend over thirty years later, but when I was nineteen and wrestling with the competing demands of filial duty and my abhorrence of war, there was no Arthur or anyone else. I was on my own but, no doubt, so were thousands of other young men.

Arthur was an economist and lawyer whose work as a lobbyist in Canberra gained him the affection and respect of a very large number of people in commerce and at various levels of government on both sides of politics. He was nearly eighty when he became my patient with a small but aggressive mouth cancer, necessitating very complicated surgery. During the remaining five years of his life he became my close friend and adviser, monitoring my progress and gently nudging me from time to time to adjust my course. I would visit Arthur at his home occasionally and sit with him discussing my ideas and plans, while he listened and offered his wise counsel in small, subtle and sometimes cryptic doses. Once, as he bid me goodbye at his front door, he handed me a paper bag containing a copy of *Who's Who in Australia*. I looked at the book, he looked at me; the only words spoken were my 'thank you, Arthur'. The next edition had an entry under my name.

There is a huge unmet need for mentoring in virtually every stratum of society. Young people especially can benefit enormously from a relationship based on trust and respect with someone older and more experienced and with the right balance of generosity, wisdom and detachment. Detachment is important because the mentor must deny himself (or herself) the emotional investment that spawns expectation. This, a product of love, is what often leads parents to being poor at mentoring their children. The issue of mentoring is still close to my heart. Even during the four years I spent as director of the Sydney Cancer Centre, I often wished that I could test my ideas with or seek the guidance of another person who had no agenda or requirement or expectation of me (other than that I would fulfil my potential and be successful), and whose wisdom I respected, whose judgement I valued, and who did not have a vested interest in the outcome of any of my decisions.

As a young man, though, I simply knew that a failure to register for National Service would be a devastating blow to my father, which would send an aftershock through the household and lead to all manner of unpredictable problems. I tied myself in knots as I questioned my true feelings and motives. Was I really a pacifist? Did I plan not to register for National Service out of arrogant pride? Was my eventual decision to go ahead and register an act of consideration for my father or an admission that, deep down, I was afraid of the consequences of not registering? I went ahead and registered; my birthday was not drawn in the ballot; for me it all came and went quietly and Australia's troops were withdrawn from Vietnam.

My dilemma had been a moral one, not a political one, and I soon realised that compared to so many of my better informed and politically active contemporaries at university, I really did not have particularly sophisticated political views. On the day the Whitlam Government was dismissed in 1975 I was in my bedroom at home building new oversized stereo speakers, listening to the events unfolding in Canberra on the radio. Next day I was playing The Beatles, Rolling Stones and Hendrix through an old Sansui amplifier that had all the backbone needed to rattle the bedroom windows and the odds and ends on the dressing table.

Religion began to play a less and less significant part in my life almost as soon as I left school. I still prayed before exams and rugby games but I didn't bother to go to Mass on the mornings of those particular challenges as I had done all the way through high school, carrying with me a sense, even an expectation, that I might fail in particular endeavours or attract some alternative retribution if I fell short in my devotions. This withdrawal from earnest Catholicism was driven in part by the attitude of my girlfriend, an intense and intelligent atheist, who expressed bewilderment and outright disgust for the treacherous hypocrisy I demonstrated by sleeping with her, then confessing this mortal sin to a priest in order to return myself to a state of grace, and then doing it all again. Of course she was right and justifiably questioned exactly what it was that I had held sacred for all these years.

The position taken by *The Catholic Weekly* in relation to Vietnam had already caused me enormous disappointment and anger. Their editorial emphatically supported the sending of conscripts away to fight and admonished young Catholics to register for National Service.

It wasn't difficult to stop going to Mass and, with little resistance, I assumed the role of a lapsed Catholic. This is a little like going onto the non-playing roster at a golf club. Catholics almost never give the game (their religion) away altogether, they just move into an inactive role that they may occupy for many years, because returning to the status of playing member takes a desire and a level of commitment and sacrifice they have long since lost the ability to muster. Deep down, however, they remain Catholic; they say or write 'Catholic' on those occasions when they need to nominate their religion and derive an odd satisfaction, even comfort, from the fading familiarity they have with the saints, the sacraments, the Virgin Mary and the ritual of the Mass, even if they never set foot inside a church again.

I really did not return to the Church with any conviction until my youngest son, James, was born sixteen years later and nearly died. Ironically, in his last couple of years of schooling under the Jesuits at St Ignatius' College, Riverview, James confided in me that he really didn't believe in God or the religious rituals in which he was expected to participate. I was initially disappointed but, since my own beliefs had evolved to deep scepticism for a time, I later felt proud of him — that he was trying to sort out his own beliefs by questioning dogma that defied science and logic rather than blindly accepting the creed he was being taught. We agreed that he should read Richard Dawkins (*The God Delusion*), Christopher Hitchens (*God is not Great: How Religion Poisons Everything*) and the work of other contemporary atheists so that he could inform his thinking. He was not interested in the conventional view any more.

For my own part, I had already observed that over the past decade or more, the incapacitating dilemma posed by mortal sin and the need to seek absolution through confession seemed to have become completely non-problematic for Catholics. Despite the fact that confession, now called reconciliation, had become quite unfashionable, everyone was going to communion, and as far as I am concerned, so they should. People seem to have finally worked out for themselves that the concept of sin is an invention of men, not God, and that it has been used as an effective way of exerting control over otherwise decent citizens, casting them as unworthy malefactors, innately drawn to evil. This has assisted the clerical hierarchy in maintaining its position of authority and power as the sullen and disapproving gatekeeper to enlightenment, spiritual fulfilment and eternal happiness, only letting through those who yield to their will.

CHAPTER 5

Discovering a larger world

DURING MY FIRST YEAR OF MEDICINE I needed to find a part-time job so that I could pay for running a car along with the costs inherent in having a steady girlfriend and an active social life. I managed to get a position at Concord Hospital as a nurses' aide, doing a couple of shifts during the week and then working more regularly during holidays.

After a day or so of training I was given an ill-fitting uniform, shown how to clock on and off, and then sent to one of the wards scattered over the hospital's rural landscape, which was bordered by stands of mangrove trees where the hospital precinct met the Parramatta River.

Ward 12 was supposed to be a rehabilitation ward but when I arrived there I found the thirty or so beds occupied by elderly men who were almost all stroke victims, some of them having been resident in the ward for many months. The exception was Doug Smith, who was rendered quadriplegic when he fell from a ladder at home. Doug was an intelligent former engineer aged about forty-eight who had lived in the ward for years. He was a huge man and we needed a hydraulic lift to get him into and out of the bath each day, his great frame hanging limp and corpulent in the lift's sling. We could have used him as a wrecking ball. Doug seemed to have a supportive family; in particular his wife, an attractive brunette about the same age, visited regularly. This quiet patient man had every reason in the world to be depressed and angry — in fact there was no negative emotion to which he was not entitled. Yet for unfathomable reasons, he projected a demeanour of stoical calm and cheerfulness and was grateful for every act of care he was given.

There was no rehabilitation to speak of for these bed-ridden veterans. Along with another nurses' aide and the sister in charge of the ward, it was my task to shower or bath these patients, feed them, attend to their toilet needs and provide 'second-hourly back care'. This duty involved turning the patients every two hours, after changing wet or soiled sheets and reattaching urinary drainage devices if necessary, and applying barrier cream to pressure areas — heels, sacrum and buttocks — to minimise the risk of pressure sores developing. These basic nursing duties, along with taking patients to and from the toilet, delivering and taking away urine bottles and bedpans, serving meals and feeding those patients who were unable to feed themselves, combined to make every shift both enormously busy and physically arduous.

On my first day in Ward 12, I was greeted by an ungodly odour and was asked to assist my nursing aide colleague for the shift — an outlandishly obese and camp young man with hair dyed a flaming red and looking like a character out of the Fellini movie *Satyricon* — to lift an elderly and emaciated man with hideous bed sores over both hips and his sacral region, into a salt bath. His bed sheet was saturated with urine and smeared with excrement, although it had apparently been changed only two hours earlier.

As we lowered this poor remnant of a human into the bath, maggots and dead flesh floated to the surface of the water from his putrid wounds. I really wasn't ready for this and it took some effort to avoid emptying the contents of my stomach into the bath with the other detritus. The entire scene was so medieval and revolting it was like something out of a horror show. To my great relief, I was not rostered on to Ward 12 for another couple of days and by then, this poor patient had perished. One could only hope that he was greeted by a kind-hearted boatman who took him across the river to his eternal reward. This poor man's plight was not the result of neglect or inadequate nursing at Concord. He had lived with his elderly wife before his admission to the hospital and the frail little thing was just unable to attend to her husband's needs and care for him. This Dickensian scenario haunted me for some time.

I continued to work at Concord Hospital on a part-time basis during my clinical attachment there as a student and, with my father's intermittent admissions for psychiatric care along with the fact that I lived in the students' quarters at Concord from fourth year onwards, my life at that time seemed to revolve around the hospital.

I was embarrassed, even ashamed, that my father was periodically a psychiatric patient at Concord and I never divulged this fact to my colleagues. Our clinical activities as students never really raised the likelihood that my peers would meet up with Dad when he was an inpatient, and I was thankful for this. I had never been one to confide in others, perhaps fearing that my family or I would be judged harshly and I would be less well thought of.

In our fourth year of medicine there were still nearly 250 students in the year. We were allocated, according to our suburb of residence, to one of the four teaching hospitals attached to the University of Sydney — Sydney Hospital, Royal Prince Alfred, Royal North Shore and Concord. Since I came from the western suburbs I was sent to Concord, which was well liked by students because it had capacious grounds with tennis courts and a swimming pool and the relaxed friendly atmosphere of a country club while still providing excellent clinical experience and teaching.

Once these clinical years commenced I found a new enthusiasm, a passion even, for study. Bedside tutorials and ward rounds with professors, consultants and ambitious young registrars were endlessly stimulating and entertaining; for the first time since I began medicine in 1970, I knew that I had chosen the right vocation. I enjoyed working in every unit to which I was attached and, for nearly a year, I chose a new specialty every month. On balance, the surgical specialties attracted me more than the medical ones, though I went through a phase of being enthralled with neurology because I liked the clinical problem solving involved. We would examine patients with various neurological signs and disabilities and try to pick where in the brain or spinal cord the problem was located or what type of pathological process was going on. I was quite good at this but it didn't take long before it became apparent that it didn't really matter where the abnormality was, because almost nothing could be done about it unless it was a small and localised tumour. Nearly everything else was, sadly, untreatable or inaccessible to surgical intervention, making the 'locate the lesion' exercises little more than an academic guessing game.

My experience with psychiatry, which initially I really enjoyed and seriously considered pursuing, could have been identical. However, I found a wonderful book, which was not among the prescribed texts and not on the reading list, called *Personality Development and Psychopathology* by Norman Cameron. This wonderfully readable volume provided a brilliantly concise explanation of Freudian psychodynamics and described the genesis of all the major types of behavioural and psychological problems like personality disorders, phobias, neuroses and psychoses and how these so-called deviations from normality reflected interruptions, obstructions or distortions of normal progression through the various phases of psychological development. A failure to successfully or comfortably negotiate the anal phase of development (toilet training), for example, may lead to the formation of obsessive-compulsive characteristics which could be imprinted into the psyche and hence the personality, and surface later as a coping mechanism during times of stress. These theories may have long since been discredited and discarded from modern psychiatry but they fascinated me at the time and explained with disturbing accuracy so much of what I recognised in myself and in the behaviour of my family and friends. Again, however, there seemed to be so little that could be done to remedy the various maladjustments that lead to that spectrum of disorders known — sometimes euphemistically and sometimes pejoratively — as mental illness.

So psychiatry became another stimulating fascination, like neurology, but I could not seriously entertain the possibility of working in a medical specialty that offered a genuine prospect of cure to so few of its clients. The idea of being able to carry out an elegant surgical procedure on someone with a life-threatening problem and possibly restore them to health forever was far more appealing. That thought, along with the positive influence of confident extrovert surgeons as role models, convinced me that I needed to be a surgeon when I finished medical school.

Fifth-year medicine commenced in 1974 and with it came the prospect of new knowledge and new experiences, some of which would be life changing. During the previous year I had lived in the student quarters of Concord Hospital, my first real experience of living away from home. Despite Concord's country club reputation, the student accommodation was utilitarian to the point of being spartan; nonetheless every day was enjoyable and I luxuriated in the space and freedom I felt being away from home.

During fifth year we were introduced to a range of specialties like obstetrics and gynaecology, paediatrics, psychiatry and dermatology, which all brought a new level of interest to my education and provided a measure of relief from the dense complexities of clinical medicine.

Early on in fifth year I was given the opportunity to become an office bearer in the Australian Medical Students Association (AMSA). For totally obscure reasons and certainly not because I had previously demonstrated either interest or knowledge in these particular areas, I was asked to take on the preposterously titled position of Chairman of the AMSA Sub-committee on Population and Environment. The quid pro quo was a free trip to Singapore and Malaysia, representing Australian medical students at an international conference.

I had never been on an aeroplane before, much less travelled overseas, so the opportunity was too good to pass up. Almost overnight, I became an expert on Zero Population Growth, quoting Ralph Nader, regurgitating statistics and voicing bleak predictions about the fate of the human race if our reproductive proclivities were not curtailed. Later that year, at the AMSA Convention in Adelaide — a five-day orgy during which scientific, ethical and professional matters relevant to medical students would, I'm sure, have been discussed in great depth had there been time — I gave a lengthy presentation on the importance of population control and even fielded questions from the floor as though I was genuinely an expert in this field. Of course I was nothing of the sort.

The trip to Singapore and Malaysia proved to be enormously educational. For men, having hair below collar length was a criminal offence in Singapore at the time, punishable by death, public flogging, having bamboo shoots driven up under the fingernails or some other brutal torture, so before setting off I visited the barber and shed my shaggy mane. I travelled to Asia with another student, Adrian Gale, who was a year ahead of me at uni and very sensible and organised. More importantly, he had an excellent contact in Singapore, a woman named Eunice Chua, the daughter of the Chief Justice.

Eunice was in her late thirties and married to a general practitioner. She worked for a Qantas holiday operator and, to our absolute joy, arranged for Adrian and me to stay with her parents in their magnificent colonial residence in a very salubrious part of Singapore called Mount Pleasant. Judge Chua, as we were invited to call him, would instruct one of his drivers to take us into the city each day and pick us up in time to be home for a classic cucumber-sandwiches-with-the-crusts-cut-off afternoon tea. There were servants everywhere, the house was like a palace and I wanted to stay there forever.

We travelled to Kuala Lumpur on an overnight train that moved at snail's pace through densely forested countryside as we sweltered in a third-class sleeping compartment containing about a dozen other bodies on hard bunks and a single small electric fan at the end of the carriage, turning with slow and unproductive reticence. Our stay in Kuala Lumpur was brief but it was made memorable by a visit one evening to a nightclub where a trio of very attractive Australian girls was performing. We struck up a conversation with the girls but it soon became apparent that Adrian and I were out of our league when two of the trio, both very pretty blondes, asked if we could help them out with diaphragms or any other contraceptive materials we might be carrying, since we were international experts on population control and they were expecting an active few days in KL.

The best part of fifth-year medicine came at the end. It was a four-month block of free time called elective term, during which neither lectures nor clinical tutorials were scheduled. Students were encouraged to seek out a clinical attachment in an emergency department or with a medical or surgical unit in a rural, interstate or overseas hospital of their choice, with the aim of gaining practical experience looking after patients as well as additional life experience.

Elective term proved to be one of the most fruitful, enjoyable and mind-expanding periods of medical school and, indeed, of my life. The options and possibilities were endless and limited only by one's imagination, thirst for travel and discovery, and the availability of a post in the desired location.

The trip to Singapore and Malaysia had thoroughly whetted my appetite for travel, so I now poured enormous energy into preparing for this adventure. Having never been to Europe I was yearning to visit places like Notre Dame, the British Museum and the Colosseum, and to see the *Mona Lisa* and real Impressionist paintings, rather than photographs of them. Elective term loomed as an irresistible opportunity to take a leap into the great world that lay outside my narrow sphere of existence.

My nurses' aide job enabled me to accumulate a good deal of money and, by mid-1974, I had enough saved to pay for my return airfare to Europe and to keep me going for about three and a half months if I kept to a very tight budget. Arthur Frommer's famous travel guide *Europe on $5.00 a Day* would be my bible.

I managed to secure a position for six weeks in a teaching hospital in a city quite close to Zurich called Winterthur. I was thrilled at the prospect, not only of visiting Switzerland, a country which had long fascinated me, but also of earning the equivalent of A$200 per week for the privilege. The authorities at the Kantonspital, or provincial hospital, in Winterthur did not seem put off by the fact that I could not speak Swiss German and I was quite confident that my passable French would see me through.

In November, I kitted myself out with a large but uncomfortable rucksack, a cheap parka which was relatively, but not completely, water repellent, enough warm clothing to see me through a European winter, and an excellent pair of walking boots. 'Lowa, mate! Can't beat 'em. Tough, lightweight, you can even dance in 'em!' the young salesman in Paddy Pallin had enthused. He was right: they lasted me ten years and I did dance in them.

I flew first to the United States to visit relatives in Sacramento, California. One of my father's sisters, Mavis, had married an American soldier after the war and emigrated to America. Mavis' husband, Nick Miller, was a philandering Greyhound bus driver who spent his money freely, had his suit dry-cleaned after one wear and generally looked down on his new relatives, whom he found unworldly and impecunious.

Although we really never saw them, we felt close to our American relatives because Dad's parents and his other sister, Patti, travelled regularly to the United States and brought back reports. I was fascinated by these exciting and seemingly exotic journeys and was thrilled when they brought home even the most meagre of souvenirs, like drink coasters or little foil-wrapped moistened towelettes from the plane or from hotels in San Francisco and Lake Tahoe.

After the unexpected birth of twins, Mavis left her husband but was well supported by her two eldest, Sharon and Oran, who both demonstrated resilience and grit, working hard at their studies and part-time jobs to educate and advance themselves, support their mother and younger siblings and pay off the mortgage on the family house. Sharon became a senior bureaucrat with the Californian government while Oran learned to fly, joined the airlines and earned promotion to the position of chief pilot with one of America's largest international airlines.

From America I flew to Europe, now equipped with a better parka and two additional books: *Tropic of Cancer* by Henry Miller and *Quiet Flows the Don* by Mikhail Sholokhov, the Russian Nobel Laureate. I somehow knew I would be different by the time I returned to Sydney and I wanted to create opportunities for change along the way.

When I landed in Brussels on a freezing windswept November day, I was, to my surprise, suddenly overwhelmed with homesickness. I was now completely alone with neither friends nor family to provide company or comfort. Perhaps it was more a sense of aloneness than homesickness.

Soon enough I found a youth hostel in the centre of Brussels, bought a couple of hot waffles from a street vendor and then set off to explore the city. I spent the next three days travelling continuously as I tried to distract myself with constant mobility to stave off the maudlin self-pity into which I would slip from time to time. Perhaps starting my European travels in Brussels was an error because, apart from the beautiful Grande Place, little in the city invited my attention. I had developed a growing sense, too, that the decision to hitchhike around Europe alone had been a mistake and that I should have teamed up with other friends from medicine who were also touring Europe and with whom I planned to meet in a few weeks. Fortunately, I was lucky with my hitchhiking, despite the fact that it was winter and standing by the roadside was bitterly cold. I soon worked out where to stand and how best to flag down a ride. Hitchhiking was so ubiquitous and reliable a means of travel at that time because European motorists were generous and, so it seemed, almost universally willing to stop for backpackers. I learned from other travellers that it was useful to hold up a sign displaying my intended destination, as if to invite drivers to bid for my presence in their vehicle — or at least give them the option of having company to Heidelberg or Zurich or wherever.

It seemed that nearly half my medical school year was in Europe at this time so I arranged to rendezvous with friends at a couple of attractive destinations. As Europe's winter progressed and the landscape turned to postcard-white magnificence, the first of these meetings was planned to take place in Innsbruck, the capital of Austria's Tyrol. Frommer's brilliant guidebook recommended a visit to the guesthouse of a cheerful, round, red-cheeked little woman named Katie Woolf in a tiny farming village called Mütters, a short drive in Katie's dilapidated Volkswagen from Innsbruck railway station.

Mütters was a dairy farming village perched on the side of a tame mountain, which provided lush grazing land for cattle during the summer months and was transformed into a ski slope in winter. The local farmers operated the lifts while their animals sheltered contentedly in ample stone and timber barns that were dotted through the village. There I met up with my old friend Mark Malouf, his travelling companion for elective term, John (Blue) Newton, who was also a friend from Med Five, and two other mates, Tom Boogert and Dave Little, who had just finished their elective term posting at a hospital in the Netherlands. None of us had skied very much before, apart from one or two weekends together in Australia — one, a chaotic production befitting a Marx Brothers movie, was memorably spent camping on the shores of Lake Jindabyne on a night so cold we crawled into our sleeping bags wearing every stitch we had with us, including ski jackets and beanies. My own initiation to the sport had been a short visit to the small bargain-basement resort of Smiggin Holes in the Snowy Mountains about two years earlier. I spent my time bombing down the short hills wearing jeans and an old football jumper, rendered partially weatherproof by a big plastic garbage bag in which I made holes for my head and arms and which kept most of the snow off during the endless spills and tumbles that punctuated my early efforts. We were short on experience, but the consensus of our intentions was to become expert skiers as quickly as possible.

That Mütters and Katie Woolf were unprepared for our visit is an understatement — we had a boisterous, hilarious, exhausting time. The reunion of five exuberant medical students from Sydney in Katie's breakfast room was raucous and regenerative for us all as we shared our stories, ate and drank till the early morning and then set off into Innsbruck to buy skiing equipment.

We all took lessons from an ancient and cheerfully authoritarian little instructor named Rudi, a legendary local identity well over seventy years of age, who taught us in his uncompromising and effective way how to ski in the classic Austrian style — skis together, weight on the downhill ski, uphill ski tip forward, chest downhill, backside into the mountain and knees bent. This technique is now regarded as being incredibly archaic and passé, particularly in North America but, once mastered, it is very difficult to unlearn and generally guarantees an efficient, even elegant, and trouble-free descent of most slopes.

We left Austria together with a plan to invade Germany and then split up to continue on our various ways. During a visit to Munich with this same group I met and immediately fell in love with a beautiful American girl named Jackie who came from Boston and was also on a backpacking vacation. I spent the next two weeks travelling with her and we corresponded devotedly for two years or more after we left Europe. The relationship ultimately succumbed to the negative influence of geography and suffered the fate to which it was predictably doomed at the outset. This initially caused me some heartache but I was only a little over a year away from meeting my soul mate so, on balance, there was little I could complain about in relation to romance.

The hospital in Winterthur where I was to spend my six-week clinical attachment in the lowly position of *Unterassistenten* (literally under-assistant) proved to be a brilliant find. The town itself was quietly picturesque and civilised and adjacent to the hospital grounds was a small forest of fir trees, mingled with birch and maple. Nearby was a magnificent private home that had belonged to a local industrialist named Oskar Rheinhart, which he had donated to the city as an art gallery. The home, called Am Romerholz, contained Rheinhart's superb private collection of Impressionist paintings. Each of the great names in Impressionism was represented by one or two beautiful and exemplary paintings. There was also a magnificent collection of early Italian religious paintings and old Flemish tapestries. I spent many hours in this wonderfully serene, decorative and historically important gallery, feeding my appetite for art and, from time to time, sketching my favourite works.

Even though as an *Unterassistenten* I was as low on the medical ladder as one could possibly go, I was hampered in carrying out even my limited duties by my lack of facility with the Swiss German language. Nonetheless, I started off enthusiastically, learning a handful of phrases and joining my superiors (and it seemed that absolutely everyone in the hospital was superior to me) in the operating theatre as a willing but mostly confused assistant. The surgical team to which I was allocated was the domain of a group of sweaty and obese general surgeons with a penchant for shouting and throwing instruments when the procedure at hand failed to go as well as it might. I was happy enough to suffer these slings and arrows (and scissors and scalpels) and to pull on retractors for hours at a time but I was otherwise unable to participate in the banter and conversation that went back and forth over the abdominal cavity.

The clinical structure was Teutonically hierarchical. Everyone was Herr Doctor this or Herr Professor that, click heels here, click heels there (everywhere a click click!) except in the case of the unit intern who came from Romania, spoke no English and whom I was allowed to address by his first name.

What might have been a desolate and lonely sojourn was rescued by the kindness of a woman named Lydia Schlagenhaufen, the secretary of the Chief of Surgery. Lydia was a middle-aged divorcee who lived alone, and who made it her task to look after visiting medical students. She spoke excellent English and was kind enough to invite me to her apartment for dinner from time to time, where she recounted stories from her past, particularly the melancholy reminiscences of failed romances. Lydia was a generous hostess and I liked both her cooking and the cosiness of her home, so it was not difficult to be a good listener.

One side of her face had been badly contorted by a long-standing facial palsy, the cause of which was obscure to me at the time. In an attempt to ameliorate the paralysis and restore her previous very attractive appearance, Lydia had undergone a number of plastic surgery procedures. These operations had been anything but successful and the result was an immobile mouth, dragged into an unsightly grimace, a stiff mask-like visage and an unblinking eye.

Poor Lydia had been a desperate romantic all of her life and, while still married and prior to the development of her facial palsy, she had had an affair that led to a bitter divorce and estrangement from her children. A subsequent string of relationships also failed; at the time of my visit to Winterthur, she was engaged in correspondence with a jail inmate who was promising her eternal happiness if she would only assist him in his efforts to have his sentence shortened.

To brighten and otherwise add adventure to her lonely existence, Lydia travelled regularly to exotic destinations and had numerous photo albums in her apartment showing a detailed pictorial record of these trips. There were many photographs of Lydia herself, always taken from her good side and often showing her posing provocatively next to a place of interest or more commonly, her favourite toy, a sports car.

Lydia's generosity and hospitality enriched my stay in Winterthur far beyond my expectations and I was energetic in exploring the surrounding countryside and towns, particularly

Zurich. It was all really too good to be true. I kept reminding myself where I was from and sent weekly aerograms home to keep Mum and Dad up to date on my adventures, omitting the disasters that occasionally befell me.

I was a willing but not particularly productive *Unterassistenten* for, although I was being paid, I continued to find the communication difficulty a real disincentive to being at work all day every day. I regularly took Fridays and Mondays off so that I could enjoy a long weekend skiing at St Moritz or Davos or some other famous location.

My European travels ended in London, which I found cold, damp and wonderful. I managed to find clean digs in Earls Court for one pound fifty a night, sharing a room with three other travellers. The rest of the boarding house was inhabited by other young out-of-towners who had come to London to find work and who could afford nothing more luxurious.

Somehow I managed to stay within budget in London and didn't feel that I had missed anything, although on a couple of occasions I chose to see a play rather than eat dinner. A highlight was a Stephane Grappelli concert in Festival Hall where I sat right behind the band for only fifty pence, leaving plenty over for a meal as well. I'd grown to love jazz during high school and I would listen to Arch McCurdy's *Music to Midnight* program on 2BL several nights a week, so a chance to see and hear the greatest jazz violinist ever for next to nothing was too good to miss.

I returned home in February 1975 thin, pale and dishevelled but clean and immensely happy, carrying a swag of souvenirs for the family and a backpack weighing nearly twenty kilograms more than when I had left Sydney but still with some money in my pocket. More importantly I had grown as a person and had my horizons broadened. Road trips are all about change and I knew that I needed to come back from elective term transformed. And so I was.

I was genuinely delighted to be home and to be reunited with my parents and siblings, whom I had idealised and missed during my travels and whose faults I had largely forgotten. But the world to which I returned, in which I had grown up — my room at home, the house itself, all of Regents Park — was all so small. Michael had already moved out of home two years earlier and Carmel, who had spent three years away while she studied nursing, had just returned. I was careful in the way I expressed my new feelings about how I now perceived this environment, but I was dislocated and distracted, wanting desperately to be back on the other side of the world.

CHAPTER 6

Prince Alfred men

I COMMENCED THE SIXTH and last year of my degree feeling ill-prepared mentally for resuming a rigorous study schedule. Nonetheless I returned to my room at Concord Hospital willingly enough and allowed reality to assert itself slowly and sweep me along like a wave. The memories of my trip were consigned to safe places in my psyche and my heart, accessible when I needed to relive them but otherwise not a constant challenge to my concentration and growing desire to finish university and start doctoring.

During my final year of medicine I continued to live in the students' quarters at Concord Hospital. There was little or no need to be at the university because the emphasis now was purely on clinical medicine and surgery. I had by now made a firm decision that, when the opportunity arose, I would pursue a career in surgery. Internal medicine with its many complex sub-specialties like endocrinology, neurology, cardiology, respiratory medicine, renal medicine, gastroenterology, rheumatology and so on seemed endlessly complicated. At Concord, with a few notable exceptions, it was the career choice of individuals who generally struck me as being introspective, dogged, unexciting, unemotional and preferring an arm's-length approach to their patients. In contrast to surgery, medicine appeared to be a discipline that demanded hours of quiet contemplation and rumination rather than action, intervention and the quest for an expeditious and permanent outcome.

In final year I continued to read novels where I could and made a decision that, even if I was unable to read a lot, I would read well, so I actively sought out important books to occupy my spare time, even if they were difficult. I also remained physically active, jogging on most days and playing a poor standard of tennis and golf when time permitted. On an occasional afternoon off I would meet friends — particularly Butch Davison and Lawrie Hayden, two students at RPA — for a round of golf at Moore Park. None of us was particularly good and our play was characterised by the hapless inconsistency of once-a-month hackers — one minute a 200-metre drive down the middle of the fairway, the next an almighty slice into oblivion. There was laughter all the way round the course and abundant enthusiasm and confidence as every shot was approached with the never-say-die expectation of a career-best result.

At that time the second hole at Moore Park ran parallel to South Dowling Street, a busy thoroughfare that consumed many of our wayward tee shots. Late one afternoon Butch sliced a very ugly drive out of the course and into the peak-hour traffic, which looked like a sea of parked cars filling both sides of the road. The ball finished its journey with a clatter as it ricocheted among the cars and landed on the grass-covered median strip.

With conviction grossly surpassing insight, or so I thought, Butch marched through the stationary cars with a pitching wedge over his shoulder as if striding down the fairway. Then, to the bemusement, disbelief and horror of motorists sitting in their cars, he proceeded to play his next shot from the median strip with three lanes of traffic on either side. It was the best shot he hit all day — in fact, it was the best shot he had ever hit in his life. Drivers and passengers in nearby cars crouched for cover during the back swing while Lawrie and I watched in dumbstruck amazement as the ball sailed across cars, trees, rough and bunkers and landed on the green. It was a magnificent sight and it only took Butch his usual five or six putts to get the ball into the hole.

I am better known among my friends for famously bad golf shots than famously good ones. An average golfer at best, I once hit a startlingly hideous early morning drive at Killara Golf Club which, as a group of my friends watched with a combination of embarrassment and undisguised schadenfreude, left the club head at right angles to the desired line of flight (memories of that wattle tree all over again) and shot between the heads of two elderly members who were sitting close together on a low wall nearby, grumpily watching our group hit off ahead of them. The ball ploughed through and partially decimated a lush rose garden which surrounded the practice putting green and rocketed like an Exocet missile across the putting surface, striking a retired judge (with no sense of humour at all, as it turned out) on the ankle at about 200 kilometres per hour. He fell to the ground with a shriek as I ran to the putting green blathering apologies and expressions of profound remorse to the accompaniment of the derisive cheers of my friends. This inauspicious tee shot still haunts me and there is really no likelihood that I will forget it since I am reminded of it whenever I see my old university chums.

Fortunately I was a better medical student than I was a golfer. I did well in my final exams and was allocated to my first choice hospital for my internship the following year. Along with my mate Mark, with whom I continued to run a parallel course, I decided that I would leave Concord's comfort, safety and predictability and try swimming in the turbulent and unpredictable waters of Royal Prince Alfred Hospital.

RPA was reputedly Sydney's, if not Australia's, leading teaching hospital. It shared an exquisitely blurred boundary with neighbouring Sydney University; this happy juxtaposition of two great institutions was a factor which contributed significantly to the success and standing of both.

The hospital had been built on pastureland in Camperdown in 1882. It was a gift to the people of Sydney from Queen Victoria in thanks for the expeditious and successful treatment of her son Alfred, the Prince of Wales, who was wounded in the buttock during a visit to Australia as a result of an unsuccessful assassination attempt carried out by a cranky but incompetent Irishman named Patrick O'Farrell.

Royal Prince Alfred Hospital also had a reputation for attracting outstanding, if not the very best, clinicians and for being an uncompromising place in which to work. Discipline among the ranks of those who worked as doctors and nurses was strict and for a long time many of the senior clinical staff at the hospital were regarded by their colleagues across Sydney and around the country with a combination of respect, fear and even loathing.

In the hospital's front hall there are several busts of RPA luminaries on pedestals and a number of antique stained-glass windows, some of which bear Latin inscriptions which represent popular aphorisms or family mottos. My favourite declares in faded script *Mortalibus non arduum.* Roughly translated, this opines that hard work never killed anyone. I was a devotee of this philosophy until the end of the year 2006, when I was given cause to consider the role that stress generated by too much hard work (stress that I did not believe existed and of which I was blissfully ignorant) contributed to the development of my brain cancer.

Over the years there has developed a code of euphemisms that was useful in describing some of the characteristics of senior clinicians who worked at RPA. The term 'complex man', for example, was used to describe anyone from a benign eccentric to an individual who was stark raving mad. An individual whose behaviour was characterised by bullying and intimidation and who treated everyone around him like dirt beneath his feet was called a 'hard man'; historically, RPA has had its fair share of these. Finally, people who combined all of these attributes or about whom nothing good at all could be said were simply called 'Prince Alfred men'.

There is a saying which, over the years has been applied to many institutions but which was especially relevant to RPA in those early days: 'You can always tell a Prince Alfred man — you just can't tell him very much.'

The hospital was an exciting melting pot where people needed only to be hard working and competent to do well. As an intern in 1976 I joined a collective of residents and registrars who were mostly male and who nearly all had long hair. A high proportion also wore some type of hairy facial adornment. In those days I liked to look like everyone else so through most of medical school I had a moustache of the drooping type favoured by Mexican bandits. Residents wore all white — including shorts and long socks during summer and long white coats in winter — while medical students wore short white coats year round.

Working as an intern for a year after graduation from medical school is not only a statutory requirement for medical registration, it is also a vital opportunity to assimilate practical knowledge and, for the first time in six years, to take personal responsibility for the welfare of patients. The transition from the role of a final-year medical student who is expected to know everything to an intern who is expected to know absolutely nothing is generally smooth and pleasurable. By this time I knew that it was time to stop being a student — I was ready to be a doctor.

During my intern year, RPA was the centre of my universe. I was initially attached to a very good medical unit with an excellent registrar and wise consultants who behaved like gentlemen and treated their patients and the staff as dignified human beings. Sometimes, though, the rules of engagement were less than gentlemanly.

On one occasion we needed to consult the thoracic surgeons about one of our patients with a chronic collection of infected fluid in the lung (an empyema), and so I wrote out the consultation sheet, collected the relevant X-rays, called the cardiothoracic registrar and stayed late that afternoon waiting for the surgeons to arrive. The consultant was a burly, big-framed man who swaggered into the ward on bandy legs, with a registrar and resident trailing behind at a respectful distance. I tried to introduce myself so that I could take him and his entourage to the patient but was brushed aside while he read the consultation, spoke briefly to his registrar and then turned on me.

'Here you! Did you write this?' he growled.

'Yes sir,' I responded, not really sure what was coming next.

'What's wrong with you people! Are you trying to kill this man? Well, if he has an operation you'll kill him. Do you understand that, you idiot?' He was shouting now and standing too close. I could smell him and I didn't like it.

'No sir,' came my timid response. 'I mean yes.'

Later I was angry with myself for this timidity. The French call it *l'esprit d'escalier*, 'the spirit of the stair', referring to the belated courage that sometimes surfaces after a confrontation (while going upstairs at the end of the night, for example, when it is no use at all), or suddenly thinking of a retort after the event that should have been fired back in response to an insult or accusation. I was struck dumb, as there was really nothing I felt I could say. Maybe I *was* trying to kill the poor man. Anyway, I had learned a lesson — that intimidation was an intrinsic part of the culture of cardiothoracic surgery at Prince Alfred. This bothered me because I wanted to specialise in surgery and knew I would be doing that specialty as a resident the next year and as a registrar a couple of years later.

I wasn't fearful of being bullied because I was confident I had enough steel in my spine to cope with whatever was dished up to me and look after myself, but I despised bullies and the whole concept of people using their power, position or size to intimidate their subordinates or those they perceived to be weaker or at a disadvantage. I had never had difficulty controlling my temper and was usually very respectful, but I had developed a sharp tongue that I was willing to use in defence of a colleague or myself.

Despite this and other very occasional negative experiences, I quickly found I loved my work and was rapidly becoming quite competent. The fact that several of the Prince Alfred surgeons fell into the 'hard' and 'complex' categories was not a deterrent and only made me more determined to do surgery.

Technical procedures posed few difficulties for me and I made sure I knew how to tie knots and hold surgical instruments correctly so that when the opportunity came for me to carry out my first operation, I was ready. I attached myself to one of the senior surgical registrars who took a shine to me and went out of his way to teach me how to operate. In this first year I performed fifteen appendectomies, a good number for an intern, each through a smaller and neater incision than the one before. I felt I was already on the long road to becoming a surgeon.

Each day of this Utopian existence was filled with interest and possibility. I relished the size and complexity of the hospital and the volume and variety of the work. I liked pretty much everyone I worked with, was surrounded by attractive young women, and had started earning a good income for the first time in my life. What could be better?

CHAPTER 7

Roast greyhound and a tender-faced beauty

I STARTED MY INTERN YEAR still living at home, but this only lasted a couple of weeks. The time to find my own place had come. With two new colleagues I moved into a rambling shambles of an apartment that was part of a grand but dilapidated house, surrounded by an equally grand but sadly neglected garden in Hunters Hill. Each of the bedrooms had a cast-iron fireplace suitable for burning coal, which we bought in big hessian bags.

My new flatmates, both interns, were a tall, slow-talking Queenslander, Tim Porter, and a laconic Melburnian, Dave Ellis. We were all acceptably tidy, paid our share of the costs reliably, enjoyed food and drink, respected each other's privacy, had a sense of humour and, probably most importantly, we were normal. It worked beautifully and was fun from the moment we moved in. The house and its four constituent apartments was owned by an ancient little man whom we knew simply as Mr Webb. Mr Webb, who looked, sounded and smelled as though he came straight out of *Steptoe and Son*, would call in regularly to collect the rent, which we mostly paid on time.

A disagreement developed at one point over the state of the living-room ceiling, which developed an almighty and ominous sag from the enormous weight of water it was supporting as a consequence of a leaking roof. We found that withholding rent payments increased Mr Webb's willingness to discuss the possibility of authorising the much-needed repairs. The issue was brought to a head when a well-directed thrust with a broom handle caused the central part of the ceiling to collapse into the living room, along with about half a bathtub's worth of water and filth from the roof space.

Life at Number 5 Mount Street was a hurdy-gurdy of frenetic hedonism moderated only by our obligation to be at work at an early hour almost every day, to remain there for long hours, sometimes the entire weekend, and to sleep. The place seemed to be full of people all the time. During or after parties, which seemed to initiate themselves with next to no prompting, it was not uncommon for Tim or Dave or me to wander off to bed in the hope of snatching a night's rest only to find our bed already inhabited by a person, a couple or a group of snoring drunks, whose identities were, more often than not, unknown to any of us.

We really brought these inconveniences on ourselves because we loved entertaining and regularly carried the rusting and flaking garden furniture inside so that we could seat twenty or more people for dinner at a long table. The quality of the cooking at these soirees was often suspect, but Mount Street dinner parties were not about cuisine — they were about the boisterous celebration of life and the consumption of large quantities of wine, usually in flagons or casks. Ordinary wine suitable for guzzling was cheap, although had we known better we could have purchased much better wine for a lot more money. Ignorance, as they say, is bliss — and sometimes economical too.

On one occasion we planned an ambitious Saturday afternoon barbecue for about thirty people in mid-summer with the idea of roasting a lamb on a spit in the garden. After I completed my Saturday rounds, which were compulsory for all interns and residents at that time, I drove to a wholesale butcher and picked up a good-sized animal (was it a cow?), sat it in the front seat of my car and strapped the hapless, headless carcass in with the seatbelt. There had been very little discussion and planning about just how we might propel a rotisserie, nor about the construction of a suitable fireplace. Nonetheless, a shallow rectangular hole was dug, filled with coke from Tim's winter stock for the fireplace in his room, and surrounded by a small brick wall, three bricks high at the ends. On this we rested a galvanised iron fencing pole which had been scavenged from the back fence and rammed unceremoniously through the long axis of the beast so that it hung over the pit. The coke took forever to ignite but gathered enthusiasm after it was fed a cup of petrol. We had no way of rotating the lamb but at least we were cooking, albeit very slowly.

Hungry and expectant guests and a handful of uninvited freeloaders slowly began to filter in. Time was advancing but after two or three hours we had barely managed to raise the lamb's temperature. This was in contrast to everyone else who, as the heat and humidity of the day began to exert their effects, became totally preoccupied with rehydrating and quenching their thirst. As our guests drank themselves into a stupor we were able to keep them happy with bread rolls and salad, but the lamb remained defiantly raw over the glowing coals, looking like it would take till the following summer to cook.

Finally, at about 8 p.m., when some people had gone home, perhaps still mystified about exactly what it was they had been invited to, and others were lying around the garden or inside the house in various states of consciousness, the lamb — which now resembled a small greyhound — was declared cooked. At this announcement, a roar of almost hysterical relief went up and an inebriated and ravenous throng charged the lamb. We hacked big chunks of succulent meat from the flanks and hindquarters and ate them with our hands with maniacal, almost desperate, enthusiasm.

We judged the barbecue a resounding success and at one o'clock the next morning were still feasting on warm lamb, farewelling friends and strangers and trying to restore the garden to its former neglected glory.

In addition to an outstanding group of interns and residents, 1976 saw the arrival at RPA of a very attractive and friendly group of physiotherapy residents, who also lived in the hospital and worked just as hard as the medical residents. Among them was Gail Bamford, a pretty and flirtatious girl from Cronulla, 'a tender-faced beauty' whose gentleness and warmth endeared her to everyone and who was destined to become my soul mate and the love of my life. We met at a hospital party and everything clicked, especially when we danced. Gail was a wonderful dancer, having trained for years in ballet; she had wanted to pursue a career as a ballerina but her parents vetoed her following this course and advised that a university degree would provide safer and more sustainable options. By the time we met, Gail had shelved her plan to be a professional dancer but she continued to attend ballet classes in the city. My parents, like everyone who met her, were captivated by Gail's warm smile and affectionate nature and encouraged our relationship.

The social scene at RPA in the mid-1970s was hectic and sometimes more exhausting than the work; during the period before Gail and I agreed that we would only see each other, I occasionally found myself double booked or obligated to fulfil other complex and unachievable commitments. We were once invited to attend a black tie twenty-first birthday party for Gail's close friend Jenny Mulvey (now known widely as Jenny McConnell, one of Australia's leading physiotherapists), but by some administrative glitch, I had to leave the party early to attend a ball with a nurse from the hospital. This did not particularly surprise any of my friends but it disappointed Gail and raised the hackles of Peter Mulvey, Jenny's father and a very straight-talking allergist who, like everyone else, was very fond of Gail. 'You're just a bloody mug!' he exploded as I made my apologies before sloping off. Never were truer words spoken.

By the end of the year our relationship was strong and settled (Gail's and mine more so than mine and Dr Mulvey's) and the next year we planned a trip to Port Vila, the capital of the New Hebrides, which was ruled by a French–English condominium government.

Gail also accompanied me to Dubbo where I had a three-month secondment as a surgical resident and where she worked as a physio. Her parents, delightful but conservative and concerned for the welfare of their daughter, knew me well by now but did not like the arrangement at all.

The first time I met Grace and Murray Bamford was at a dinner at their home. They were lapsed Presbyterians, Irish and initially sceptical of the intentions of a Catholic peasant from the western suburbs. But my stocks rose sharply, I was later told, when I withstood the trial by ordeal set by Dr Bamford, a kindly and astute general practitioner (and, at eighty now, still one of the best all-round doctors I have met). I had to match him joke for joke and drink for drink, all the while contributing to the family conversation, trying to use the correct cutlery and not spill food down my front. Then followed a cigar-smoking ritual after dinner which nearly caused my demise when I inhaled grandly on a cigar as fat as my forearm ('Yes, Dr Bamford, smoke 'em all the time,' I lied when offered one). It took superhuman self-control to stop myself coughing both of my lungs across the table into his lap.

By the end of 1977 my commitment to a career in surgery was total. To achieve this aim I needed to negotiate the first big barrier to surgical training: the Primary Examination, a difficult exam in the medical sciences with a high failure rate. Anatomy, pathology and physiology were examined comprehensively, necessitating (for me at least) a thorough review of these subjects if I was to have any hope of being among the thirty per cent who passed. Successfully sitting the Primary was an absolute requirement before a resident could be selected for advanced surgical training.

Work was very busy, particularly during my rotation in cardiothoracic surgery, the character-building exercise for which I had been preparing mentally since my intern year. Sister Soutar, who was in charge of the ward, was an uncompromising, birdlike little creature, almost impossible to please, who fed on residents and registrars after she terrorised them into submission. Mirroring this reign of terror on the medical side were the surgeons, one of whom, my boss Sandy Grant, conducted his ward round at 7 a.m. each day. It was the task of the resident to have examined and reviewed all the patients — chest, abdomen, legs (to exclude clots in the calf veins), temperature, blood pressure, urine output, X-ray results — and to know the results of all blood tests before the round. In particular, patients who had had heart valve replacements very often needed to be treated with a blood-thinning tablet called Warfarin to prevent clot formation around the valve. Warfarin changes the blood's clotting time and this was measured by a test called the Prothrombin Index (PI). The cardiothoracic resident's job was to know the PI of each of the relevant patients so that when it reached the therapeutic range (the level that confirmed that the drug dose was correct and that it was doing its job), the patient could go home.

I was determined to make a good impression during this three-month attachment and I worked very hard at being on top of things. I rode a pushbike to work each day and made sure that I arrived early enough to have a shower, change and get to the ward by 6 a.m. It was very difficult to be on the ward before Sister Soutar but occasionally I fluked that little victory. The cardiothoracic service was a superbly organised and highly professional unit and, despite the undercurrent of intimidation and episodes of overt bullying that took place, I developed deep respect for the clinical skill of the surgeons and their disciplined work ethic. I knew, however, that I did not want to be like them.

Roast greyhound and a tender-faced beauty

*

During our early resident years inter-hospital sport was still very popular and RPA, because of its size and large number of residents, was always very competitive. Hospital rugby was popular and from time to time the teams boasted ex-first grade and even international players.

Preparation for the short inter-hospital competition was relatively low key, with some players given to interrupting their training for a smoke, but the games were played with a passion and commitment befitting a much higher level of competition. Most players were willing but not as fit as they were in their younger days so there was always a possibility that injuries, both mild and serious, could occur.

On one occasion the Prince Alfred team, of which I was a member, played a trial match on the St John's College football ground, which lies between the beautiful sandstone college building and the Faculty of Veterinary Science buildings of Sydney University. Tragedy struck when a scrum collapsed and one of the PA front rowers, Alan Farrell — a close friend since the time we started medical school — was rendered quadriplegic. He cried out in anguish from the bottom of the heap of bodies, unable to move his limbs and, no doubt, terrified.

Alan was saved by the presence of mind of those immediately around him, particularly Bob Hampshire (an outstanding player himself and later to become a well-known Sydney psychiatrist) and Bill Patrick, a surgical registrar at the time. Together they held Alan's head completely still and averted a catastrophe. The injury saw the end of hospital football but fortunately, the ending was a happy one. Alan was transferred to the spinal unit at Royal North Shore Hospital where he remained in a quadriplegic state for six weeks. Slowly, and to the relief of his concerned but serene wife, Tina, and many friends, he began to recover and later went on to have an operation to fuse some of the bones in his neck. With enormous effort and determination he returned to full activity, continuing to be a fearless skier and even taking up kayaking, with only a few minor deficits in his functioning. This was, in every way, a miraculous and courageous recovery.

As 1978 unfolded the prospects for very significant life changes loomed large. I planned to sit the Primary in March, so with a group of friends from PA — including Butch, Lawrie, Tim and Dave Little — travelled to Melbourne to undertake an intensive study course to prepare for the exam. We lived with other aspiring young surgeons from around the country in International House, one of Melbourne University's residential colleges, on a beautiful tree-lined avenue in Parkville. This was a time of intense study combined with rampant social regression, demonstrated by a level of adolescent behaviour that would have been an embarrassment to most boarding schools. In short it was the best fun we had experienced since elective term, and it was a good thing for all when our six weeks in Melbourne ended and we returned to our various cities to sit the exam. The Primary was notoriously difficult and sometimes barely a third of those sitting passed. I felt reasonably confident of passing at the end of these months of study and disciplined preparation and just wanted it to be over.

Roast greyhound and a tender-faced beauty

Gail and I were closely bound by this time. I was successful in the exam and went to work soon after as a locum in her father's general practice, in order to save money for our planned travels overseas later that year. I also worked with the Radio Doctor Service, which provided after-hours emergency cover for general practices across Sydney. This was necessary but soul-destroying work, which made use of two-way radios carried in the car with a magnetised aerial slapped on the roof. It was usual for each doctor on call to cover a particular part of the metropolitan area during the long overnight shifts; all too often the calls were from poverty-stricken supplicants with the chronic diseases of age, abject self-neglect and profound social isolation. Frequently there would be calls from narcotic-addicted patients seeking their nightly pethidine injection, usually supported by a letter written years before on a now-crumpled, torn, dirty or stained piece of paper by some doctor or other certifying that Mr or Mrs X suffered from chronic and intractable pain and required regular injections of narcotic and requesting that whoever read the letter might kindly provide the necessary medication. These pathetic individuals, mostly living in squalid surroundings, troubled me deeply. I could not bring myself to give an injection that fed the addiction, but in giving a small dose of saline and a couple of Valium tablets I felt I was betraying the hapless patient and their hopeless circumstances.

I couldn't wait to finish my stint as a radio doctor but I desperately needed to save for the marvellous adventure on which Gail and I were about to embark. Gail worked as a physiotherapist and was for a time employed by an orthopaedic surgeon who had an enormous practice which, along with conventional surgery, involved admitting large numbers of patients with what were alleged to be work-related back injuries to a hospital in which he held a financial interest and implementing weeks of bed rest and traction for their complaint. Gail hated this work and, to no one's surprise, the specialist was struck off the medical register some years later.

By May, and again to the disapproval of her parents, Gail and I were ready to set off for the rest of the year on a trip that would be the making of our relationship. I had resigned from Prince Alfred and, instead of applying for a surgical training position, decided to take what a number of friends and colleagues described as a foolhardy gamble: returning to Europe to see more of the world and absorb a little more cultural enlightenment.

Gail's dad shared his view of our plans with me. 'I don't believe that you should have the honeymoon before the wedding,' he remarked, but not without warmth in his voice and with a subtext that read, 'just make sure you look after my precious daughter'.

Our parents farewelled us at the airport in a gesture of familial bipartisanship; already the foundations of a strong friendship between the two families had been established.

CHAPTER 8

Naked in Paris

AT THE HEIGHT OF EUROPE'S summer we visited Gail's uncle, aunt and grandmother in the village of Malahide, just north of Dublin. The prospect of a visitation by a favourite niece travelling with a Catholic boyfriend clearly posed a few difficulties for these charming folk, who were more concerned about the likelihood of alienating Gail's elderly and very conservative grandmother, known as Mamma, than having their own Presbyterian feathers ruffled.

Malahide is a beautiful little village on the coast and Gail's relatives, Hugh and Clonagh Burrows, live in a large and comfortable home that still boasts a splendid garden. Before our arrival I had read a comprehensive little monograph on Irish history along with the Leon Uris novel *Trinity*, which explores the period of the Irish uprising with undisguised bias and the typical Uris combination of drama, heroism and romance played out with broad-brush historical accuracy. As our plane descended towards Shannon Airport across a patchwork of verdant pastures I felt an unusual combination of comfort and excitement — oddly as though I was coming home.

I was unsure of the origin of these emotions although, during my student days, I had read some of Carl Jung's work and I liked his theory about the collective unconscious and the thought that I had (within my psyche or my soul or both) an inherited blueprint of experiences and responses which had been passed between individuals and across tribes and generations for hundreds of years. In fact, my Irish roots were real and not all that distant since my great-great-grandfather, James O'Brien, had left County Cavan in 1850 in the hope of finding a new life, and sailed to Australia on a ship called the *Anglia* as a lone twenty-one-year-old, a part of the great Irish diaspora that saw two million Irish citizens emigrate during the years of the famine and immediately after. He travelled to Tamworth and must have been industrious because although he only worked as a farm labourer, within a few years he had saved the necessary money to pay for the passage of his parents, three brothers and a sister, who in 1856 arrived in Sydney on a ship called *The Lloyds*. They all moved to Gunnedah where they successfully farmed the land they selected in that region.

In Dublin the problem of Gail's Catholic boyfriend was solved by accommodating him in a borrowed caravan parked next to the house — for the purposes of sleeping only, a decision having been made that he was otherwise welcome to enjoy all the privileges of a normal guest, that is, the opportunity to shower and take all meals inside the main house. Gail and I laughed about this arrangement and, in truth, Hugh and Clonagh were remarkably hospitable and kind, even expressing their embarrassment at the need to house me in the caravan in order to satisfy Mamma's traditional morals. It mattered not in the slightest to me. I was made welcome in every other way and was thrilled to be there.

Hugh was a passionate sailor and, pleased to have extra crew on his yacht, took Gail and me sailing on the Irish Sea one bitterly cold summer's day. The weather was horrendous and we came home wet through and utterly freezing. Under my sweater and jeans I had worn the thermal underwear that I planned to use later in the year when we were skiing. These I hung over the clothesline after we returned home late in the afternoon and had warmed up with a couple of hot whiskies, the perfect recovery drink: a measure of Irish whiskey, lemon, a sugar cube and a couple of cloves in boiling water — magic! Next morning, Mamma saw my long underwear on the line and, a little bemused, asked Gail if it was common for Australian men to wear long underwear in the summertime. Perhaps she was concerned that her granddaughter was travelling in the company of some namby-pamby Catholic weakling who couldn't cope with a little sailing on a bracing Irish July day.

We moved on from Ireland to Paris where we spent the next six weeks totally immersed in all things French. We undertook a course that was described as a fine arts course but really amounted to an intensive introduction to French culture, run by a small organisation which proudly called itself the Paris American Academy.

Located on the Left Bank in the Rue des Ursulines, a little street off the Rue St Jacques, the Academy attracted well-heeled Francophilic divorcees, retirees and college undergraduates, mainly from New York and Los Angeles, hoping to soak up a big dose of 'Parisiana' during the American summer holidays and have some of their work accredited to their degree.

Gail and I were accommodated in a run-down one-bedroom apartment on the Boulevard Raspail, in the centre of the trendy and exciting Montparnasse district. Like me, Gail had visited Paris once before and we were both now thrilled to be living in our favourite European city.

Each morning began with a two-hour lesson in French language, followed by another two hours of history or art history. The afternoons were spent on elective subjects — painting and photography for me, ballet and cooking for Gail. At night we explored the city, eating out with others doing the course, or ate at home — a simple meal of food purchased from one or more of the numerous small shops that we passed on our way back from classes. France is said to be a nation of shopkeepers and, at that time, much of Paris bore out this generalisation. We would also often stop on the way home at one or other little bar and have a kir: a mixture of crème de cassis and cheap dry white wine. Still after thirty years, it is one of our favourite aperitifs.

On weekends there were excursions to places of interest in Paris or visits to more distant locations like Chartres, Caen and Mont Saint Michel, as well as a grand tour of the magnificent chateaux of the Loire Valley. We all travelled in a bus for these excursions and wonderful bonds of friendship and camaraderie developed in the group of about thirty people. We became friendly with a retired NASA engineer named Roly Bliss and his wife, Louisa. Roly and I would spend many of our free afternoons walking the streets with our art supplies until we found a suitable location and then set up and spend hours drawing and painting street scenes, buildings or monuments. Roly loved to finish these sessions together with a couple of glasses of red wine, which he called 'von rouge' when ordering.

Those in our group who chose painting as an elective were obliged to attend life drawing classes twice a week. To my disappointment our model on each occasion was a mournful-looking woman of late middle age who appeared badly in need of a bath and a decent meal — and who no doubt also needed the small amount of money paid to models. She stood naked on a low table in the centre of our atelier next to a one-bar radiator, trying to warm herself while a dozen or so novice artists sat at their easels sketching away, some clumsily and some with remarkable expertise.

Despite all the drawing I had done as a boy, my efforts were little more than mediocre. The drawings I produced were in proportion but static and flat, lacking life and volume. Nonetheless, I felt thoroughly contented — sitting in a studio in Paris, drawing and painting from life, light years from Regents Park, my father's troubles and the poor wretches calling for their nightly pethidine fix.

If Paris was a paradise of possibilities for those inclined to painting and sketching, it was an equivalent Utopia for photographers, and I revelled in the opportunity to record my impressions with Kodak Tri-X film and to spend the afternoons developing and printing black and white images of Parisian street life. Gail equally enjoyed her unfettered freedom to participate in ballet and cooking classes. It was, in every way, a dream holiday and happily the antithesis of our recent years of rigorously disciplined study and clinical work.

We have returned to Paris on a number of occasions since then, each time visiting familiar quarters and discovering new and fascinating spots, but I still feel that we have barely scratched the surface. To engage with Paris fully, fluency in French is useful but not obligatory. It is probably more important that one is prepared to experience some of the grime and danger that characterises the older and more authentic quarters. Recent excellent books by Andrew Hussey (*Paris: The Secret History*) and Edmund White (*The Flaneur*) are wonderful aids to the appreciation of the complex history and geography of this wondrous metropolis. The latter book suffers from White's preoccupation with the development of gay culture, but both writers describe a Paris smouldering with erotic and intellectual energy, made for the aimless but interested stroller (the *flaneur*) who wanders the ancient backstreets and alleys taking in the sensual delights of the city, perhaps with detachment but more than likely ever ready for engagement — a visit to a favourite café or bar or gallery, or an encounter in a fondly remembered brothel or with an old lover.

I wrote home regularly and was always delighted to receive return aerograms from Mum and Dad and friends, who were all carrying on comfortably with their lives. To my relief Dad was enjoying an extended period of mental peace.

We travelled around Europe in a little Renault Six, which we spotted on the street one day displaying a prominent 'For Sale' sign on the front and back windows. I wrote my name and address on each side and, sure enough, next day I was visited by the car's owner, Albert Armand, a fast-talking Moroccan who was happy to exchange the car and its papers for the equivalent of about A$200. This was the beginning of a bureaucratic headache that would curse us and determine our actions for most of the next six months.

The car itself was exactly what we needed. It had a quirky gear lever that projected from the dashboard but it was mechanically sound and consumed almost no petrol. Beyond a speed of 90 kilometres per hour the Renault was prone to anxiety attacks and this nervousness seemed readily to transfer itself to the driver, so Gail and I decided that we would drive no faster than that speed and happily relegated ourselves to the shoulder of the autoroute or secondary roads. We preferred using secondary roads anyway because they offered more scenic and leisurely driving, and paying autoroute tolls would take bigger bites from our budget than we were prepared to sustain. The problem with the car was that it was registered with tourist numberplates in Belgium. Further, the registration certificate, called the *carte grise* (grey card), carried the name Louis Toujon, the former owner, not Armand from whom we bought the car. We had no proof therefore that the car was ours; the Belgian tourist registration had lapsed and we still wanted to drive around the Continent for six months, crossing customs and immigration checkpoints at every border. In addition we needed to sell the car at the end of our stay because the money we hoped to recoup was integral to our budget. Clearly we would have to get the vehicle re-registered, but what would be a straightforward exercise in Sydney became a complicated game of snakes and ladders, made especially difficult by the fact that it had to be conducted in French. At the end of our Parisian sojourn we decided to drive back to Belgium and throw ourselves on the mercy of the Belgian authorities in the hope that, in their charitable wisdom, they would help us out of our difficulties.

This hope proved to be one of the more extreme examples of futile optimism that I had ever conjured. The Belgian police proved as adept as the French at the Gallic shrug of indifference, palms upturned, bottom lip pushed forward as if to say 'Help you? I might if I gave a damn.' We were instructed that our best option would be to take the car back to France and try to get together the necessary paperwork to have it registered in our name. Like so many other near-impossible tasks, this made all the sense in the world. We hunted down the appropriate piece of paper, called a *certificat du vent* (a certificate of sale), filled it in with our details and sent it to Louis Toujon at an address in Canada asking that he add his details and return it to us, care of the American Express office in Nice, with all haste. Toujon was an academic from Toronto who had purchased and used the car during a six-month sabbatical in Brussels. We were confident that, if he ever received our letter, he would be responsive to our plight.

We continued on our way feeling like fugitives and experienced a sense of impending doom mixed with nervous guilt at each border crossing. The attitude of customs officers ranged from obsessive officiousness to laissez faire indifference, but our papers were never scrutinised closely enough for anything out of order to be detected.

We toured the length of Italy and Greece and back again, and spent two weeks exploring the Italian and French Riviera, stopping every few days at the American Express office in Nice to check for a response from Toujon. As the days passed and nothing arrived we sensed that our hopes would not be realised and that we had no choice but to get on with our travels.

As we drove out of Nice for the last time, feeling empty and uncertain, Gail stopped the car outside the American Express office, double-parked with the motor running as I went inside one last time. To our combined amazement and joy the much hoped-for letter from Louis Toujon was waiting to be picked up. Inside was an apologetic note from Louis (good old Louis!) sympathising with our predicament; more importantly, he had enclosed the signed *certificat du vent*, indicating that he had sold the vehicle directly to us.

We now had to take this certificate to the Prefecture of Police in order to obtain a *carte grise* showing that we were the registered owners. That document would allow us to re-register the car in France and obtain standard black French numberplates.

But the fates would not permit this odyssey to end yet, as we soon learned that the car did not comply with French regulations. We needed to exchange the standard white headlights used in Belgium for the yellow lights required in France and purchase a safety triangle, which was compulsory emergency equipment in all cars in France. These minor matters were easily sorted out in a garage in Paris but, in the process, it became apparent that the car carried a number of significant defects rendering it both unroadworthy and unregisterable. The car failed its inspection, which was carried out by an unsympathetic stony-faced little man, who was deaf to our entreaties, and Gail's frustrated and uncharacteristic observation that he was a *petite merde*, in a desolate and freezing town just outside of Paris called Chilly-Mazarin. (Gail and I still say 'Chilly-Mazarin' to each other on bitterly cold days.)

Further repairs were carried out and then we had to confront the same inspector again. We pulled our coat collars up and our hats down in the hope of avoiding recognition but perhaps even this was unnecessary, since our man was not given to eye contact and offered only a minimum of grunted conversation. The little Renault sailed through the inspection with flying colours and in doing so avoided the Fawlty Towers-like thrashing with a tree branch that I had planned for it if we came up short again.

While our transport tribulations were being addressed we were back living in Paris, this time with Steve and Vivi, a couple we had met in Greece. Steve was English, Vivi French, and they generously invited us to stay a while in their little apartment. During this visit, the iconic Belgian singer Jacques Brel, a long-time favourite of mine, sadly died of lung cancer. We honoured his passing with an appropriate wake, and late in the evening, after many toasts, Brel music gave way to the Rolling Stones and we danced till the early hours.

Our eight months of travel through Europe was a time of shared adventure, happiness and education, but I disappointed Gail as the trip ended when I failed to ask her to marry me. I had no doubt about my love for her but I was unready to make the final and permanent commitment that was necessary to guarantee a happy and successful marriage.

We decided to follow separate paths for a time so Gail stayed on in London to pursue her dancing while I returned to Sydney to take up a position as a junior surgical registrar, with the hope of securing a surgical training post at the end of the year. The year away from Prince Alfred and months of travelling combined to reinvigorate my desire to continue my training and return to a settled life.

CHAPTER 9

Darwin and a Strauss waltz

PART OF MY FIRST YEAR BACK involved a secondment to Darwin Hospital (later to become Royal Darwin), which at that time consisted of a cluster of single-storey buildings on a grassy peninsula overlooking the beach, not far from the centre of town. I was still in my fourth year from graduation and relatively junior in terms of training and experience. Before going to Darwin I spent six months as the junior registrar on the professorial surgical unit at Prince Alfred; I was the last registrar of soon-to-retire Professor Sir John Loewenthal, one of the giants of surgery in Australia and an immensely important figure at Royal Prince Alfred and Sydney University. Loewenthal had built powerful and productive departments of surgery in both institutions, had the ear of politicians and had been unchallenged as a leader and patriarch for decades.

The six months I spent with Loewenthal and the other academic surgeons in the professorial unit were brilliant in every way. I took my work very seriously and was a diligent registrar.

Loewenthal treated me with fatherly approval and generosity. My work involved mainly vascular and transplantation surgery, at which I became capable, and I found both interesting and fun. I was looking forward to the opportunity of putting into practice some of the new skills I had learned and hoped I would cope well with the surprises and bizarre challenges that Darwin regularly produced. A friend and colleague, Brian McCaughan, had been there two years ahead of me and had heroically operated on the minced liver of a car-accident victim, saving the patient, despite never having performed a liver operation before.

It was not long before I collected my own procession of battered victims — run over by speedboat propellers, gored by buffalos, flattened by speeding vehicles of every description, sometimes having fallen from the back of a truck or car and then receiving a double dose as the driver backed up to see who fell out.

Darwin was an odd place at that time and seemed to be populated by a funny mix of people, some trying to escape from something, others trying to sneak into the country: libertines, dilettantes, alcoholics, potheads, sociopaths and the group to which I belonged, outsiders transplanted from cities all over the continent who were working there temporarily and trying to decide which of the other groups they would join. The culture was a mixture of tropical bohemian, relaxed civility, boofheaded, blokey Australiana and Wild West lawlessness.

The hospital buildings, generously surrounded by lawn, bougainvillea, oleander and palm trees, were dated but well maintained, airy and readily open to the elements. The local Indigenous people frequently gathered in shaded areas on the grass to eat and talk, often with their relatives who were patients in the hospital. Some had exotic names like Mango Chutney, Electric Motor and Billy Crocodile. One older man, who carried the grand appellation Captain Bishop Number One Marango, once came to visit one of his seven children who were conveniently, logically and, presumably, lovingly named Barramundi Number One, Barramundi Number Two, Barramundi Number Three, and so on.

The surgeons for whom I worked were a strange mix also. They included a laid-back yet competent Victorian named Jon Wardell, who was teacher and friend to each of the Prince Alfred registrars. Living next door to Wardell and his family, eating, drinking, travelling and camping with him and helping him tend his tropical plants, were among my most pleasurable experiences during my Darwin secondment. There was also an amusing and eccentric little Indian surgeon who, in quite the reverse of the way surgical training normally works, constantly expressed his keenness to learn as much as he could from the visiting registrars and who also proudly claimed he could do a thousand push-ups. No doubt he felt that it was a handy skill for a surgeon to have. The senior man was a beefy Englishman who was completely bald, had a prominent harelip and was cursed with a bad stammer that caused his speech to deliver itself in a fusillade of explosive staccato. He was the epitome of bluff and bluster yet had a kindly streak and always encouraged the registrars to 'have a go', especially when it saved him coming in late at night. Finally, there was an unpopular surgeon who specialised in using a microscope to inspect children's ears under general anaesthetic and releasing tongue-ties, which seemed to occur in epidemic numbers among the young children of white people with health insurance in Darwin.

This particular surgeon, in an act that reflected either dreadfully poor judgement or suicidal tendencies or both, decided to carry out an operating list on a day very close to Christmas, when the other surgeons had decided to postpone their operating so that the staff could have a day off and enjoy a party. While a score or more of Darwin's children were having their tongues freed up or ears examined, a disgruntled group of technicians and orderlies decided to tap dance heavily across the top of the doctor's car from front to back, claiming that the damage was due to a freak hailstorm which came and went in minutes, and then proceeded to fill his briefcase with sugar.

The outraged surgeon lodged an immediate complaint with the hospital's superintendent, who summoned the alleged culprits to his office for interrogation. There was very little risk that any wrongdoing would be proven because, as luck would have it, no witnesses chose to come forward and the group of suspects was bent on convincing the superintendent that the surgeon in question had been stealing the hospital's sugar for years and that they had finally caught him and should be congratulated. In the absence of evidence to the contrary this must have seemed like a plausible enough story and the perpetrators were exonerated.

One of the duties of the Prince Alfred registrar was to fly to the town of Gove, situated several hundred kilometres to the east of Darwin, near the Gulf of Carpentaria. The Gove visit involved conducting an outpatient clinic, identifying patients who needed surgical treatment and then scheduling their operations. Those operations would be undertaken weeks or months later, possibly by the next registrar. After the clinic the registrar, who was treated like a visiting dignitary for the day and made to feel very important, would have lunch and then carry out the operations booked for him, more than likely months before, by his predecessor.

I had no idea at all about what would confront me. Upon my arrival I was greeted by a hospital car and a good deal of bowing and scraping, which although it embarrassed me I quite liked. They did everything but call me 'Bwana' as I was conducted to the hospital, directed to the outpatient department and asked what I would like to have for lunch in the most solicitous and deferential fashion.

I still didn't know what was on the operating list and felt a combination of excitement and nervousness at the prospect of being the surgeon in charge of a number of cases. The schedule in outpatients involved seeing a small cohort of relatively routine surgical patients with straightforward problems, some requiring an operation (which I duly arranged) and others requiring reassurance or an additional visit for review in a few weeks. I asked a number of times during the clinic if I could see the operating list and eventually it was produced. I read the list of names, ages and planned procedures with a combination of relief and anxiety. First, a middle-aged man with an inguinal hernia, followed by a middle-aged woman with varicose veins in one leg, and finally a two-year-old boy with an undescended testicle. A what? Not only had I never performed an operation for an undescended testis, I had never even seen one done! I knew that undescended testes were at high risk of turning malignant, so it was a necessary procedure.

I perused the operating list, trying to look as casual as I could, then turned to the sister-in-charge and asked in a nonchalant fashion whether or not there was a medical library in the hospital, implying that instead of just sitting around waiting to start work I could read a little, purely to pass the time. I was told 'yes, of course', so as soon as she left, I grabbed my plate of egg sandwiches and walked very quickly and, with a rising sense of urgency, directly to the library. I scrambled through the shelves and soon found what I was after — a textbook on operative surgery, although it was about sixty years old and missing a lot of pages. Thumbing through furiously I came to the relevant section and made notes as I read. My challenge was to find the pea-sized testicle in the boy's groin then to deliver it with an adequate blood supply to his scrotum. I knew that this would be tricky and the last thing that I wanted to do was harm the little patient, whom I had not yet met. So I was mightily relieved when I found a subsection entitled 'Staged Procedures', which described what should be done if the testis could not be delivered to its rightful position in the scrotum in one operation.

All of this took much longer than I had anticipated and, as I went over and over the operative diagrams, I was interrupted by a knock on the door and a call from the operating theatres that the first patient was on the table and the anaesthetist was ready. Anxious not to appear an incompetent fool (even though I might have been one) I resisted the temptation to bring the textbook to the theatre.

The first two cases went well. I was adept at hernia repair and varicose vein procedures, and this seemed to put the anaesthetist into a good mood. He had the placid, phlegmatic manner of someone who had been competently plying his trade for years, contributing nothing more and nothing less than what was required to get the job done and no doubt he had witnessed every type of error, misjudgement and act of clumsy ineptitude that young surgeons were capable of enacting. His bone-dry sense of humour and general disinterest made me comfortable and confident that I should simply go about my task as well as I could and not try to convince him that I was better than I was.

Midway through the case of the undescended testicle I found myself confused about the anatomy and worried that I might have compromised the blood supply to my patient's little gonad, so I stopped momentarily to consider the options. My anaesthetist colleague had been monosyllabic at best throughout the list but he now leaned over the drapes and asked, 'Not sure what to do, son?'

'Just thinking,' I replied, my mind racing as I tried to recall the textbook diagrams.

'Tell you what I'd do,' he continued.

'Yes?' came my response, almost pleading.

'I'd use a nine iron.' He chuckled quietly, turned back to his equipment and twiddled a couple of knobs.

I released a big sigh (a truckload of anxiety rose into air), thanked him for his advice and decided that the situation clearly warranted a staged procedure. Brilliant! After confirming to my satisfaction that the testicle was viable I tucked it into the top of the scrotum and retreated as expeditiously and elegantly as I could, all the while nodding and murmuring to myself, but really for the benefit of those watching (not one of whom was I fooling) — things like, 'yes, that's good, very good. Yes I'm happy with that.' I closed the wound neatly and retired to the tearoom to enjoy a much-needed cup of tea.

I finished the operating session pleased that I had at least fulfilled the first commandment of the Hippocratic Oath — 'First do no harm'. At least I hoped I hadn't done any harm.

The six-month secondment to Darwin proved to be yet another watershed period of growth and learning. Towards the end of my tenure I learned that my application for a surgical training position at RPA had been successful. More importantly, during this time, my hesitancy and caution about marriage slowly dissipated, like a veil being lifted, and I finally saw with crystal clarity how lucky I was to have met and become romantically involved with Gail. She was far too pretty and smart to wait forever, so I asked her to marry me and we agreed that 16 February 1980 would be a suitable day. Our parents were as relieved as they were elated. Minor hurdles needed to be negotiated but Gail and her parents graciously consented to have the wedding celebrated by a Catholic priest. My suggestion was that Father Les Cashen (who had formerly been appointed to St Patrick's Cathedral at Parramatta and was chaplain of the Marist Brothers during my school days, and was now rector of St John's College at Sydney University) might be an ideal celebrant. According to the rules of the Church, it was necessary for Gail and me — Gail in particular — to attend instructional sessions aimed at educating the non-Catholic partner in the fundamentals of the Catholic faith and establishing an agreement (which was non-binding in practical terms) that any children we might have would be brought up Catholic. This, of course, was an issue entirely for the parents and I was at pains to thank Gail for her consideration and to reassure her, from my point of view, that an obligation on her part was neither assumed nor implied. I was not at all concerned that she would find Les Cashen's advice and instruction offensive, intimidating or incomprehensible.

At our first meeting Les asked whether or not we had had dinner and when I replied in the negative he explained that he had already eaten and therefore would be drinking a glass of port while we might find sherry more appropriate. Neither of us was a fan of sherry but, in the absence of a kir, it proved a very satisfactory aperitif and icebreaker.

Twenty years later, with three children baptised Catholic and the two boys attending a Catholic school, Gail decided to convert to Catholicism quite of her own accord, in an act of unselfish love which would allow her to participate in religious activities with the family more closely.

I was aware that Gail's parents had some reservations about the strongly Catholic flavour of the ceremony they were about to fund so, rather than have the service in a church, we decided that the Great Hall at Sydney University would provide a grand piece of neutral territory. It suited the occasion magnificently and when Gail and her father walked into the Hall and down the aisle as Offenbach's beautiful 'Barcarolle' rang out from the grand organ, she was the apotheosis of 'graceful femininity'.

The only minor disappointment was my own performance in the bridal waltz, a quirky version of the 'Blue Danube' performed by a group called The Stanza Trio; despite numerous practices and the fact that I was a fair dancer anyway, I found it impossible to detect any three-four time. Fortunately my shuffling effort went unnoticed as my parents staged what must have been one of the best Strauss waltzes ever performed in the Union Refectory. Before long the dance floor was full and it remained that way all night.

Because we had not long returned from our European travels, we decided on a relatively simple honeymoon and spent a week in Hong Kong followed by a week in Sydney learning to scuba dive. A week proved to be more than enough in Hong Kong. We went with a shopping list as everyone did in those days and presumably still does — watches, cameras and electrical goods for ourselves, family and those friends with gall enough to ask. Rather than shopping around, carefully researching prices and comparing them from shop to shop, I became a little over-excited and, confident I was being both an astute shopper and an effective haggler, bought everything I planned to buy on the first day. Then, to Gail's bewilderment and very occasional impatience, I spent the subsequent days going from place to place trying to confirm that I had gotten a good deal on each item (which I almost never had!).

In retrospect I cannot imagine what life might have been like if I had not married Gail. Our three decades together have made me a better person, and with her I know I am a good husband and father.

CHAPTER 10

Trainee surgeon and proud father

BEFORE OUR WEDDING my position as an accredited surgical trainee had commenced and I found myself allocated for the first six months of the year to cardiothoracic surgery. Again I was determined to work hard, learn as much as I could and avoid finding myself on the wrong side of the intensely choleric senior surgeons. By this stage my confidence had grown and a tendency to irreverence surfaced more frequently than during my previous stints with the cardiothoracic team.

Great emphasis was placed on cleanliness and sterility in the operating theatre suite and my bosses, in their usual threatening way, took every opportunity to impress upon the staff the need for hand washing and all other aspects of infection control. I was surprised therefore one day to be standing next to Mr Grant at the scrub sink outside the operating theatres and to see that he was washing with a bandaid on his hand. A resident and a student stood on the other side of him also scrubbing and so I thought I would risk an inquiry. 'What have you got under that bandaid,

Mr Grant?' I asked as I lathered my hands and forearms with antiseptic foam. Sandy, considerably taller than I, looked down at me from his height and responded, 'Shut up, you!' I waited a minute or two and then tried to move the conversation along by asking in a relaxed chatty tone, 'Mr Grant, did you see that article in the newspaper that said if all Australian men stood side by side with their penises on their heads, they'd all be the same height?' The resident and student exploded with muffled laughter into their masks as Sandy, nonplussed and caught off balance, did a double take and growled back, 'I thought I told you to shut up!' 'Yes, Mr Grant,' I responded, sounding as compliant and respectful as I could. His mood was surprisingly good throughout the case that followed and I still suspect that inside his mask he had smiled.

In fairness, I enjoyed being Sandy Grant's registrar and there was much to admire about him, but my favourite was Doug Baird, the unit head. Doug was smooth, narcissistic, meticulous in everything he did, charming and generally even-tempered but, like his partners, he was also a demanding perfectionist who on occasions was given to pettiness and pedantic outbursts. He was generous to me and showed me continuous encouragement, inviting me to his office from time to time to discuss my progress and to recommend that, if I were to consider a career in cardiac surgery, he would like to assist and support me. I was keen to keep my options open at the time but was deeply thankful and honoured that I had his confidence and friendship. Sadly, Doug died of liver cancer when he was only fifty-six, when my career in head and neck surgery was well established. His vision and leadership are still missed at RPA. Before his death, our paths would regularly cross at a private hospital in which we both worked. He would go out of his way to show interest in whatever operation I was doing and to make complimentary remarks about my handling of the technical aspects of the case.

Training in general surgery involved a four-year program broken into eight terms of six months, with the aim of covering the various sub-specialties of general surgery in sufficient depth to achieve technical competence, sound judgement, and a thorough knowledge of surgical diseases and how to investigate and manage them, along with the ability to manage trauma and critically ill patients.

Both the requirements of the training program and the service obligations of the hospital necessitated one or more six-month secondment terms away from the hospital, usually in a rural area or possibly in Darwin or New Guinea. Despite the hospital's reputation for providing outstanding surgical training, the program at that time was poorly organised. Instead of each registrar having a sequence of terms mapped out at the beginning of their four years of training to be sure that all specialties were covered and to allow for the pursuit of a particular interest, decisions about which term an individual registrar would do next were made on an ad hoc basis. Nonetheless, the volume and complexity of work that came to Prince Alfred and its affiliated hospitals, along with the quality of surgeons who provided the teaching, guaranteed that a very high standard of surgeon was produced. Younger consultants and senior registrars continued to contribute to the teaching of trainees who were constantly quizzed and progressively — sometimes firmly — moulded into shape.

My six-month stint in cardiothoracic surgery was followed by two general surgical terms at Prince Alfred, which involved working with two of the more complicated and difficult individuals on the staff. I had problems with one in particular, whose tendency to mean-spirited surliness and bullying rubbed me completely the wrong way. I made sure that I stood my ground at each episode of conflict but these were intermittent and short-lived; my working environment was otherwise harmonious and enjoyable.

During the first year of my surgical training I made my first tentative steps into the world of clinical research. I carried out a small retrospective study of a group of patients with a disease called bullous emphysema, which affects the lungs. People with this disease develop cysts, or bullae, which can become very large and effectively replace normal lung tissue with non-functioning air cavities, incapable of contributing to the oxygenation of blood. Occasionally these cysts also burst, leading to the collapse of the lung. One of the treatments of bullous emphysema is surgical removal of the lung cysts, which allows the compressed and displaced lung to expand and function properly. The aim of the study was to examine the benefit of this surgical intervention by measuring lung function before and after the operation. The problem I had was that not all patients had their lung function recorded properly before surgery and a number had not had any measurement after surgery either. With a good deal of encouragement but very little direct supervision and help from the consultants who actually treated the patients, I did my best to chase up the results and to organise breathing tests for the more recently treated patients.

Strictly speaking I was not at all confident that the information that I was collecting was reliable nor that the conclusions from the study were sound. Nonetheless, I pressed on: I dragged all the data together, along with some before and after X-rays, tabulated the results, put together a plausible story that I could present at a surgical meeting, and then had it published in *The Australian and New Zealand Journal of Surgery*. It was my first ever publication and, although aspects of the methodology would not really stand up to close scrutiny today, I was proud to have completed the project and to have a publication with my name on it.

This exercise taught me the importance of keeping accurate data and I determined right then that, irrespective of the specialty in which I would finally work, I would develop a database which would allow me to collect all the clinical and pathological information on my patients and conduct careful follow-up, so that I could analyse and report it and compare my treatment results with those described in the medical literature. I could envisage no other way of guaranteeing to myself and my patients that my work was absolutely first class and the equal of anywhere in the world.

In the first two years of my training I had the opportunity to work with the hospital's senior surgeon, who had a large thyroid practice, and the principal head and neck surgeon. They both treated me well although their personalities were quite different; in fact the unit was an unhappy marriage of polar opposites and they disliked each other intensely — one gruff, conservative, fastidious but kindly, the other eccentric, full of caprices and with a quirky, even bizarre, sense of humour. Importantly, both were very good surgeons and although neither was a natural teacher, I learned a great deal from them both and was stimulated to consider pursuing the relatively new and ill-defined specialty of head and neck surgery.

I was scheduled to have a term away from the hospital and Rabaul in Papua New Guinea was the nominated destination. However, around this time, Gail learned that she was pregnant and the safer option was clearly to stay in Australia, so we opted for six months in Wollongong rather than New Guinea. I was anxious not to leave my pregnant wife, nor to take her to the wilds and uncertainties of life in Rabaul. My desire to stay in Australia for what I thought were sound reasons caused some annoyance to a couple of the senior surgeons, who griped among themselves that I should do as I was being told but they did not make their views known to me.

One of the attractions of being at Wollongong Hospital during this important time was that my sister Carmel was the nurse in charge of the main nursery and we were all looking forward to her providing both care for the baby and support for Gail.

So with Gail's pregnancy well advanced we headed for Wollongong and in the early hours of a morning in October 1981, Christopher Adam O'Brien was born by emergency caesarean section. Gail and I had gone to the hospital in the afternoon hoping that our little baby would be delivered that evening after induction of labour. I had with me a bottle of champagne which I planned to drink with the labour ward team and our obstetrician; instead I shared it in a subdued fashion at 4 a.m. with a couple of baffled cleaners, the only people around at that time, following our baby's difficult birth, resuscitation and transfer to the neonatal unit.

At the end of this Wollongong posting we returned to our little house in Balmain, proud parents of a beautiful little blond-headed baby boy whom we called Adam.

The following year I found myself once again as registrar in the professorial unit. The head of surgery was now Professor Jim May, a supremely elegant and successful surgeon with a very large private practice who had decided to leave the secular world of merchant medicine to take on the Chair of Surgery at Prince Alfred. Jim was quiet and phlegmatic but he possessed a dry and wonderfully wicked sense of humour and he became (and remains) a close friend and valued mentor. Jim's reputation as a teacher and surgeon was second to none. His unique method of teaching surgery involved allowing his registrar to perform virtually every operation while he stood on the other side of the operating table carefully retracting, assisting, guiding and encouraging in such an unobtrusive yet coherent fashion that the registrar was inevitably lulled into believing that his own skill was solely responsible for the operation being conducted smoothly, bloodlessly and successfully. Of course, everyone wanted to work with Jim May and I knew that I was fortunate to have a whole year as his apprentice. Also in the unit was Professor Ross Shiel, whose principal interests were tennis and transplantation surgery and who had been working diligently for years in the laboratory and with animal models to build the scientific and clinical case for the establishment of a liver transplant unit at Prince Alfred Hospital. His tireless work was rewarded and vindicated in 1982 when the Federal Government funded the establishment of the Australian National Liver Transplant Unit at RPA. There was already a vast experience in kidney transplantation at the hospital, which was a logical and necessary offshoot of the large and very busy kidney dialysis service.

This year in the professorial unit gave me an opportunity to consider carefully which surgical specialty I might pursue. I was still hearing words of encouragement from Doug Baird and another of the cardiac surgeons, but their group was a large one and I did not want to join the roster as just another heart surgeon performing what I judged to be a limited range of operations, albeit in a highly professional environment.

I had a similar view of other sub-specialties, so after much thought and discussion with those whom I trusted, I decided that I would pursue head and neck surgery. This relatively new discipline, not really recognised as a specialty in its own right, involved the management of cancers of the mouth, throat and sinuses along with diseases and tumours of the salivary glands, thyroid and parathyroid glands and the management of benign and malignant lumps in the neck. The majority of malignant lumps in the neck are secondary cancers in lymph glands, which have spread from primary cancers involved in the lining of the mouth and throat or the skin of the head and neck.

Later in my career when I explained to people what head and neck surgery was all about, I was at pains to be quite clear that this discipline did not include cosmetic surgery or brain surgery. 'If I see the brain, I've gone too far and need to back up,' I would say.

I had really enjoyed my six months in head and neck surgery, working with a surgeon who was ageing and whose techniques were rapidly being overtaken by more modern approaches as a revolution in reconstructive surgery had commenced. All of this, along with the potential to become the leader in the specialty in the hospital and in Sydney, made head and neck surgery an attractive and exciting career option for me.

CHAPTER 11

Rat catcher becomes surgeon

IN THE SECOND HALF of the year Jim May suggested that I might consider spending my fourth and last year of surgical training doing research instead of another clinical rotation. I had by this time carried out a large number of operations and my training logbook, in which these procedures were detailed, was impressive for the number and complexity of operations I had performed. This was important because if I was to spend my last year doing research, there was a risk that the examiners of the College of Surgeons would judge my overall training as being inadequate. Of equal importance was the need, irrespective of the assessment of the College, to be as well trained as possible simply to be a totally competent surgeon.

It was Jim's recommendation that I spend 1983 doing microvascular research with the aim of gaining a higher degree, a Master of Surgery, in order to build my curriculum vitae and academic credentials and also to learn a vital new skill which would better equip me to become a complete head and neck surgeon, skilled in both tumour removal and reconstruction. With very little hesitation I jumped at the opportunity that I was being offered and I was grateful to Jim for showing this confidence in me.

At the time Gail and I were still living in our small terrace house in Balmain. We bought it immediately after marrying but it needed a lot of work. The land was tiny and fronted onto a very narrow but pleasant residential street with good neighbours all around. On one side was a pleasant couple, probably in their late thirties, who flew the Eureka Stockade Flag from their front balcony, quietly sold marijuana to customers who came and went discreetly at all hours of the day and night, and whom we hardly ever saw. On the other side was an older woman living alone, a character from Balmain's working-class heyday who smoked and coughed incessantly and was never seen without her hair in rollers and fluffy pink slippers on her feet. Across the road lived a gay couple, Rex and Eric, who had met and fallen in love when they were patients of the cardiothoracic unit at St Vincent's Hospital, one there for a heart operation and the other for lung surgery. They were a friendly couple who regularly held noisy parties and invited us along. Frank Sinatra's hit 'New York, New York' was a gay anthem at the time and when, on a Saturday afternoon, it started to ring out along the street, we knew that there would be a big bash that night.

When we bought it, our Balmain house had an outside toilet, which did not bother us at all because it was our plan to carry out renovations immediately and get rid of what we thought was a particularly squalid and outdated amenity. 'How could they stand to live like that?' I remember remarking to Gail. 'It's the first thing we'll get fixed.' We had spent a lot of time scrubbing and cleaning when we first moved in but inevitably and imperceptibly, the former owner's dirt slowly became our dirt and it was over a year and a half before we had an inside toilet. In the meantime guests were occasionally inconvenienced and embarrassed when the toilet paper ran out and a plaintive cry for more from the back yard interrupted kitchen conversation.

In our compact cottage everything was very close together; this had both advantages and disadvantages. We had a small dinner party one evening and the guests included Gail's old friend from physiotherapy Jenny McConnell and her husband, Peter, along with another friend from PA, Brian McCaughan, who planned to do cardiothoracic surgery. Our taste in wine at the time was still relatively undeveloped so we always had a cask of white wine in the fridge for quaffing, reserving bottled wine for special occasions. At this particular dinner, for inexplicable reasons, I had anticipated a heavy consumption of red wine so I bought three moderately expensive bottles and removed their corks mid-afternoon to let them breathe. Because money was tight I held back on buying white wine and purchased only a single bottle of Riesling.

I was surprised and a little concerned to see the bottle of Riesling nearly disappear on the first round of pre-dinner drinks. So I quietly retreated to the kitchen with the bottle and refilled it from a cask of entirely different wine. No one was the wiser when I returned to the living room and topped up empty glasses. We then sat down and I tried to encourage everyone to start on the three bottles of red that I had opened and which were sitting on a side table. There was, to my dismay, no interest in the red wine at all and everyone pushed their glasses forward with comments like, 'No thanks, Chris, we'll stick to the white, if you've got any more.' 'You really should try this red,' I urged, 'but, yes of course, I've plenty of white!' and then I retired to the kitchen once more with the near-empty Riesling bottle, opened the refrigerator and started to fill it. There was noisy conversation in the dining room when I walked through the beaded curtain into the kitchen but the fridge was located just inside the kitchen doorway. As I was filling the bottle there was a momentary pause in conversation and a startling and embarrassingly loud glug, glug, glug could be heard coming from the kitchen.

'Just bring the cask in, O'Brien! You're not fooling anyone,' called the irreverent McCaughan, and raucous laughter filled the room. Sheepishly, I stuck my head through the beads and said, 'If you guys were more sophisticated and knew how to drink red wine I wouldn't be in this predicament.'

The little Balmain house had a tiny bricked courtyard and a garden overgrown with bamboo but it was cosy and very liveable. The bathroom and laundry badly needed renovation; along with the installation of an inside toilet. This work would cost about $10,000, so I borrowed the money and our improvements proceeded ever so slowly.

My new research job afforded me ample time to be at home and I was delighted that long hours and emergency calls did not keep me from spending this important time with my wife and new son. This created a problem of its own, however, since my salary had dropped dramatically when I ceased working as a clinical registrar and was doing no overtime. I tried to earn a little extra money assisting some of the Prince Alfred surgeons but this arrangement did not sit well with them and I had few opportunities to augment my income. Ironically, my change of status and drop in income coincided with a significant pay rise for registrars, making my net loss even greater, but I had already decided that the benefits of doing a year of research, both academic and domestic, would far outweigh the negatives.

My life as a researcher started with several obstacles to overcome, not the least of which was the fact that there was no microsurgery laboratory in which I could work, nor was there anyone to teach and supervise me. It would be my job to create the lab and, to a greater or lesser degree, supervise myself. I was offered space in the bottom floor of an old building, the Blackburn Building, on the grounds of Sydney University, which was perfect because it also housed the administrative offices of the clinical academics affiliated with both the university and RPA as well as a number of other laboratories.

The space was large and well lit with two good-sized offices, ample bench space and a room with shelving for storage, but it had not been used for some time and it was filthy and in need of significant re-equipping if I was going to turn it into a microsurgery laboratory. I was given a small budget to assist with the purchase of instruments and which would later also be used to buy experimental animals, so I started hunting and gathering expeditions with the aim of scavenging equipment and furniture for my new empire. An ancient operating microscope was rescued from a storeroom in the operating theatres and, once thoroughly serviced, it performed with admirable efficiency. I discovered another in even better condition but about to be replaced, theatre staff assured me, so I liberated it too.

While the lab was being restored to some kind of order and upgraded to suit my needs, I travelled to Melbourne to learn how to do microsurgery. There was really only one place to go and that was the microsurgery research laboratory established next door to St Vincent's Hospital in Melbourne by my famous but unrelated namesake Bernard O'Brien, a world pioneer in microsurgery. The laboratory was very well funded and equipped and at any one time, two or three overseas fellows were undertaking research projects there, mainly operating on rabbits, with the assistance of the numerous technical and scientific staff who contributed to the smooth and productive running of this outstanding facility. I did not have an official appointment as a fellow and really just visited for three weeks to learn the ropes but during that time I was treated hospitably and generously by Bernie, his brilliantly talented offsider, Wayne Morrison, and all the staff. In subsequent years, when my modest research was recognised as having been successful and useful, I was amused to learn that my name and photo had been put up alongside those of the official fellows, identifying me as yet another successful product of the laboratory.

I quickly became adept at sewing together tiny blood vessels, using tiny instruments and tiny sutures. While in Melbourne, I lived in a very basic room provided by the hospital and tried to use my spare time studying for my final exams but I badly missed Gail and Adam and flew home on the weekends, even though it was expensive.

After three weeks I had learned what I needed to know and had also convinced one of the lab's technicians, whose role it was to assist the fellows in their microsurgery, that she might find a visit to Sydney interesting. As it turned out the move suited her plans perfectly and she transferred to Sydney and spent the rest of the year working with me. This additional salary took my budgetary needs to a new level but Jim recognised that technical help was vital; somehow the cost was absorbed in a way I did not understand and did not particularly want to know about.

There were two main projects that I planned to complete for my master's thesis. One involved operating on blood vessels of dog hind legs while the other involved experiments using 1 mm diameter tubes to create bypasses in the back legs of rats. Rats of course were much smaller than the rabbits that I had practised on in Melbourne but it was not difficult to become proficient at sewing their smaller arteries and veins. Although this was a level of surgical complexity that I had never anticipated, the importance of microsurgery in head and neck reconstruction was increasing by the day and I knew that acquiring this new skill would be invaluable, irrespective of the outcome of my experiments.

Until Liz, my laboratory assistant, arrived from Melbourne I had to do everything for myself, including anaesthetising and taking care of the dogs and rats on which my early operative procedures were performed. The rats were called hooded rats because of the colouration on their heads and, being relatively tame creatures, it was quite straightforward to anaesthetise them once I learned the technique. A target animal was selected from the group huddled in their wire cage, lifted by its tail to the bench nearby and suspended to encourage it to grasp the edge of the bench by its front paws. This exposed the belly into which I would plunge a small needle, delivering an appropriate dose of Pentothal into the abdominal cavity. The animal would lapse into a safe and relaxed slumber for thirty minutes or more. I would then have to shave the fur on the abdomen and groins, incise the skin and isolate the tiny blood vessels using the microscope for magnification and the very fine instruments which were especially designed for microsurgery. Part of the experimental method was to place short lengths of vein or Gore-Tex tubing (Gore-Tex is a type of Teflon now used very widely in outdoor wear), only 1 mm in diameter, as a bypass graft across a segment of artery, joining the ends with sutures that were barely visible to the naked eye. One of the questions I hoped to answer was whether or not this synthetic material was as reliable as a piece of vein in acting as a bypass conduit.

The rats I worked with were generally the same size but occasionally a different breed would sneak in among the black and white hooded variety. On one occasion the standard cage was delivered to the laboratory with an enormous dark brown rat in it, along with three other smaller rats huddled defensively in the corner. I suspected the giant was terrorising his three companions and decided to anaesthetise him first. That was easier said than done: as I tried to pick him up by the tail he rounded on me with a snarling grunt and tried to bite my hand. He came so close that I was then wary of trying again. I tried to pick up one of his companions but again, as my hand drew near he leapt from his side of the cage and tried to grab me. It was impossible to put my hand inside the cage safely and so I left them alone and chose some other animals. Next morning when I came to the laboratory I found that particular cage open and three dead bodies lying in the straw at the bottom. Worse, the murderous giant had escaped and was lurking somewhere in the laboratory. Most diffidently I crept around the laboratory searching on top of and under every bit of furniture but without success. For the next two days I entered the laboratory with considerable caution, expecting to be leapt upon by a big angry rat at any time. By some dim-witted oversight I didn't think to set a trap but instead spent a lot of time searching the laboratory for him with a big lump of wood in my hand. Eventually, with all the courage and cunning I could muster, I was able to corner the mutant demon one day, club him into submission and then administer a lethal dose of anaesthetic.

As my research proceeded successfully I was able to write a number of scientific papers which were published in Australian and international journals, causing my superiors considerable delight because these publications represented an objective measure of the soundness and relevance of the work and also added modestly to their own CVs. The microsurgery laboratory, now well organised and equipped, also functioned very well as a teaching facility and some of the other junior registrars took the opportunity to come and acquaint themselves with the techniques of microsurgery. My own experience to date had been exclusively gained with experimental animals but one of the plastic surgeons, David Pennington, kindly invited me to assist him from time to time in the operating theatre in order to give me experience with clinical applications of the techniques of microsurgery. The benefits that flowed from the establishment of the laboratory were many and varied and, in some cases, neither predicted nor sought.

I wrote my thesis as I went along so that by the end of the year, as my experimental work finished, I would be able to complete it and submit it on time. This was a very busy period because it also marked the end of my surgical training and in May I was able to sit my final fellowship exam. This examination is a searching rite of passage during which absolutely anything related to surgery can be examined. There are several written papers and oral examinations including clinical exams, short cases and long cases, which require evaluation of real patients followed by detailed discussion of the nature of their disease and its appropriate investigation and management. The various exams stretched over a week or more and were preceded by an intensive one-month course conducted at the various teaching hospitals around Sydney every day from early morning till late afternoon. The daily program consisted of lectures, viva sessions with pathology and anatomy specimens, and practice clinical cases conducted by consultants and senior registrars from the hospitals, all giving their time pro bono in the same way that all surgical teaching is carried out through the year. My old friend Tim Porter, with whom I had lived at Hunters Hill in our early years, was on the course with me and would sit the exam at the same time. Mark Malouf and a number of my other friends had sat and passed already because my travels to Europe with Gail in 1978 had put me a year behind.

Although few of them were close friends, in the group of a dozen or so doing the fellowship course and about to undertake the exam there rapidly developed a close bond of camaraderie so that, when we completed our last exam, great sighs of relief were shared and we adjourned to a pub in the city to enjoy a well-earned beer. For many it was the first drink for months as abstinence from alcohol was regarded as sensible practice in the months before this, the most searching and important exam of our lives. Along with other young trainees who had sat specialty exams like orthopaedics, urology, ENT and the like, we were then expected to convene at the College of Surgeons building in Macquarie Street to await the announcement of our results. The examiners had been meeting all afternoon, correlating results of written and clinical exams, reviewing logbook documentation of surgical experience, and discussing individual candidates whose performance was inadequate or borderline, with the aim of being absolutely fair while still maintaining the high standards of the College and not allowing an individual to pass if he or she had not reached the requisite level of theoretical and practical knowledge.

The College building was relatively small and the candidates gathered in a very tight foyer at the bottom of a steep and impressive staircase while wives, girlfriends and some parents waited outside. At the top of the stairs stood Peter Carter, the College secretary, wearing his academic robe, while in the adjacent drawing room the Court of Examiners in their gold-trimmed college gowns were chatting and awaiting the arrival of the successful candidates. Each of us had an examination number and Carter imperiously began calling the numbers of those who had passed, neglecting the numbers of those who had not. Each successful candidate was then invited to ascend the stairs and join the examiners for sherry in the drawing room.

This was a nerve-wracking ritual and, as we heard our numbers called, there were broad grins, handshakes and pats on the back. A number of people had sat this difficult exam on several previous occasions and I could not help but be moved by the sight of those who had failed quietly slipping out the door, the loneliest of figures, while the rest of us strode up the stairs exhilarated, unburdened, ecstatic.

Those who did not pass were left to ponder what might have been and to rake over their situation, where they went wrong and what they would do next, sometimes in the arms of a tearful wife with the puzzled little faces of their children looking on, or quietly walking alone back to a car searching their minds and hearts and asking whether they had the resilience to bounce back and do it all again when the next opportunity to sit the exam came up in six months' time.

It was really the best of times and the worst of times. The sense of relief, release and freedom experienced after passing the final fellowship examination is unique in its intensity, almost indescribable and something really only understood by those who have been through it. I still needed to complete my research year, submit my thesis and plan the next steps in my professional life, but a great weight had been lifted and my readiness to practise as a surgeon and to continue on my career path had been acknowledged.

CHAPTER 12

London via a deceased estate

WHILE I WAS PREPARING for my fellowship exam, trying to conduct technically demanding experiments sewing together tiny blood vessels and pieces of Gore-Tex, and acting as chief rat catcher all the while, we were quickly going backwards financially and were barely able to cover the mortgage and the repayments on our loan for the renovations on our house in Balmain.

We were planning on going to Europe and the United States the following year while I pursued more training in head and neck surgery, and we decided that the best course of action would be to sell the house and buy something cheaper so that we could rent it while we were overseas but not lose our foothold in the expensive Sydney property market. The Balmain house had limitations anyway — the tiny paved courtyard really didn't give Adam enough room to play and the upstairs bedrooms were only accessible by a steep and narrow staircase. Adam learned to negotiate this very early, sliding down on his belly feet first at great speed and with no difficulty at all, but we needed more space and were constantly on the lookout for an alternative home.

This was not a time of heartache and privation at all, because once my exam was out of the way and with my research year bounding along successfully, Gail, Adam and I were a happy little family having great fun and with plenty to look forward to, especially when we learned that there was another baby on the way.

Fortune continued to smile on us and one day I drove past a good-sized semi-detached house overlooking the water in Drummoyne with a 'For Sale — Deceased Estate' sign in the front yard. From the outside it looked absolutely ideal for our needs so, equipped with my guile and negotiating skills, I met with the real estate agent handling the sale one morning and inspected the place. The house was large and spacious inside with many original features but in need of total redecoration — new kitchen, new bathroom, everything — as it had been the home of a miserly widow who lived there alone in frugal self-denial for over fifty years.

'How much are they asking?' I asked, very nonchalant and trying not to sound particularly interested.

'Seventy thousand,' the agent answered, more nonchalant than I and (apparently) even less interested.

I sighed and made a show of mulling things over in a 'couldn't care less' fashion and then came back with, 'Would they take sixty-eight?' He'd started to respond before I had finished asking the question: 'Yep, they'll take sixty-eight.'

I was thrilled, but as I drove home to tell Gail, a belated flash of insight told me that maybe I hadn't driven quite a hard enough bargain. Oh well, live and learn. But this episode smacked of the shopping technique I had used in Hong Kong a few years before. Maybe I was a slow learner.

Our Balmain house sold quickly, returning us a modest profit; we bought the Drummoyne semi, moved in and I set about redecorating it. Our next-door neighbour was an old plumber who willingly helped me rebuild the bathroom. His name was Ray and he came from the old-fashioned school, having in his tool kit nothing much more than a range of sledgehammers which, despite his ageing and sinewy frame, he used vigorously to bash rough holes in everything so that they looked liked they had been created by gun fire. I hired appropriate tools, replaced the floor, and bought and installed a new bath and washbasin while Ray welded copper pipes and fitted the taps and my sister Carmel's husband Phil helped me to retile the whole room. It was a masterpiece! All the while we lived in the house like cavemen; little Adam was constantly filthy, scratching round on the old floorboards that had previously been covered by lino and newspapers from the 1940s. Eventually we were the proud owners of a freshly painted and carpeted home with three generously sized bedrooms and a level and grassy back yard, which was perfect for our little boy and his much-anticipated sibling.

We had managed to improve our physical surroundings significantly while restoring our finances to viability, in time for me to continue as a senior registrar in head and neck surgery at RPA and prepare for the birth of our little daughter, Juliette Isabella, who arrived in February 1984. Soon after her birth Juliette was found to have a heart murmur due to a small congenital defect, but our initial fears were eased when we were told that the small hole between the two upper chambers of her heart was not life-threatening and would close spontaneously, and it did.

There was, and still is, a long-accepted tradition in Australian surgery that young surgeons wanting to specialise and learn the newest techniques should travel to an overseas institution in the UK or USA for a year or two of additional training. I wanted to go to both places so we arranged for the house to be rented to some nurses from the hospital and organised a job and accommodation in London.

In the middle of the year we set off to England where I would work in the head and neck unit of the Royal Marsden Hospital in London. This old institution, sitting proudly on Fulham Road in Chelsea, had a great reputation, though a little beyond its deserving, and there was an affiliated institution with the same name in Sutton, just out of London.

I was given the position of honorary clinical fellow in head and neck surgery. The British are masters at conferring titles upon their subjects and just as readily adding the word 'honorary' in front of the title to avoid any confusion on the part of the recipient that a stipend might come with the position. There is always a risk that when one accepts a job without pay it is not a real job and doesn't actually involve any work, so one of my challenges was to be sure that I got plenty to do and became an integral part of the team.

When we left Australia we had nothing in the bank but I carried with me a grant of $15,000 from Sydney University, equivalent then to £9000, which was intended to sustain us for the year. This of course did not compute but we were delighted to be going to London and, with the reassurance provided by credit cards and an overdraft, looked forward to this new adventure.

When we arrived at the airport on our departure day our baggage was grossly over the allowable weight and I was concerned that we would have to pay a big penalty for this. I loaded the bags onto a trolley, hung other bits and pieces off my shoulders and around my neck and then took Adam in one arm and Juliette in the other. I suggested to Gail, our parents and other family members who had gathered to bid us farewell that they should retire for a couple of minutes and then approached the check-in counter looking harassed, exhausted and like a man with the weight, not only of his family, but of the world on his shoulders, and threw myself on the mercy of the young woman sitting at the computer.

The ploy worked a treat — as I trudged forward with the doleful demeanour of a pack mule that had had a lifetime of whipping, I could tell that she had started taking pity on me before I had even reached the counter. She found us good seats and charged no extra for the many kilos of luggage we checked in. I sincerely hope that in subsequent years, this woman has enjoyed good health, found true love and won the lottery at least once.

Gail and I boarded the plane full of excitement and expectation, happy at the prospect of being a compact foursome. Adam was two-and-a-half years old and Juliette five months and neither took much interest in the books and colouring pencils given to them by the (mostly male) flight crew. ('When was the last time you saw a five-month-old baby colouring in?' I might have asked.) We survived the long flight well and were met in

London by Mark Malouf, who was living there while spending a year working with England's top varicose veins specialist, and Tim Porter, my Hunters Hill flatmate who was now married and also living in London with his wife, Jan, while he pursued additional training. It was a heart-warming reunion and a great help as we settled in.

Our accommodation consisted of a small one-bedroom flat, one of four in a brick building behind a larger stone structure called Bernard Johnson House and separated from it by a generous square of lawn and an elegant garden full of summer blooms. We had an apple tree and blackberry bushes which both yielded a continuous and abundant crop through the summer and from which Gail, relishing the opportunity, baked delicious pies almost weekly.

It was a blissful time and we shared the buildings with other young families who, similarly, had come to England so that one or other parent could undertake further medical training. Gail, feeling the full weight of responsibility of having to care for two little children with limited resources while I was at work each day, was elated to have Jan Porter, Tim's wife and a very close friend, living just metres away. They and the other women, including two other Australians, supported each other with generosity, resourcefulness and boundless good humour during that year.

When we arrived in England it was mid-summer. With a number of the clinical staff away from the Royal Marsden and not much happening, I was advised to take Gail and the children on a holiday. So we bought a decent car, vastly superior to the humble Renault we owned six years earlier, and headed for Europe. In a few days we reached Vienna where we stayed with an Austrian couple, Andreas and Gretl Kees, who had become good friends back in Sydney while Andreas was doing research, during which he spent a short time in the microsurgery laboratory.

Sixteen years later, when the head and neck fellowship positions had been established at RPA and were very popular, we sat in the dining room one evening with our children and a newly arrived young fellow from the United States, Jeff Adams. Jeff came from Seattle, and he sat opposite me with his wife, Sue, and two young children, earnestly seeking information about what his duties and responsibilities would be over the ensuing twelve months.

'Jeff,' I said, 'your first duty is to look after Sue and make sure you spend plenty of time with her and the children.'

'And then?' he inquired, still waiting for me to spell out what he thought would be a backbreaking schedule.

'After that, you need to get to know Sydney well and to see some of Australia.'

'And what then?' he persisted.

'After that, you can spend some time learning to be a head and neck surgeon and doing a little research.'

By the time that conversation took place I was an experienced surgeon and enjoyed immensely the fact that other young surgeons wanted to travel from America, Europe and New Zealand to work with me and learn. It was my strong view that overseas fellowships of this type should be life changing, character building and fun — a time of personal and professional growth during which family relationships should be enhanced, not neglected.

*

Bernard Johnson House sat on a busy but picturesque street called Fortis Green in a small town called East Finchley, on the Northern Line of London's Underground, close to Hampstead and a village called Muswell Hill. The latter had attracted recent notoriety because one of its inhabitants had developed the habit of inviting young men home for dinner, neglecting to mention to his guests, or rather victims, that they were actually on the menu for the night. On a more uplifting note, Muswell Hill had an excellent bike shop and I was able to buy a terrific little bicycle with training wheels for Adam's third birthday, which we celebrated in October of the year of our arrival.

Our small flat had a single bedroom and a living/dining room of similar size that naturally became a playroom for the children in the colder months. There were also a small bathroom and a kitchen, both of which were perfectly adequate for our needs. The entrance to our dwelling was guarded by a voracious electricity metre that ate fifty pence coins with gluttonous regularity. If it was underfed, the entire flat would be plunged into darkness at the most inopportune moments. We soon got used to having plenty of coins available so that the children's bath time and our dinner parties were not interrupted by blackouts and their attendant confusion. Adam and Juliette played happily in the delightful garden with the other children living there and together they formed a merry little band. They were particularly thrilled when it snowed through the winter and they all joined in building a number of very handsome snowmen.

Nearby was a large and verdant park called Cherry Tree Wood, in which there were tennis courts and a well-equipped playground, which had in its centre a lofty slippery dip with a long ladder leading up to the top of the slide but no cage for protection at the top. Gail would regularly walk Adam and Juliette to Cherry Tree Wood with friends and allow the children to play in the playground. On my first visit to the park I was happy that this spacious and leafy environment was so conveniently located for Gail and the children but I was aghast to find out that Adam had learned to scale the ladder of the slippery dip and that, unassisted by an adult, he would climb to the top, get himself onto the slide and then descend at a great rate over and over again.

'That looks incredibly high! I don't think he should be allowed up there on his own,' I chided Gail when I looked at the slide. 'Come on, mate, hold on to Daddy. I'll take you down the slippery dip,' I said, taking charge and, so I believed at the time, restoring some safety and order to the situation. Adam climbed nimbly to the top just in front of me so that my arms were on either side of him and, when we reached the summit, I sat on the platform and put him on my lap. 'Much safer don't you think, sweetie?' I called to Gail, standing below holding Juliette.

We set off down the slide but as we slid down, Adam's little foot slipped between my legs, catching his sneaker on the slide and causing his leg to twist under mine. I did not appreciate what had happened but when we reached the bottom he was whimpering and holding his leg. There was nothing much to see when we pulled back his jeans but his shin was tender and a little swollen. He sensibly declined the offer of riding on a different piece of apparatus with his interfering father and we drove to a nearby hospital as soon as we reached home. The poor little fellow had a spiral fracture of his tibia and his leg was wrapped in a plaster cast, which extended from mid-thigh to toes and would remain in place for four weeks.

Gail was gracious enough not to take advantage of her clearly ascendant position as I apologised to her and little Adam for my rash and arrogant overruling of the quiet competence with which she nurtured and cared for the children while I was off all day pursuing my own ends. Another lesson for me. Live and learn — it never ends.

To our relief we were advised the fracture was unlikely to cause Adam any long-term ill effects and he was very quickly getting about, a little awkwardly, but otherwise with only minimally reduced mobility. In fact, he was so mobile that three weeks later he was playing soccer with his leg still plastered, in the garden with the other children, when he fell and sustained a similar fracture above the elbow of the opposite arm. Another plaster was applied, this time from mid upper arm to hand, and we believed it was only a matter of time before we were visited by a rabid social worker carrying a court order claiming that we were unfit parents and that our little boy would have to be taken away for his own safety.

Thankfully, nothing of the sort ensued, Adam recovered completely and very kindly developed total amnesia for his mishap on the slippery dip. What's the saying? Time heals all wounds? Yes, that's it.

Living in London was enormously expensive and so our entertainments were as simple and inexpensive as we could arrange — walks on Hampstead Heath, visits to the markets around Covent Garden, picnics in Cherry Tree Wood and regular dinner parties with our neighbours. Next door were Lloyd and Ros Dorrington (the Dorros) from Queensland. Ros didn't like London and kept a picture of the dream home she wanted to build, a wide-verandahed Australian homestead, stuck to the wall over their dining-room table and spent every day yearning for sunshine and pineapples. Upstairs were Vince and Margaret Cousins from Melbourne, while Tim and Jan had a flat in the main house.

I caught the tube each day to South Kensington, reading a novel or *The Guardian* on the way, and soon learned that the British commuter is a highly private and restrained creature. The men, in particular, would sit their briefcases on their laps and pull their newspapers up close to their noses with the apparent intention of obstructing unauthorised and unwanted scrutiny of the paper by a neighbouring passenger (unlikely because they all had newspapers) and also to obliterate from their own view anything that might upset their safe and private little world, like a pregnant woman needing a seat or a mother with a baby. So insulated and absolved from any need to interact with fellow passengers, the stoical Brit would sit in patient and preoccupied silence. If the train stopped in a tunnel or between stations for some reason, the silence would intensify but, if any conversation took place at all, it was conducted in the most dignified of quiet whispers. As the train neared central London and tourists, mainly noisily uninhibited Americans, boarded the carriage in increasing numbers, the true and rightful owners of the train would signal their discomfort with waves of exasperated newspaper rustling and disapproving looks. It was also the time of the miners' strike and so at the entrance and exit of each tube stop pinstriped executives were forced to thread their way through a phalanx of picketers collecting money for their cause in yellow buckets. To me, insulated with a thick Australian skin (and a thick coat in the winter), it was all theatre.

Work at the Marsden was busy and it only took a little while for me to establish a space for myself in the head and neck unit, which was top heavy with registrars and senior registrars from ENT and plastic surgery, all with their elbows out to help preserve their patch. I claimed my space with little difficulty and without confrontation or ill feeling when they realised that I was well trained, competent and, on balance, more experienced than they were.

The Marsden's reputation as an outstanding cancer hospital was of long standing and patients frequently came from far and wide seeking a last-ditch cure, having experienced failed initial treatment elsewhere. They made their pilgrimages from places like Greece, Egypt, Portugal and Gibraltar, while others only had to venture one or two tube stops.

My bosses were Henry Shaw and Nick Breach. Henry was the unit head and a charming senior ENT surgeon with excellent standing in England and overseas, but with modest skill in the operating theatre and a reputation for being a little tight with money. Nick was a dexterous, left-handed plastic surgeon with a broad grin and the stammering diffidence of Bertie Wooster.

At the time, a cruel but often apt riddle asked, 'How does one define an English surgeon?' Answer: 'A pinstriped suit full of bullshit!' Neither Henry nor Nick fitted this stereotype but some of the inflated senior registrars did.

I met with Henry and Nick separately early in my stay and sought their advice about suitable research projects that I might be able to undertake but, since neither of them was particularly strong academically, little other than their encouragement and wishes of good luck were forthcoming. The most helpful person in this regard was a pathologist who worked at the Sutton branch of the Marsden, Richard Carter. He was a dapper and meticulous bachelor who was known internationally as a productive scientist of the highest quality and who generously invited me to participate in his work and also to write a number of papers with him.

Among the senior registrars with whom I worked, I became especially friendly with Barry Jones, a flamboyant extrovert whose talent and bearing marked him as the golden-haired boy of British plastic surgery and a superstar on the rise. Barry and I instantly became friends, thoroughly enjoying every minute we spent together in the operating theatre, the outpatient clinics and clinical meetings and also many frivolous occasions away from work. He has become London's society plastic surgeon, discreetly modifying, augmenting and generally enhancing the fair faces and feminine parts of numerous well-known English flowers, not to mention jet-setting itinerants. Well over twenty years later we remain the closest of friends.

I was very fortunate at the Marsden and gained invaluable experience by operating on patients with more advanced and complicated cancers than I had seen in Sydney. I was also able to utilise my microsurgical skills in a real-life non-laboratory setting because, in contrast to the practice at Prince Alfred Hospital, the reconstructive surgeons at the Royal Marsden had embraced the relatively new technique of microvascular free tissue transfer. This involved moving islands or blocks of tissue from the arm or the back or the hip, along with the related blood vessels, to a defect in the head and neck region (the mouth, the throat or perhaps an area of skin) and then sewing the relevant artery and vein into larger vessels in the patient's neck in order to provide the new tissue (called the free flap) with the blood supply it required to survive in its new position. This technique had been pioneered in Melbourne by Bernie O'Brien and (working quite separately) one of his contemporaries, Ian Taylor. The Chinese had already developed a unique operation which made use of an island of skin, taken from the inner aspect of the forearm along with blood vessels, which provided an especially useful free flap because the tissue was thin and pliable and the vessels were large enough to guarantee a very high rate of success when sutured to their new blood supply.

There is no doubt that I was fortunate to be working in this busy and fertile environment at such an early stage in the 'free flap revolution'. New parts of the body — skin, muscle and bone — which could be harvested with their feeding artery and draining vein with little or no disability or incapacity to the donor site, were being described all the time as researchers re-examined the body's anatomy with a newfound enthusiasm and sense of inquiry, hoping to identify new flaps and add to their reconstructive options.

My parents: a very young and pretty Maureen Healey with her strapping beau, Kevin O'Brien, early in their courtship. This photo was taken around 1950 by a street photographer near the GPO in Sydney.

Mum holding Carmel (aged about three months) with Dad, me (three) and Michael (five) at our home in Regents Park in the western suburbs of Sydney.

My First Communion at St Peter Chanel convent, Berala. I'm in the front right. We were a devoutly Catholic family and I would kneel by my bed every night to say my prayers before going to sleep.

Christmas with the family, 1965. Left to right: Michael, Grandma O'Brien, Carmel, me, Grandfather O'Brien, Mum and Dad. In later years, Dad slowly grew depressed and would drink too much on social occasions.

My teen years were dominated by sport, and in 1967 I proudly led the team on a lap of honour as captain of the premiership winning Parramatta Marist Under 15s rugby league team.

In 1969 I was elected school captain of Parramatta Marist Brothers. I thrived in my senior school years, and was awarded several honours including being named the school's outstanding sportsman-student.

One of my favourite pictures of Gail. I took this photo during our time in Paris in 1978 as she was preparing for a ballet class. A wonderful dancer, Gail considered pursuing a career in dance.

After four years together, Gail and I finally married in 1980 (much to the relief and elation of our parents). Here we are on our honeymoon in Hong Kong. I cannot imagine what life might have been like if I hadn't married Gail.

This photo was taken at Concord Hospital in 1975 for our Medical Yearbook. I kept this bizarre moustache in one form or another from 1970 till about 1992.

With my close friend, Mark Malouf, in London in 1984, where I worked in the head and neck unit of the Royal Marsden Hospital.

With Gail and the kids — Adam, James and Juliette — in the garden at our house in Drummoyne. I was always determined to never jeopardise my commitment to my role as a husband and father for the sake of my career.

With medical school friends (from left) Lawrie Hayden, Alan Farrell, Tom Boogert and Ian Davison. A number of my most treasured friendships started back in university.

In 2000 I had the rare honour of being invited to join the Council of the American Head and Neck Society. I also received a presidential citation from Jesus Medina, President of the Society, for my contribution to head and neck surgery.

I received a Doctorate in Medicine (MD) in November 2004 for my work on the management of metastatic cancer in the neck from the now sadly deceased Kim Santow, who was then Chancellor of the University of Sydney.

The launch of the Sydney Head and Neck Cancer Institute at a grand gala ball in Sydney in 2002 was a great success in every way. Here, Gail and I are with Professor Marie Bashir AC, Governor of NSW, who accepted my invitation to become patron of the institute, and her husband, Sir Nicholas Shehadie.

Accompanying HRH Prince Charles on a tour of the Sydney Cancer Centre, one of only a few official engagements the Prince attended during his brief visit to Sydney in March 2004.

At Government House, Sydney, in 2005, after being invested as a Member of the Order of Australia (AM). James, Gail, my dad and Juliette were all there to see me receive the medal, which was presented by Professor Marie Bashir AC.

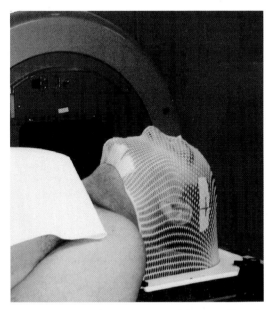

Lying on the radiotherapy treatment table with an immobilising mask in place about two weeks after my first operation to remove my brain tumour. Now it was my turn to experience what so many of my own patients had gone through.

With Prime Minister Kevin Rudd at a fundraising lunch in May 2008. He had pledged $50 million support for the Sydney Cancer Centre just before the 2007 Federal election and confirmed that commitment that day.

Christmas 2006 with my family, one month after my initial operation. From left: Adam, Gail, me, Juliette and James. My priority has been to stay cheerful and positive, and to encourage those around me to share my optimism.

CHAPTER 13

The Deep South

AFTER A YEAR IN LONDON, during which our limited financial means necessitated our developing a sizable bank overdraft, we prepared to travel to the United States where I planned to undertake a second clinical fellowship. Our belongings were packed into tea chests and we farewelled friends, work colleagues and associates in a round of parties that occupied two or three weeks. Before I left the Marsden, Henry Shaw invited Gail and me to lunch at a well-known Italian restaurant called San Frediano, just across Fulham Road from the hospital. To my surprise he presented me with a cheque for £150 and thanked me for helping with the treatment of a number of his private patients. In fact, Henry contributed little to the management of any his patients, public or private. He would scrub and gown himself carefully, elaborately drape the anaesthetised patient and draw careful lines on the skin to mark his planned incision and then, with a sigh of resignation, give a little cough, adjust his glasses with his gloved hand, thereby rendering himself non-sterile and unable to participate in the operation, and then excuse himself, muttering something about having to make a phone call. Before he left the operating theatre he would wish the team luck and ask that we join him in the pub nearby at the end of the day. As charming and tight as his reputation maintained, he gave me the privilege of paying the bill at the end of our meal.

At first glance London, England and Birmingham, Alabama may seem to have little in common other than the fact that English is spoken (sort of) in both places. Closer examination and experience soon revealed that the two cities have absolutely nothing in common apart from the fact that by the end of 1986 the O'Briens would have lived in both places. I secured the position of head and neck oncology fellow in the Department of Surgical Oncology at the University of Alabama Birmingham (UAB) after I met the department head, Charles Balch, while he was on sabbatical in Sydney. Balch's plan was to become America's expert on malignant melanoma by writing a textbook on the subject in which he combined his own series of about eighty patients with the five-hundred patient experience of Professors Gerry Milton and Bill McCarthy in Sydney and then subjected the combined data to statistical analysis.

We met at a clinical meeting in Sydney and Balch asked me what my career plans were. When I said that I was interested in doing head and neck surgery he turned into a fast-talking salesman and extolled the many merits of working at UAB, particularly with Bill Maddox, the senior head and neck surgeon. The fellowship at UAB was one of twelve accredited by the joint training council of the two head and neck societies in the United States. I had written applications to a number of institutions but the responses were not encouraging other than to say that I would be welcome to fly over for an interview. With no guarantee of a position and additional airfares likely to add further pressure to our financial situation it seemed sensible not to look a gift horse in the mouth and I accepted the UAB fellowship.

All I knew about Birmingham, Alabama, was that it figured prominently in the news during the decades of America's race riots and that Birmingham's conservative radio announcers led the burning of Beatles records when John Lennon tangled himself terribly in his own hubris by claiming that The Beatles were more popular than Jesus Christ.

In contrast to London, Birmingham offered the prospect of a reasonable salary and a comfortable apartment in a complex of dwellings that included tennis courts and swimming pools as well as the opportunity to experience a new way of life, different values and an often idiosyncratic culture, if culture is the right word.

Gail and the children were excited about this move and not really sorry to leave England: despite its comforting familiarity, life there was physically challenging on our skimpy budget, and winter with its short, damp days and lack of sunshine had been long and depressingly dreary.

An early positive point of contrast between Birmingham and London was the fact that the UAB staff had arranged accommodation at a motel for us for a couple of nights and further, provided us with maps and a list of apartments which might suit our rental requirements and which we could inspect the day after our arrival. These small kindnesses, along with the regular assurance that 'Y'all are real welcome here!' gave us confidence that we would quickly grow to appreciate Southern hospitality and the physical comforts of middle-class Americana.

Birmingham was hot and humid when we arrived and Gail and the children were relieved when we finally dragged our belongings into a large air-conditioned motel room, complete with a minibar and a big colour TV. Through the window of our room we could hear a group of young girls playing in the motel swimming pool as they called each other by name in their syrupy drawls — Candy, Brandy and Cindy. Gail and I looked at each other and laughed. We had arrived in the Deep South and we were sure we would enjoy the ride, irrespective of twists, turns, ups and downs.

We found a comfortable modern apartment with two big bedrooms, two bathrooms and spacious living areas. The rent seemed modest by Australian standards but the apartment was unfurnished and we needed to either buy or rent furniture. The latter was a novel and, at least initially, more attractive option with each item just a few dollars per week. By the time we had chosen enough furniture to appropriately and comfortably fit out the apartment the rental cost did not seem excessive but within a month it was quite clear that our ambitions and desires were well beyond our means so we sent back all but the absolute necessities — one couch instead of a four-piece suite, a small dining table and four chairs, one mattress on the floor of each bedroom and a single medium-sized colour TV. It didn't matter — we were very comfortable and Adam, nearly four years old now, and Juliette, almost eighteen months, delighted in the space and relative luxury.

We managed to negotiate yet another car purchase: an older Plymouth in excellent condition and every bit as good as the cowboy salesman claimed. When we went along to the car yard it was a scene straight from Steinbeck's *The Grapes of Wrath*. The head salesman gave us his earnest attention for a moment or two then handed us on to a tobacco-chewing hick whose previous work history was anyone's guess and who had just started selling cars that day.

'Y'all take it easy on my pardner Jimbo here, folks, he's new at thisa here business, so break 'im in gentle won't ya,' the boss winked as Jimbo, wearing cowboy boots and jeans, led us to a varied collection of cars with prices and signs in salespeak emblazoned on their windscreens in red and blue — 'Low miles', 'A beauty!', 'Your dream car!' and so on it went. Jimbo could be described as a 'car-sellin' green horn' but he tried with folksy ineptitude to do his best.

'We got us a yeller car over here and if'n it don't suit y'all, we got us a coupla blue cars over yonder.' Then, his voice rising as if he had a genuine treat in store, he gushed, 'I gotta li'l red sporty number out back.' Turning to me with a conspiratorial wink he added, 'If the li'l lady will letcha take a li'l looksee.' I was getting impatient by this stage and had no confidence whatsoever that Jimbo the cowboy had the slightest idea about cars. 'Listen, Jimbo, you've been real helpful but I need a safe, reliable station wagon for my family and I'd really 'preciate it if we could speak to your boss again.' The other salesman came back and, with his syrupy drawl, congratulated Jimbo and us on our good work so far. He took over the sale, showed us exactly what we needed and could afford and we drove the car home that afternoon.

With a tight budget once again we were limited in our entertainments and so we often found ourselves on picnics, or window-shopping on a Saturday afternoon at the Galleria or other shopping malls. The choice of movies in Birmingham was limited and its subject matter was narrow and skewed. The current release in the Rambo series played for about six months while we were there but the picturesque and charming Merchant Ivory production *A Room With a View* finished after three nights.

Adam and Juliette attended a delightful little local kindergarten and effortlessly picked up Southern accents. Gail was made welcome by a group of friendly and funny Englishwomen who were part of the large expatriate network that had developed through the university community. For me, the professional environment was as fertile and stimulating as I could have hoped for. UAB had a comprehensive cancer centre that had been built at the behest of former governor, George Wallace, who, when his wife Eileen developed breast cancer, was dismayed to learn that she could not be treated adequately in Alabama because of the lack of cancer treatment facilities which were comparatively plentiful elsewhere in the country. The UAB Cancer Center had an outstanding reputation, as did the hospital's cardiac service.

The quality of heart surgery, including transplantation, in which Birmingham rated number two or three in the country, was a product of the visionary efforts of Dr John Kirkland, a cardiac surgeon who came to Alabama from the Mayo Clinic because he saw immense opportunities and a large neglected population.

As an institution UAB attracted outstanding clinicians and researchers and operated with a level of quality and efficiency that belied the quaint and folksy language of its workforce. By the time I reached Birmingham, Charles Balch had moved to the M.D. Anderson Cancer Center in Houston, an enormous and wealthy institution affiliated with the University of Texas and ranked, along with the Memorial Sloan-Kettering Cancer Center in New York, as one of the best cancer centres in the world.

Balch's departure before my arrival proved to be of no great consequence since Bill Maddox, the senior surgeon and my principal teacher, was exceptional and proved to be the role model I had hoped to find at the Royal Marsden. Maddox was wiry and suntanned and regarded by many as the best surgeon in the South. His understanding of anatomy and pathology was phenomenal and he was Jim May's equal as a technical surgeon.

He played at being a Southern larrikin but he was intelligent and a gentleman, scrupulously honest and an excellent teacher. On the rare occasions that a complication occurred, Bill would short-circuit any head-scratching or attempts to shift the blame to the patients — who in Sydney were occasionally told that their problem arose because they were 'bleeders' or 'bad healers' — by simply declaring, 'I did bad surgery, simple as that. That's why we have a problem now and why this man won't do as well as he should. Bad surgery, and I gotta do better.' Bill Maddox's disarming candour, along with his innate comprehension of head and neck cancer and technical brilliance, caused my admiration and affection for him to grow as the weeks and months passed. It was only his overt and, in some ways, contradictory racism that made me qualify my feelings towards him.

Next to the university hospital where most of our work was undertaken was a Veterans Administration (VA) hospital where UAB residents carried out much of the surgery. Most of the patients in the VA hospital were in poor health from alcohol and nicotine abuse and most were also dirt poor and living only on their veteran's pension. A high proportion of the VA patients were black and we would visit the hospital from time to time to see new patients or review the ones operated on by the residents in our department under the supervision of Bill, myself or another consultant. If, as we waited in the foyer for an elevator, the doors opened and the lift was occupied by a black person, Bill would not go in, preferring to wait for one occupied by whites or one that was empty altogether. He came to work one day in a new car, which I admired; when I asked him whether he traded in his old one Bill said no, he had given it to his maid. I knew she was a black woman and so I commented, 'That was generous of you, Dr Maddox,' but he parried my remark by replying, 'Well, she didn't have one.'

He once took me, along with my father-in-law Murray who was visiting us at the time, to play golf at a famous course called Shoal Creek, which was magnificently designed and tended and regularly used in major championships. Bill had invited another old friend so there were four in our group. Because of an arthritic hip, Bill rode in a cart, with Murray and the fourth player taking it in turns to ride with him, while I walked with our black caddy Rudolph. He was spotlessly attired in white overalls and carried a bag of golf clubs on each shoulder and refused to let me carry my own. At the end of the round Rudolph was entitled to a fee of around $100 but Bill gave him an extra $150 and thanked him warmly for his assistance.

I was unable to sort out to my satisfaction exactly what Bill's attitude to black people was. Did he despise them? Did he tolerate them only when they played a role of humble subservience, based on the notion that they were fundamentally inferior?

Racist conversation was common throughout the offices at UAB, particularly among the white secretarial staff, who frequently used the term 'nigger' to describe black people, whether they were patients, co-workers or sportspeople whose names cropped up in conversation.

I was struck by the irony of attending football games played by the legendary University of Alabama Crimson Tide in a stadium of 80,000 cheering people, nearly all white, when the most athletic players were black. One of the Alabama heroes during that time was a brilliant and dynamic line-backer named Cornelius Bennett, who attracted glowing praise from even the most rabid bigots and whose devastating tackle of the Notre Dame quarterback during an historic victory was captured in a photograph that filled the front page of every newspaper in the city. Bill Maddox and I periodically talked about how he viewed black people and I was cautious to approach the subject from the point of view of gentle inquiry and without any comments that may have sounded judgemental. Coming from a country whose indigenous population has one of the highest infant mortality rates in the world and where the ancient culture of its Aborigines has long been under threat from the scourges of poverty, alcohol and social disadvantage, I didn't think I was in a position to be taking the moral high ground. 'I know it isn't right,' Bill said on more than one occasion, 'But that's the way I was brought up.'

Birmingham at the time ranked very high on the national homicide league table, particularly in the northern part of the city, where most violence occurred among blacks and was drug related. Gail had an early and unexpected racial experience when she took Adam and Juliette one day to visit a paediatrician whose name she found in the telephone book and who had an excellent reputation, according to a woman with children living in a neighbouring apartment. Gail arrived to find a very busy waiting room, full of black people. Taken aback but otherwise undaunted, she found the children a seat and made her way to the receptionist who, trying to be helpful, raised her eyebrows, gave an understanding smile and asked, 'Are you sure you've come to the right place?'

Gail told me that evening that she found this a challenging question but both she and I were proud of her response. 'Dr So-and-so is a paediatrician, isn't she?'

The receptionist replied, 'Yes, she is.'

'Well, I've come to the right place,' Gail responded.

The paediatrician was an elegant and capable woman and an excellent doctor. With a knowing woman-to-woman smile she asked Gail at the end of the consultation whether or not she would be back. 'Of course I will,' said Gail.

As it happened Adam and Juliette were robustly healthy and required almost no medical care during our eighteen months in Alabama. When questions of health arose, however, Gail and the children were happy to visit this practice and soon became accustomed to the stares, nudges and comments whispered behind the hands of other young patients and their parents in the waiting room.

Although Charles Balch had left Alabama for Houston, he had laid some foundations which assisted me enormously, particularly the hiring of a data manager for the Department of Surgical Oncology who arranged for all of Bill Maddox's very high quality clinical records to be transferred to a computerised database. This resource was made available to me for clinical research and, with Bill's support and blessing, I wrote a number of papers, analysing his experience with a range of cancers and operations, all of which were published in the American medical literature. The existence of this database, which I later helped to modify and streamline, also allowed me to solve a major challenge that I brought with me from home.

When I left Sydney at the beginning of this overseas sojourn in mid-1984 one of my goals was to learn how the world's leading cancer hospitals were dealing with the challenge of collecting clinical data on head and neck cancer patients and, if I could, I hoped to bring back a copy of a suitable database.

I had been surprised and disappointed to learn that at the Royal Marsden no such system existed and that, to carry out clinical research, I had to trawl through medical records which were as incomplete, appallingly kept and unreliable as those back in Australia. The quality of documentation in the medical charts was superior in America but even at New York's famous Memorial Sloan-Kettering Cancer Center, I was stunned by the inadequacy of the clumsy database slowly being established by a senior head and neck surgeon who just happened to have greater understanding of and facility with computers than his colleagues.

The UAB head and neck database was imperfect but readily adaptable to my needs; when I returned to RPA I was able to develop it further and create a computerised system in which it was possible to record every operation, all pathology, every complication, every episode of disease recurrence, and every episode of radiotherapy and chemotherapy treatment along with ongoing follow-up.

The establishment of the RPAH head and neck database is one of a handful of initiatives of which I am proud and I am indebted to the vision of Charles Balch, the generosity of Bill Maddox, the assistance of a woman named Judy Smith, who worked as the data manager in Surgical Oncology, and the advice of a brilliant biostatistician, Seng Jaw Soong, for helping me conquer this small mountain.

Despite Bill Maddox's technical brilliance in the operating theatre, the reconstructive techniques employed at UAB were quite old fashioned and there had been no attempt to utilise newer techniques involving free flaps and microvascular surgery. After I had been there a month or so I asked whether Bill would be comfortable with me trying some of these newer reconstructive techniques on the patients we treated in the university hospital and at the VA hospital. Bill and his associate, Marshall Urist, a protégé of Charles Balch who had taken over as head of Surgical Oncology, both agreed, although their scepticism told me that I would have to be very careful not to put a foot wrong with these early cases.

There are really two potential pitfalls with free flap surgery that can lead to failure. Firstly the flap tissue, be it bone, muscle or skin, needs to be lifted from its site of origin with great care, leaving its attached blood vessels intact. Secondly, these blood vessels must be sutured with great accuracy to the other vessels in the new site to guarantee that the transplanted tissue has a reliable blood supply. The point at which the two vessels are joined is called the anastomosis, and the trick is always to create a technically perfect anastomosis that will not block off with blood clot. Rough handling of the vessels or poor technique can lead to failure, resulting in a cold, dead flap that must be removed and then replaced with fresh tissue. A success rate of about ninety-six per cent is expected, so there is very little margin for error and any failure is dramatically obvious for all to see. Fortunately, the early cases at UAB in which I used the free flap technique were trouble free.

I found aspects of America's health system less trouble free; at first I struggled to accept the extent to which dollars could impact on the health of individual patients.

One afternoon in the head and neck clinic I saw a poorly educated white woman from a farm in one of the more remote rural parts of Alabama. She had been introduced to the once-common habit of 'snuff dipping' when she was a child and now, as an unkempt and simple soul in her mid-sixties, she came along complaining of an advanced cancer sitting on the top of her left lower gum and extending into the groove between the gum and the cheek. This clearly malignant growth had started to eat into the jaw and had spread to one of the lymph glands in the upper part of her neck on the same side. It was an advanced cancer but eminently treatable.

Snuff is a mixture of fine tobacco and slaked lime, a lump or wad of which is wedged into the space between the gum and the cheek, just where this lady's cancer had developed, then kept there for hours and hours, sometimes all day and even overnight. An identical form of carcinogenic stimulant wrapped in a betel leaf is so widely used in India that oral cavity cancer is one the most common forms of malignant disease in that country. The habit of betel nut chewing in New Guinea causes the same problems.

The woman who came to the outpatient department with her mouth cancer from rural Alabama, not surprisingly, had no health insurance but this did not immediately preclude her from receiving treatment at UAB. Each year, a small proportion of the hospital's budget was allocated to the care of needy patients and it was necessary for the clinicians wanting to treat those patients to obtain authorisation from the chief of the department.

The head of surgery was an austere and taciturn man named Gil Diethelm (apparently the son of a Swiss psychiatrist), an excellent surgeon but a tough disciplinarian. I assisted Diethelm from time to time and had a good relationship with him, so I was comfortable about expressing my disappointment when, in response to my inquiry about bringing this particular patient into hospital and treating her mouth cancer, he responded that the year's allocation for treating indigent patients had already been spent and therefore she could not be admitted to hospital.

The woman was sent away with the advice that she should present herself at one or other community hospitals outside of Birmingham in the hope that someone could help her. In fact, there was not the slightest chance that she would find anyone competent enough to treat her cancer in a community hospital and so our inability to give her the care that she required may have amounted to a death sentence.

Three months later, I was again working in the head and neck outpatient clinic when the same woman came back. By this time her cancer had spread through the cheek, creating a wide, ugly and malodorous opening between her mouth and the skin of her cheek. Her emaciated condition indicated that her state of nourishment was appalling and she demonstrated to me that she could only eat by holding a moist, smelly rag up to her cheek to cover the hole. Moreover, the lump in her neck had grown to the size of an orange but, amazingly, she was not terribly troubled by pain.

The poor wretched woman was in desperate need of assistance and it was conjectural whether or not she would benefit from any active therapy at all. I rang Diethelm's office, seeking permission to bring her into hospital. Without any hesitation I was given the all-clear because we had entered a new budget cycle so, with the horse well and truly bolted, I was made most welcome to close the barn door.

This woman's clinical course and outcome were possibly determined as soon as she developed the first little spots of cancer in her mouth but, regardless of that, I was stunned by the callous indifference and blatant stupidity of a health system which allowed the neediest of patients, with a treatable condition, to be turned away from a wealthy institution only to have the same patient welcomed back when the condition was untreatable but the financial circumstances suited better.

On another occasion I was phoned by an administrative clerk working for a Health Maintenance Organisation (HMO), a type of health fund which has a contractual arrangement with a hospital to cover the treatment costs of patients who are members of that HMO, either because they pay directly for that insurance or because it is paid by their employer. This particular administrator advised me that they would cease paying for the care of one of my patients and that any additional time in hospital would be at his own cost because, by their reckoning, he had been there long enough to have recovered fully from his originally planned operation, a procedure called a neck dissection, which involved removing malignant lymph nodes in the neck. The operation had gone well and he would have been on track to be discharged from the hospital at the appropriate time but, through no fault of his own or anyone else's for that matter, he developed a perforated stomach ulcer on the third day after the neck dissection, necessitating a second major operation and, of course, additional recovery time.

The administrator from the HMO needed a lot of convincing that this was a new, unforeseen and life-threatening illness which carried a whole new set of treatment and recovery implications. Once I agreed to write a detailed report to the HMO, they were happy to extend the patient's hospital stay but it was made quite clear to me that they would continue to monitor his progress and their ongoing liability very closely.

I really didn't need any convincing that the provision of medical care, particularly at the very high level expected and demanded by so many Americans, could be cripplingly expensive and needed to be administered in a way that took into account both the need for patients to receive the best possible care and the need to get maximum value out of every dollar spent on that care. But I wondered what the tens of millions of individuals who were outside the tent of privilege felt about their plight.

The American medical fraternity is an inclusive one and many major institutions are populated, to one degree or another, with non-Americans who have been able to convert their intended short stay of months or a couple of years into a permanent and rewarding professional existence. Most Australians who work in the US are invited to stay because we seem to have the right combination of cheery adaptability, excellent training and willingness to work hard that is valued in America and attracts the attention of decision makers and leaders in US institutions.

Gail and I had no intention of staying in Alabama. The thought of raising Adam and Juliette in that environment was inconceivable but the department head, Marshall Urist, made noises about there being a place for me at UAB if I wanted to stay. Towards the end of my first year, he arranged for my promotion to the level of Instructor, the bottom rung of the academic ladder (but far superior to *Unterassistenten!*), which came with a much-needed pay rise.

The additional money and slightly elevated status made the last six months of our time in Birmingham more comfortable and enjoyable but, having achieved all I set out to do, Gail and I decided that it was time to take our family back to Sydney.

CHAPTER 14

Making a difference

WE RETURNED TO SYDNEY penniless and with only debt to our
name, having built up a significant overdraft and almost worn the
numbers off our credit cards. There was no doubt that the previous
four years had been very costly but I was confident that the financial
sacrifices that we had made really represented a sound investment in
a professional life and career which would reward me for the
remainder of my working life and underpin a happy return to family
life in Sydney. We also brought back a wealth of experiences and
memories and new friendships. There has been a long history of
young Australian doctors venturing overseas with their families in
order to increase their knowledge and skills and this has been a
strength of medical practice and research in Australia. This outward-
looking ethos and the accumulation of new knowledge and
experience which it inevitably generates has contributed over the
years to the delivery of high-quality and up-to-date care to Australian
patients when it might be expected that our geographical isolation
would make us struggle to keep up with the rest of the world.

Most young doctors who have travelled abroad for further training experience a period of uncertainty before their return, unless they had managed to arrange a guaranteed job before heading home. We have tended in Australia not to take a particularly professional, strategic or proactive approach to the recruitment of outstanding young clinicians, rather appointing individuals on an ad hoc basis after they organise their own overseas training, learn new skills and, with their families, do it tough for a couple of years. We respond by magnanimously granting them the privilege of working with their betters, instead of embracing them enthusiastically and encouraging them to put their new skills and knowledge into action for everyone's benefit.

Appointments to the staff of Prince Alfred, like nearly all public hospitals in New South Wales, were historically made on the basis of attrition. It really was not possible to appoint a new young specialist until a retirement, unforeseen accident or other phenomenon of nature created a space. This ridiculous precedent-dependent system of replacing people one for one has meant, of course, that small departments are condemned to stay small forever, irrespective of their quality and productivity, while large departments remain large even if they are unproductive and entirely self-servicing.

To get a job on the staff of Prince Alfred as a specialist I needed to wait for the retirement of the senior surgeon, John Goldie, who had been my teacher and boss when I did thyroid surgery as a registrar. So I spent 1987 in an interim position as the clinical superintendent of surgery, a senior registrar post which required me to undertake some basic administration but gave me the flexibility to pursue my interest in head and neck surgery.

Both Jim May, as head of the division of surgery and Diana Horvath, the medical director, facilitated and supported my appointment to this position and my smooth transition to the role of attending surgeon in the Department of Head and Neck Surgery at the beginning of the next year.

Although I had specialised in general surgery I had not worked as a general surgeon since 1982 when I was a registrar, and it was my intention to do nothing but head and neck surgery for the rest of my career. At the commencement of my practice, I had business cards printed with 'Head and Neck Surgeon' on them. If a patient with a general surgical problem was referred to me, I simply diverted the patient, with the permission of the referring doctor, to a general surgeon. It was my intention to send a loud and clear message to everyone that I had returned, that I was well trained in a highly specialised area and that it was my intention to practise head and neck surgery exclusively and in a way that demonstrated all the positives associated with contemporary techniques and methods of practice.

Historically, head and neck surgery had a terrible reputation. Patients tended to present with advanced disease and the operations they needed were viewed as being mutilating and often ineffective while reconstructive techniques were similarly unsophisticated and prone to failure, necessitating multiple procedures, long periods of hospitalisation and recovery and the likelihood of very significant functional impairment at the end of it all. Moreover, patients who survived this onslaught tended to die in large numbers because their cancers rapidly returned and, frequently untreatable at that point, caused a slow, painful and grisly death.

Making a difference

By contrast, I had learned how to perform radical operations which were designed to preserve important anatomical structures rather than sacrifice them and then to reconstruct the operative defect that I had created by using a flap of new tissue of appropriate volume and texture — aiming, in a single operation, to restore the patient to full function as soon as possible.

These advances were dramatic and a few years after my return, using the clinical database that I established, I was able to demonstrate objectively that modern surgical techniques were associated with a significantly shorter length of hospital stay, a much lower complication rate, fewer overall operations, better function and a higher rate of survival than a historical population of similar patients.

It was both gratifying and exciting to return to my alma mater with the knowledge and skills which could potentially make a difference not only to a particular discipline in surgery but also to the wellbeing of many patients. However, my enthusiasm to share this new knowledge and bring about change at RPA caused me to overplay my hand.

My desire to throw out a treatment philosophy and its attendant techniques that I saw as being archaic and not in the best interests of patients was seen by the older surgeons as reflecting my arrogant pride more than anything else. I particularly wanted to introduce a quality assurance program in the head and neck department so that open discussion of complications and outcomes would force change and lead to improvement. But these initiatives were seen as unnecessary and threatening and were consequently met with resistance, which added to my impatience. I could have done all of this much better, more gently and more humbly but the retrospectoscope almost always gives a crystal-clear picture and hindsight begets wisdom.

My colleagues did, however, recognise the great benefit of supporting the establishment of our database and were readily persuaded that, if this venture was to be successful, we would have to employ a full-time data manager to collect, audit and analyse the clinical information. We needed a salary of around $25,000 per annum to employ someone at the appropriate level but finding this money would be challenging and require creativity.

The RPA head and neck unit included two head and neck surgeons, my senior colleague and myself, as well as an older ear, nose and throat surgeon with a keen interest but little experience in head and neck surgery, a well-trained and recently appointed plastic surgeon who was expert in the techniques of free flap reconstruction, two radiation oncologists and a medical oncologist. From this group, nearly all contributed money from their own pockets, allowing us to accumulate $20,000. This allowed me to go to Diana Horvath to ask if the hospital budget could contribute the remaining $5000, arguing that the benefits from establishing this database would far outweigh the costs and help to make our head and neck service a leader. Diana accepted the argument, found the additional money and we were on our way. The following year the position of the head and neck data manager was written into our budget and the position has not been vacant for twenty years.

During my year as clinical superintendent of surgery I was invited by Bill McCarthy, the head of the Sydney Melanoma Unit (SMU), to join the unit because he felt that my skills in head and neck surgery might make a useful contribution. The SMU had developed a reputation for being the largest and best melanoma treatment unit in the world, building by leaps and bounds on the clinical service commenced by now deceased Professor Gerry Milton at Sydney Hospital in the 1960s.

I recall vividly that when I was a medical student, melanoma seemed to be an uncommon disease but one associated with almost inevitable death. By the time I joined the SMU, melanoma had joined cancers of the colon, prostate, breast and lung to be among the top five malignancies afflicting Australians and, as the disease was increasingly being identified in its early stages, survival rates were improving all the time.

One of the treatment paradigms for managing melanoma at the SMU around this time involved the pre-emptive removal of nearby lymph nodes associated with melanoma on the skin, even if there was no obvious abnormality to see or feel. It was believed, incorrectly as it turned out, that this would reduce the likelihood of melanoma spreading throughout the body and thus increase the chance of survival. About fifteen per cent of melanomas occur on the skin of the head and neck, so there was clearly a potential role for a surgeon trained in newer techniques of neck dissection and reconstruction.

Bill McCarthy's abrupt and often undiplomatic manner belied the generosity, inclusiveness and vision with which he carried out his role as leader of the unit. I was grateful to him for the opportunity he offered me and over the years I worked hard treating these melanoma patients, along with all the other patients in my practice with other forms of head and neck cancer, and writing numerous papers on the subject of head and neck melanoma using clinical data from the SMU database. In 1991 I wrote a paper that I later presented at the annual meeting of the American Society of Head and Neck Surgeons, detailing the treatment and outcomes of almost a thousand SMU patients with melanoma of the head and neck. When the paper was published in the *American Journal of Surgery* later that year, it was the largest series of patients from a single institution with this particular disease ever published.

The invitation to join the melanoma unit gave me a rare and brilliant opportunity to add value in a clinical setting where it was much needed and to develop what would become the world's largest personal experience by a surgeon in the management of patients with head and neck melanoma. It was in this particular aspect of head and neck oncology that I first established an international reputation, resulting in several invitations to attend meetings, symposia and conferences as a visiting speaker and to write textbook chapters on the subject. Attending local and international conferences to present my work, or work carried out in collaboration with colleagues, soon became one of the most rewarding and gratifying aspects of my professional life. In particular, when my presentations were based on my own experience and the information that had been carefully accumulated in the database that I had established at RPA, I was able to speak with authority and honesty.

As I settled into my clinical activities at the hospital and we returned to life in Sydney Gail, Adam and Juliette rapidly adjusted to being at home. Adam, now five, and Juliette, three, each had a

Southern twang to their speech and even though they had made wonderful friends overseas and fitted in very well, they were delighted to start mixing with Australian kids once again.

This period of our lives was exciting and fun but I was very conscious that my 'career' was only one component of a life in which I was already playing a number of roles: husband, father, teacher. I was determined that I would never jeopardise or sacrifice my commitment to these other roles for the sake of ambition or advancement in my professional life.

CHAPTER 15

Running late in an imperfect world

BY THIS TIME, MY MOTHER had retired and she and Dad had sold the family home in Regents Park to retire to the Blue Mountains. If Dad had had his way, they would have moved to Tasmania but even he recognised that it was illogical to do what so many other retiring couples do: that is, head off to a place which at first glance seems new, cheap and exciting but which is unfamiliar, requires considerable adaptation and is remote from friends and family.

Wentworth Falls in the Blue Mountains fulfilled all the necessary criteria and they found a pretty brick home with a large garden which Dad could fill with all the kitsch treasures he liked and together they would establish new lives among fellow retirees, living on Mum's generous teacher's superannuation and Dad's repatriation (war veteran's) pension. Because of the accumulation of Dad's various war-related disabilities his pension had, over the last decade or so, reached the maximum level and he was regarded as being totally and permanently incapacitated.

Rather than being embarrassed or depressed by this label, he revelled in it and the fortnightly payments that contributed significantly to their full, if relatively modest, lifestyle.

I was so happy to see them settling in to their new environment, taking pride in their little house and garden and meeting new and interesting people with whom they could establish new friendships. They joined the local Catholic Church, the golf club and every other club, society and group to which they were invited. Dad naturally gravitated to ex-military men with whom he enjoyed sharing stories and drinking — especially the latter — while Mum decided, at the age of sixty-five, she would return to competition tennis.

Having grandparents to visit in the mountains was a new treat for the children, although they were elated anyway to be back in Sydney and surrounded by family on all sides. We had settled back into our little Drummoyne house, well preserved by the tenants who rented it from us while we were away, but we knew that before too long we would need to move into a bigger place.

The year as clinical superintendent provided a relatively straightforward and uncomplicated way of settling back into Prince Alfred Hospital and into life in Sydney. We had come back to Australia in debt yet we still needed to buy a car, probably two in time, and to start paying bills.

My comprehension of the financial world was limited at the time, but when we sold our house well on the back of a booming housing market and then bought a larger one nearby, increasing our debt level, only to be forced to near breaking point by seventeen per cent interest rates, I received a quick lesson and a wake-up call. Thankfully, I was the owner of a recession-proof job so while the rest of the country enjoyed Keating's 'recession we had to have' at least I remained employed and earning enough money to pay our mortgage, but not enough to clear the debt which we had accumulated over the previous three years and certainly not a cent to save.

Our debt level was modest by any measure and never really a source of major concern for Gail or me. I was aware, however, that our current state of relative comfort, along with our desire and need to live in a decent home and educate the children, was entirely dependent upon my good health and ability to work. This would be an issue that would intermittently exercise my mind, although I felt no particular concern and looked to the future with optimism, expecting that the years I had invested in research and overseas study in clinical work would pay off handsomely in a dozen different ways in the future.

By the beginning of 1988 I had been appointed as a visiting medical officer in head and neck surgery and my practice had commenced. Doug Baird, still the head of cardiothoracic surgery, generously invited me to consult on a sessional basis in the rooms that he shared with his partners in the cardiothoracic unit. The two senior cardiac surgeons were marginally more civil to me in my new role as a fellow specialist, while others among the surgeons went out of their way to be helpful and encouraging.

One aspect of my work for which I felt ill-equipped was the duty of being on call for emergency surgery. Everyone had to do emergency call, usually one night a week, depending on his or her specialty. I had really only done head and neck surgery for six years, entering the abdomen only for the purposes of harvesting a segment of bowel that I could use as a conduit to replace the gullet if I had removed it for cancer. In general these evenings on call were neither arduous nor particularly complicated and I benefited greatly from the help given to me by very good registrars, Phil Walker, Hugh Lukins and Henry Hicks among them, and also by a colleague, Michael Stephen, an outlandish extrovert and larrikin but a brilliant abdominal and vascular surgeon who came to my aid on two or three occasions when I was up to my elbows in blood and my armpits in strife. When trouble was looming, I would try to notify Michael before I started an operation and he would arrive with alacrity and boundless cheerful energy. Instead of taking over the operation, he would graciously stand on the other side of the table as an assistant, noisily enthusing about the great job I was doing, while he recovered the situation, unscrambled the omelette I had been trying to deal with and left me with minor tidying up to do.

When I started my practice Gail acted as my secretary for the first six months, playing receptionist during consulting sessions, answering the phone, making appointments and carrying out the billing and receipting when the first of the paying customers started to filter through the door. We both enjoyed this time as, yet again, it was a shared enterprise, literally our family business. Until I stopped work in November 2006, Gail acted as practice manager, overseeing in a most competent and meticulous fashion all of the financial aspects of my activities. Someone had to because I had no idea and didn't really want to.

These early days were exciting and fun and I never deviated from my plan to do only head and neck surgery, being sure to pass on patients with other problems to better-qualified colleagues.

I have no doubt that my performing reconstructive surgery irked a number of the plastic surgeons around town who felt that I was encroaching on their turf, but my own colleagues at RPA were gracious enough to be either supportive or silent. Initially, I collaborated closely with my plastic surgery colleagues at Prince Alfred, inviting them to participate in the treatment of my patients. This worked well and I still strongly support the team approach to the management of head and neck cancer patients, but from time to time I was asked to postpone operations to accommodate the unavailability of the plastic surgeons. This could sometimes lead to the tail wagging the dog and I became concerned that the postponement of treatment was not in the patients' best interests, and that I would eventually lose my own reconstructive skills if I did not keep using them. I continued to perform microvascular reconstructive surgery and I encourage all of our fellows and recently appointed head and neck surgeons to develop that skill as well, simply to make themselves more complete surgeons.

We were fortunate at RPA to have avoided the turf battles that dog other areas of surgery and other institutions and which reflect a meanness of spirit that brings credit to no one. The right of an individual doctor (or surgeon) to work in a particular field or carry out a particular procedure should depend only on skill and competence, not on the label or title he carries.

My practice grew quickly. In addition to consulting at the Sydney Melanoma Unit at RPA and my office in the RPA Medical Centre adjacent to the hospital, I opened consulting rooms in Hurstville, mainly to make it easy for patients from the south coast and Canberra to see me. I was appointed to the clinical staff of St George Public Hospital as a head and neck surgeon and thoroughly enjoyed the new, friendly and slightly less frenetic atmosphere there.

When the sparkling and grand St George Private Hospital at Kogarah was opened near the public hospital in the 1990s, I transferred my Hurstville office to rooms there. At St George Private I shared a spacious office with my close friend and colleague Dave Pohl, an ear, nose and throat surgeon and one of the best otologists in the country. We shared the rooms at St George Private amicably for more than ten years until the diagnosis of my brain tumour forced me to close my practice.

The period since my withdrawal from clinical practice has given me an opportunity to consider the way the practice was conducted. I have not needed to apply large measures of analysis or Catholic guilt to reach the conclusion that there is much I could have done better.

I found it enormously difficult, if not impossible, to run on time and there must have been occasions when this tested the goodwill and equanimity of my patients to the limit. More often than not I found myself running an hour behind within two hours of commencing a day of consulting. I would start the day by doing rounds at one or more hospitals and always had a list of phone calls to return when I arrived at the rooms. I seemed to commence almost every consultation with an apology — 'I'm sorry you've been waiting ...' Throughout the day I would need to call patients to give them results and respond to inquiries from patients, referring doctors and other doctors seeking advice or guidance about clinical matters. As my administrative duties increased, a thousand issues at the Cancer Centre needing to be solved or decisions needing to be made would add to the day's interruptions. And there always seemed to be two or three emergency patients at every consulting session.

I tried wherever possible not to interrupt consultations to take calls, but this was almost impossible. I do regret that additional time spent by patients in my waiting room not only created a range of inconveniences — parking fines, missed buses and trains, lateness in picking up children — but on top of all this, accentuated the anxiety and fearfulness about what the visit might uncover or what bad news might be in store.

On numerous occasions I invited patients to share their concerns with me about the anxiety they experienced in the lead-up to a consultation. The emotional experience was so uniform it was as if each person had read the same script. They would go along happily for the three or four or six weeks in between visits and then, as the day for their appointment drew nearer, there would be a crescendo of fear which, in a small number of cases, would reach almost intolerable levels by the time the person sat down in my consulting room. I tried as well as I could to ease the anxiety but it was still not uncommon — particularly among concerned spouses — for there to be a little cheer or a few tears of relief when all was pronounced clear.

I now know the feeling only too well. A progressive gathering of dark clouds overhead as apprehension grows and anxiety builds, all dissipated in a matter of seconds with an exhaled 'Whew!'

A problem that went hand in hand with a practice that seemed to be bursting at the seams was the constant need to be adding patients to my operating lists. Sometimes a patient would arrive at my office with a suitcase — always a worrying sign — expecting to be admitted to hospital for an operation the next day, having been told by the referring doctor, 'Just go down there to Sydney to see Professor O'Brien. I'm sure he'll put you into hospital straight away, so make sure you take your things.' Sometimes this was sound advice and worked in everyone's favour, but more often than not, my operating schedule was already packed to the limit. Yet somehow we were nearly always able to find extra time for those badly in need of urgent treatment.

The increasing load of patients, particularly those who needed operations — especially long and complex operations — created difficulties in both the public and the private hospitals at which I worked, but the problems were quite different. At Prince Alfred, my all-day operating list began at 8 a.m. and finished at 6 p.m. Any work carried out after 6 p.m. meant that the nursing staff helping me needed to be paid overtime but also it meant they suffered the inconvenience of arriving home late to spouses, loved ones and children and being more physically spent than a normal day's work would demand. Additional patients in the public setting represent a cost which, when applied not only to the nursing staff but to all the staff concerned, might be considerable. By contrast, patients added to the operating lists in private hospitals represented additional income for the hospital and were more welcomed than discouraged. There was a limit, however, because nursing numbers in the private hospitals tended to be lower due to the natural inclination in the private sector to run with leaner staffing levels to keep costs down. So there was never an imperative to finish by a particular hour in the private hospital because I was adding to the hospital's revenue rather than simply chewing up resources, but it did mean that the nursing and anaesthetic staff who were unlucky enough to be working with me simply stayed on until the work was done.

The necessity to carry out a large number of operations effectively and expeditiously in the public sector occasionally meant that I could not invest the time in teaching that I would have liked to. The registrars and fellows were invariably much slower and more uncertain when performing operations and, principally through inexperience, would usually have little sense of time management. Sometimes they would stand at the operating table poking about, scratching here and there, with no sense at all that the clock was ticking and that the operation needed to be progressed and even completed. Balancing the need to teach — sometimes standing at the operating table with the registrar and directing every cut and every stitch and sometimes standing back from the operating table watching the young surgeon operate and simply commenting from time to time — with the need to get through the work so that the patients received the treatment that they needed, was a challenge throughout my working life.

CHAPTER 16

Chasing trains and turning the corner

As Adam and Juliette grew older Gail and I decided that our little family of four was almost too neat — two in the front and two in the back of the car and four around the table. We decided that our lives needed more unpredictability — but more importantly, Gail simply wanted another baby, so we decided to have a third child.

In October 1989 our wish was realised and our new son was born. It was Gail's third caesarean section, and came after a difficult pregnancy where placenta praevia caused episodes of bleeding, forcing Gail to be hospitalised repeatedly and confined to bed for weeks. This was not easy for her and in my role as a busy surgeon, looking after Adam and Juliette and getting them off to school each day was only made manageable by the generosity and constant assistance of Gail's mother, Grace, her sisters and a number of close family friends. A complex schedule of dropping off and picking up the children, along with the preparation and delivery of meals requiring only heating, was constructed and enacted with military precision and supported by constant infusions of love and good humour.

About ten days before James was due to be born Adam's eighth birthday loomed. I was determined that we would celebrate it properly and that I would buy him a Triang electric train set from Hobbyco, a shop in the city. One Thursday night, when I knew the shops would be open late, a close friend picked up the children and oversaw their dinner and baths while I raced from a day's operating into the city to do the birthday shopping. By the time I made it into town it was after 8 p.m. and with the shops due to close at 9 p.m. the pressure was really on; worse still, I was poorly prepared. I really didn't know where to find Hobbyco although I was fairly sure that it was in one of two places in George Street (Sydney's main street). I drove, with a fair degree of haste but otherwise obeying all road rules, to my first-choice location, parked illegally and then jogged up and down a couple of blocks searching in vain for the shop that sold electric train sets for little boys turning eight. Unsuccessful, I dashed back to the car, performed an illegal U-turn and headed uptown to the second place I thought the shop might be. As I drove through the heavy traffic I finally spotted the store — but by now it was five minutes to nine. I stopped in heavy traffic opposite the shop, performed another illegal U-turn and parked outside Hobbyco. As I jumped out of the car, prepared to race into the shop and snatch up the first train set I could find, I heard a siren and saw the reflection of flashing red and blue lights in the shop window. A young policeman climbed out of the passenger side of a police car and slowly approached me as I slumped across the roof of my car. The adrenalin that had kept me going since 6 a.m. now dissipated and my sense of urgency and determination was reduced to disappointment, soon to turn to defeat and dejection.

'Evening, driver. You were observed performing an illegal U-turn about fifty metres up the street,' came his declaration, calm, measured and unarguable in its accuracy. I just didn't have the physical or mental strength to argue or try to explain why I was in the city charging up and down the main street like a madman in the half hour before the shops closed. The weeks of Gail's hospitalisation and of trying, like a one-armed juggler, to keep a dozen balls in the air and not let any of them fall, had finally caught up with me in the form of an earnest young police officer. All I could think was, 'let's just get this over with'.

He asked to see my licence and examined it for what seemed an inordinate length of time. He wrote out an infringement notice that confirmed I would be liable for what seemed at the time to be an excruciatingly large fine, along with the loss of points from my licence. This all seemed to take forever and when I looked at my watch I saw that it was after 9.15 p.m. As I fumbled in my trousers pocket for the car keys I looked up and saw that Hobbyco was still open. It was now 9.20 but I raced into the shop anyway. In a final and possibly futile attempt at achieving my goal, I dashed from shop assistant to shop assistant crying, 'Trains! Quickly! Electric trains! Where are your trains?' Within five minutes I had left Hobbyco with a good little train set and they shut the front doors behind me.

Perhaps I should have laughed or victoriously punched the air. Instead I sat in the parked car for a long time feeling lonely and incapable, not at all proud that my shopping venture had been successful, but depressed and disappointed in myself that I seemed to be coping poorly with my various responsibilities and that, in the process, I had been reduced to a disorganised, shambolic madman who had lost all perspective and effectiveness. It was a low point.

When I arrived home to thank and relieve the friend who had supervised their evening, Adam and Juliette were sleeping soundly, blissfully comfortable and secure. I crept into their rooms, kissed their angelic little faces and felt my stress and melancholia quietly dissipate.

Next morning was another day. It always is. Adam was thrilled with his present and Juliette, ever with a generous little heart, joined in and encouraged his elation. The image of their beaming faces was imprinted on my mind all day. It was worth it.

Chris and Gail O'Brien proudly announced the birth of James Michael O'Brien, a brother for Adam and Juliette and a third grandchild for Maureen, Kevin, Murray and Grace, in late October 1989.

Although James was a full-term baby, he developed breathing difficulties shortly after delivery. Nursery staff responded quickly but when we were told there was a minor problem Gail and I did not appreciate the complexity of the issue nor the gravity of the crisis into which we would spiral over the next twenty-four hours. James had a very unusual problem for a full-term infant. He had severe pulmonary hypertension, meaning that the blood pressure in the blood vessels in his lungs was high and it was becoming increasingly difficult for his blood to circulate through the lungs and pick up oxygen. He was transferred to the neonatal intensive care unit and placed on a ventilator, with oxygen fed into his lungs via a tube that had been passed into his tiny mouth, through his voice box and into his windpipe.

Over the next forty-eight hours the pressure required to inflate his lungs, the oxygen needed to achieve satisfactory oxygen levels in the blood and the drug doses needed to support his circulation progressively climbed until they reached the highest levels James could tolerate. Gail was still recovering from surgery and was desperately fearful for her new baby. Although I was confident in the skill of the medical and nursing staff looking after James, each time they contacted me there seemed to be worsening news and the need to take another therapeutic step down a pathway that seemed to be leading inexorably to further complexity, the next complication and an increasingly gloomy outlook.

In his little humidicrib James looked so tiny and vulnerable; with so many tubes and needles penetrating and exiting every part of his body he looked like he was in the middle of an octopus fight. I confided in one of the neonatal intensive care registrars that if I had a patient with this number of tubes and requiring this level of support — maximum pressures on the ventilator, maximum oxygen and maximum levels of inotropes (drugs that support the cardiovascular system) — I would be counselling the patient's relatives to prepare themselves for a death. There seemed nothing to be optimistic about. But the registrar sympathetically reassured me that, underneath all this, James was a big strong baby boy with brand new organs, not a frail or elderly person with organs failing and at the end of their use-by date. It was sage advice.

By the third day after his birth, despite maximal therapy, James continued to deteriorate. Gail was up and around by this time and we would spend hours together sitting by his crib, hoping for a positive sign. As hopes of his recovery seemed to fade by the minute, we steeled ourselves for the worst and decided to have him baptised. It was Saturday afternoon and I asked the nursing staff to contact the hospital chaplain. Fifteen minutes later there arrived a cheerful and reassuring priest named James Collins — James Michael Collins, he emphasised, suggesting that it might be a sign. He conducted the baptism; as the afternoon wore on the numbers on the monitors, which impassively bore witness to the measurable parameters of this tiny life, continued to go in the wrong direction. Then, when all seemed lost, two things happened, almost but not quite simultaneously.

David Henderson-Smart, the brilliant and pioneering head of the neonatal intensive care unit, telephoned Canberra for permission to use a restricted, relatively experimental drug called prostacyclin, a rarely used vasodilator — a drug capable of relaxing blood vessels, allowing them to expand and thereby lowering pressure. 'I've got a pretty crook kid here and I need to give him prostacyclin,' Henderson-Smart explained in brusque understatement to some bureaucrat 300 kilometres away. That's all I heard of the conversation. Around that time my sister Carmel and her husband Phil arrived from Wollongong.

Eventually, at about 5.30, I asked Carmel to accompany me to the little church down Missenden Road to attend six o'clock Mass. My lapsed-Catholic status had continued uninterrupted from my university days until Gail and I were married. Adam's birth turned the option of becoming a regular Mass-goer again into an imperative, as we wanted him to grow up Catholic and attend a Jesuit school which expected that the boys they enrolled came from families who observed the rules of the Church, attended Mass regularly and participated in the sacraments.

The Mass had just begun as we entered St Joseph's and picked our way along a crowded pew and found a space. I looked towards the altar and was stopped momentarily by the sight of a long, white rectangular banner which hung from the front wall of the church and declared, in blue and gold painted letters, 'He Lives!' I could not look at anything else for the rest of the service. I fell into the responses effortlessly and quickly settled into the rhythm of the all too familiar ritual. It felt right.

Carmel and I walked back to the hospital in silence but no longer feeling the empty and oppressive hopelessness that had earlier burdened our hearts. As we entered the intensive care unit we were greeted by Gail who, for the first time in four days, was smiling. 'He's a little better,' she said quietly, eyes brimming and cheeks wet with tears. We hugged for a long time.

It was another six days before James was moved to the nursery, still needing oxygen, and six weeks before he came home with us, but his progress from that point was steady and without setbacks. Adam and Juliette were ecstatic to finally take delivery of their new little brother, who has since grown to be a funny, uninhibited and musically talented extrovert.

CHAPTER 17

A heaven of blackred roses

My parents seemed to acquire a new lease of life when they moved to Wentworth Falls. With busy social lives in a delightful and picturesque environment, they basked in their long-awaited nirvana like desert pilgrims who had finally reached their oasis. The feeling is the same after any long and arduous journey, or even after an extensive and messy home renovation that seems to be taking forever. When it's all over and normality is restored, the scars, discomfort and anxiety seem to disappear quickly, leaving only memories and experiences. Mum and Dad's relatively blissful existence lasted for nearly ten years. They experienced all that mountain life had to offer, travelled overseas and even bought an old motor launch that they moored in Sydney and which provided them with a number of opportunities to interrupt the contentment offered by their idyllic existence with episodes of chaotic misfortune and hilarious incompetence. Nonetheless, the old timber cruiser, *Clancy*, provided Mum and Dad with hours of fun even when they spent the entire weekend simply sitting on board and drinking gin and tonic.

The year 1995 was to be the last year of my mother's life. She had always enjoyed robust health and was proud of her cast-iron constitution and apparent indestructibility. If either of my parents was going to die before the other, Dad would have been everyone's first bet, with Mum an apparent certainty to reach one hundred. But earlier in the year she developed lower abdominal pain which, after investigations, was found to be an ovarian cancer. This malignancy has only a forty per cent survival rate, is aggressively invasive and can quickly involve the surrounding organs and tissue spaces, effectively gluing the bowels into a malignant mass that is generally impossible to remove completely and which can readily obstruct the flow of intestinal contents.

In the space of one year, my mother endured three operations and a long course of chemotherapy that made her hair fall out and caused her to lose a lot of weight along with her trademark vitality and resilience. Her experience was the epitome of 'going downhill'. She would stay with us in Sydney from time to time to make it easier for her to attend doctors' appointments and undergo further treatment and scans. On those evenings, I would occasionally assist her as she retired for the night. In bidding her goodnight, I sometimes watched quietly while she removed her silver wig and, looking so frail and vulnerable, knelt beside her bed to pray that she might be relieved of her cross and allowed to live. It was distressing to watch how solitary her battle had become for, despite the love and support with which she was surrounded, the fight was hers alone to win or lose. It was like watching a wild animal that had been mortally wounded fall to the ground, then stagger to its feet only to fall and stagger up again as its life slowly ebbed away.

For much of the year she was able to enjoy eating with us and join in dinnertime conversation with the children with great gusto. She had always liked parties, conversation and a vigorous discussion, loudly expressing her point of view and hoping that she would find opponents and contrarians because it was more interesting and fun if people disagreed with her. But eventually she was admitted to Prince Alfred Hospital with a bowel obstruction for which nothing could be done surgically and, over a period of weeks, she slowly deteriorated.

My father, effectively sidelined and ignored by her treating specialists (perhaps he wanted it that way to make it less difficult for himself), tried as best he could to negotiate the emotional hurdles. Dad remained attentive, spending hours at Mum's bedside, but he was helpless and overwhelmingly sad. Any attempt to coax conversation from him met with only short-lived success.

I had been working at Prince Alfred as a consultant head and neck surgeon for seven years by this time and I would try to call in on Mum in the afternoons or early evenings when I had finished consulting and operating, and usually read to her for an hour or so. I suspect that right to the very end she was disbelieving of her fate and expected that she would, in time, recover and go home. She wouldn't give up but, as nature took its course, the reins were taken from her hands and she became an increasingly apathetic passenger. Unable to eat, and with a tube passed through her nose into her stomach to drain gastric and intestinal fluid that could not otherwise follow its usual course, she was given just small quantities of fluid via an intravenous drip to reduce the likelihood that thirst would add to her other discomforts.

I read to her from Carol Shield's *The Stone Diaries*, which she enjoyed. Mum would lie quietly and in utter stillness, her eyes closed but alert and ready to comment or seek clarification on a point or ask questions at any time. There were several intimate passages, which in the circumstances made me uncomfortable and a little embarrassed, so I paraphrased these on the run as adroitly as I could. Sometimes this ruse necessitated my feigning a sneeze or the need to blow my nose to give me time to think of an appropriate alternative for the text that I found uncomfortably sexual. I found this unusual experience unsettling and questioned myself about why I felt the need for this subterfuge. These inhibitions, however, did not detract from the joy I experienced at having the opportunity to spend these quiet moments with my dying mother and I knew that my presence and the sound of my voice made her feel safe and gave her some comfort.

One afternoon Grandma Healey, Mum's elderly mother, came to visit her. She was brought to the hospital by Allison, one of Mum's younger sisters and herself an intelligent and independent woman in the Healey mould. Poor little Grandma Healey was almost ninety-five, shrunken and stooped with an acutely curved spine so that the top of her head pointed forward rather than to the sky and her eyes were directed constantly at her feet.

I witnessed her profound sadness as she took my mother's hand and bent forward slowly and awkwardly to kiss her cheek — a stricken mother herself, heart broken in the presence of her dying child. Emotion rose in my chest and throat and my eyes filled with tears at this raw and almost animal expression of helpless grief. It was like watching a mother animal of any kind nuzzling and pawing a dying calf or pup, helpless and bewildered.

Over those days I watched her slow deterioration as weakness and exhaustion turned to listless apathy and then unconsciousness. On the day she died I was in Canberra with Gail at a medical conference; I had said goodbye to her two days beforehand as she lay in a coma in Prince Alfred.

My mother died a month before her seventieth birthday, having enjoyed sixty-nine healthy, happy and productive years of life that were characterised by a boundless energy, intelligence and enthusiasm which energised everyone around her. She probably experienced the type of death described by Charlie Marlow, the principal protagonist of Joseph Conrad's short novel *Heart of Darkness*. Marlow had said, 'I have wrestled with death. It is the most unexciting contest you can imagine. It takes place in an impalpable greyness with nothing underfoot, without spectators, without glory, without the great desire for victory, without the great fear of defeat, in a sickly atmosphere of tepid scepticism, without much belief in your own rights and even less in those of your adversary.'

We buried my mother in the little Wentworth Falls cemetery on a day that belonged more to winter than the beginning of summer. The sky rained cold and bitter tears, sending family, friends and mourners scurrying for cover in a chaotic and irreverent dispersal. As rain teemed down we stamped and stumbled around the muddy grave site — seeing the ritual through to its end, but ultimately distracted and needing to return home with Dad to give him comfort and to warm ourselves up with cups of tea and a necessary litany of Maureen

O'Brien stories. The funeral service itself was sad but not tragically so. Dad, desolate and uncertain about what the future without his life partner would be like, sat in the front of the church while Michael, Carmel and I each shared our thoughts and feelings in individual eulogies.

I was able to put to good use one of the e e cummings poems I had learned at school. Long forgotten, I had only rediscovered it in May of that year when, on a trip to Boston to attend a meeting, I found a small book containing a hundred selected poems of e e cummings, who had lived and worked in Cambridge, near Boston.

The poem was perfect for the occasion and it is reproduced here, set out in its original format, with the rare use of punctuation and capitals that characterised cummings' work.

if there are any heavens my mother will(all by herself)have
one.   It will not be a pansy heaven nor
a fragile heaven of lilies-of-the valley but
it will be a heaven of blackred roses

my father will be(deep like a rose
tall like a rose)

standing near my

swaying over her
(silent)
with eyes which are really petals and see

nothing with the face of a poet really which
is a flower and not a face with

hands

which whisper

This is my beloved my

(suddenly in sunlight

he will bow,

& the whole garden will bow)

I do not know of a more beautiful poem, nor of one more apt. On that sad day the imagery of this magnificent and melancholy tribute, given to me by my English teacher, Malcolm Harrison, nearly thirty years earlier, resonated perfectly in the little Wentworth Falls Catholic Church.

The first weeks and months of single life for my father were confused and confusing. He was, predictably, smothered with support from every quarter, particularly from the many couples who had become close friends of both Mum and Dad during the previous ten years. He went through a phase of being regarded as an eligible widower by several of the widows and spinsters in the area. Invitations to dinner parties and functions progressively took on the tone of undisguised matchmaking.

We visited frequently, certainly more often than when Mum and Dad happily lived in the mountains together. He also made the journey to Sydney as often as he felt able but there was no mistaking the profound sadness and loneliness that pervaded every minute of his day and every attempt to distract and occupy himself. Men cope much less effectively than women with the loss of a partner and, with my father's old history of anxiety, depression and bouts of heavy drinking, he was now, separated from the strongest and most influential person in his life, at high risk of a rapid and painful implosion.

As it turned out, he survived, and even intermittently thrived, as a single man in his late sixties. He was able to find female company for the purposes of sharing the enjoyment of dinners, plays and concerts but, from all the available evidence, there was little joy in the various outings he undertook and slowly he withdrew from the society of close friends around him and mourned the loss of his wife every day.

After a year or so Dad began to take advantage of his enhanced financial situation, the result of his inheriting Mum's retirement funds, and he began to see himself as a prosperous country gentleman. He regularly used his out-of-town membership of the Royal Automobile Club and would hire a limousine to convey him from Wentworth Falls to Macquarie Street while he would sip champagne, pay the driver $200 and spend the next few days rattling around the club like it was a second home, tipping the staff generously for their service and the various kindnesses they were happy to bestow on him. Apart from his tendency to over-imbibe each evening, Dad's behaviour was impeccable and the staff at the club no doubt felt both fond of and a little sad for him.

These regular visits to Sydney gave him real enjoyment and also the opportunity to see and entertain friends in 'his club'. He complemented this lifestyle with a number of trips to America to visit relatives and friends, and to Europe. There were plane rides, cruises and bus tours during which he would invariably make new friends, but he never found a woman to replace his wife and partner of fifty years. Dad's burden of grief was made worse because both of his sisters also died around this time. They had been smokers and suffered crippling chronic emphysema for most of their adult years, which led to their ultimate deaths from respiratory failure in their early seventies.

That my father survived this tragic period of his life was a pleasant surprise to all who knew him and a testament either to his inner strength or his ability to shut out reality and focus on the immediate demands of his own world.

CHAPTER 18

RPA's real-life drama

THE ENVIRONMENT AT Royal Prince Alfred Hospital underwent a dramatic and exciting change in 1995 when the hospital authorities were approached by the management of Channel 9, who proposed filming a reality television program in the hospital using RPA's own doctors, nurses and patients. The idea had come from a very popular British television program called *Jimmy's*, in which St James's Hospital in Leeds allowed itself to be laid bare. The concept was brilliantly simple yet had the potential to be enormously popular and successful. The program would focus on specific patients and their families, filming them as they moved from admission to discharge and traversing hope, fear, pain, relief and despair.

What was needed was a large teaching hospital that catered for mothers and babies, had a busy emergency room and undertook complex surgery like heart operations, organ transplants and major cancer operations. One or two other hospitals in Sydney had been approached but had, for reasons best known to themselves, declined the offer and forgone the opportunity. It was indeed a marvellous opportunity for RPA which from time to time found itself under the sword of Damocles, as health planners and bureaucrats were inclined to pull from their bottom drawer an old blueprint which called for the neutralising or dismantling of the hospital to satisfy one political caprice or another, or simply to wipe a hated enemy off the map. It was also a chance to reverse the longstanding scepticism and lack of trust that characterised the relationship between the medical profession and the media. Doctors were in constant fear of being misrepresented and public hospitals also were wary of giving journalists too much freedom in their environs.

The new relationship between RPA and Channel 9 broke new ground but the CEO of the Area Health Service still had ultimate editorial control over what went to air. In the early days of the show, a young woman with a clipboard from the hospital's public affairs and marketing department was present whenever a doctor was filmed speaking to a patient or relatives. In fairness this was new territory for everyone, but I did initially take exception to being chaperoned by a young and very inexperienced agent of the Thought Police who was given the duty of making sure I 'didn't say or do anything wrong' (their words, not mine). In retrospect, we all got through the phase of being paranoid and over-cautious reasonably quickly. Eventually, everyone relaxed and recognised that there was no need at all for such precautions, apart from the obvious and important need to obtain the written permission of the patient or the guardian of the patient for filming to take place.

RPA has gone on to become Australia's most popular and longest-running reality television program, broadcasting its fourteenth series in 2008. I became involved with the *RPA* program during its second season of filming and it was only then that I began to fully appreciate the importance of the show to the profile and future of the hospital as well as its value as an educational medium for patients and the general public. For the first time, with reality television already well established as a credible and spectacularly popular genre, the experiences and travails of real patients were played out for the world to see. I never ceased to marvel at and admire the courage of patients and their families who allowed some of the most intimate and private moments and days of their lives to be subjected to the scrutiny and judgement of one and a half million people or more each week. The motivations of patients for participating in the program were, of course, many and varied but, most commonly, there was a desire to assist others. 'Maybe someone else will learn from this,' was the most frequently articulated reason my patients gave for allowing themselves to be filmed. In a small number of cases there may have been a desire for celebrity but, given the choice, being a patient on reality TV would not be most people's preferred means of achieving that end.

The success of *RPA* has been dependent on three critical factors: the willingness of patients and their families to have their privacy invaded and to share their story with fellow human beings; the willingness and ability of the staff of RPA to have their professional world infiltrated and laid open to the closest scrutiny; and, in that setting, their ability to continue to perform in the most professional and caring manner. Finally, the program has relied mightily on a consistently ethical, professional and open-minded ethos on the part of the production staff of Channel 9 and the video and sound crews.

The show was never supposed to be about clever doctors showing off their skills or individual surgeons demonstrating a new or tricky operation in the hope of building their profile and practice. It was all about the patient's journey — the difficult decisions, the discomfort and pain, the worry, heartache and even grief.

Since 1995 *RPA* has contributed to demystifying many of the complexities of the medicine that is practised in Australia's big teaching hospitals. It has given doctors an opportunity to be seen as caring and professional human beings and to show just how much nursing and allied health staff contribute to the care of patients. It is impossible to calculate how many and in what way individual lives have been affected by the show but many people must have found reassurance in what they have witnessed and perhaps even gained the courage to go along and see their doctor about symptoms that they had been ignoring or overlooking through fear or ignorance.

The viewing public have clearly found the program fascinating and entertaining, and responded most positively as, year by year, the producers of the program have returned to the hospital and ratcheted up the complexity and the confronting nature of the stories and images that are put to air.

RPA has won two Logies, both for Best Reality TV Program, in 2000 and 2003. I was fortunate enough to attend the award evening on two occasions. As a festival of flesh and frivolity it is, in my limited experience, difficult to beat. I had never before seen so many attractive young women wearing so little. In 2003 I was given the honour of receiving the award from the master of ceremonies, Eddie McGuire, on behalf of Channel 9. Executive producer Danny Milosavljevic and I threaded our way through a sea of tables and celebrities in Melbourne's Crown Hotel ballroom and bounced onto the stage to be greeted by Eddie and the now sadly deceased Steve Irwin, who had just finished clowning with a large snake. My moment of fame was a thrill; I accepted the Logie and made a short and, I hope, dignified speech of thanks on behalf of the patients, RPA staff and the production team. I restrained myself from sending a goofy cheerio to Gail and the children, waited for Danny to make his remarks and was then whisked from the stage for publicity photographs. My moment of fame was over in a flash.

There followed a number of parties at which often outrageous spirited misbehaviour and flirtatious revelry were the order of the day. It didn't take me long to recognise that I didn't really belong at any of the parties or with any of the people who attended them and I was happy enough, after a congratulatory drink with Danny, to retire to my room for the night and fly back to Sydney early the next morning.

Over the years, for one reason or another, I seem to have figured frequently on *RPA*, always with patients with head and neck problems, some minor and relatively straightforward and others very complicated and requiring lengthy, complex and (in terms of the potential for failure in front of television cameras) high-risk operations.

Quite a number of the patients whom I was fortunate enough to treat became well known on the program and developed their own following of viewers who were anxious to trace every step of their journey. The first of these was a warm-natured and delightful woman with big sad brown eyes named Dolores Stephens. Dolores, aged about sixty and previously a heavy smoker, thought that she was perfectly healthy until she found a lump about the size of a large grape in her neck one day and went off to seek the advice of her family doctor. She was referred to a specialist who arranged a needle biopsy of the lump and that test confirmed that it was a cancer, probably a secondary cancer from a primary growth in the throat or the back of the mouth. Further investigation revealed a malignant tumour in her throat, adjacent to her voice box, on the same side as the secondary lump.

Dolores came to see me with a chest X-ray, which thankfully was clear, and a CT scan of the head and neck region. Our initial consultation and discussion had taken place in my office in the RPA Medical Centre, but for the purposes of filming her journey for the television program we repeated the consultation in one of the clinic rooms in the hospital. We went through the scans and I discussed with her, as clearly but as gently as I could, the gravity of her situation. In particular I explained that to treat her cancer adequately she would need to undergo a radical and debilitating operation called a laryngectomy, which means removal of the voice box and part of the surrounding throat. She would also require a neck dissection to remove the malignant mass in her neck and the related lymph glands. Dolores was an intelligent woman and readily understood what was being explained to her, along with what she could expect after the operation. Nonetheless, this news and the images it conjured up must have caused her a crushing sense of fear.

The principal alternative treatment at the time was radiotherapy, which would involve six weeks of treatment to the throat and neck with no guarantee that the tumour would be gone by the end of treatment. In the decade since Dolores had her surgery, radiotherapy has increasingly been combined with chemotherapy in the treatment of advanced cancers of the throat. The benefit of this combined therapy is that it is more effective than radiotherapy alone and can very often obviate the need for surgery thereby helping to preserve the important functions of speech and swallowing by conserving the anatomical structures that are responsible for these functions.

Dolores consented to a laryngectomy and then underwent a series of consultations with people who would, hopefully, assist her to recover well from the operation and achieve maximum rehabilitation. These included our speech pathologist, social worker and another man, aged only about forty, who had also undergone a laryngectomy. This man had achieved excellent recovery of his speech and was able to talk to Dolores about what she might expect in the post-operative period and also how she might go about learning to communicate again.

Dolores was a remarkably positive person but it was distressing to see her go through all this alone. Her husband, whom I only met once, had stayed at home in Gilgandra and would telephone the ward nurses from time to time to keep up to date on his wife's progress. I had explained how I expected events to unfold and invited his inquiries but saw very little of Mr Stephens over the ensuing weeks.

When Dolores was admitted to hospital for surgery we had another patient in the head and neck ward who was also recovering from a laryngectomy carried out a week earlier by one of my colleagues. He was a cheerful Italian barber named

Cesar D'Angelo and his kind and sympathetic nature drew him to Dolores. In the absence of any immediate support, she was delighted to have the reassurance and friendship of this kindly and gentle man, conveyed in silence but with scribbled notes and a mutually manufactured sign language. The *RPA* filming crew captured a beautiful moment the evening before the operation when poor Dolores finally succumbed to the pressure of all that was happening to her and began to weep in big deep sobs at the end of a discussion with an anaesthetic registrar, who had spent some time explaining what would take place the following morning. I came into the room just as her comrade, Cesar, came to her aid and, weeping himself, took her in his arms and cradled her head against his chest. They cried their tears together — hers of resignation and, probably, terror; his of affectionate sympathy and sadness for his friend and perhaps for his own changed state and new voiceless life. I witnessed this vignette by pure chance as I stopped in briefly to say good evening to my patient and that I would look forward to seeing her in the morning, but it was one of the most beautiful and tender scenes that I have ever witnessed — the human spirit open, kind, vulnerable and brave.

Before the operation commenced I had a brief talk with Dolores in the anaesthetic room outside the theatre. It was my habit to do this anyway just to give the patient final reassurance and also to invite any last questions. This little discussion was usually filmed as it then led logically into the subsequent procedure. At the end of our brief talk Dolores simply said, 'I'm all yours.'

Dolores's laryngectomy went smoothly and the filming team, totally professional as ever, maintained a distance which compromised neither sterility nor dignity yet gave them the access they needed to record the images that the viewer would want to see.

Post-operatively, there were no complications. On the tenth day, Dolores needed to have a special X-ray, which involved her swallowing a contrast agent (a dye) to allow me to make sure that there was no leak along the suture line that was used to close the upper part of her gullet after removal of the voice box. Clinically, she seemed so well that I was confident that there would be no leakage of the dye but I was still apprehensive and Dolores was too. She was pensive and appeared to be praying quietly as her procedure was carried out and the X-rays were developed. To the relief and joy of everyone, the X-ray showed that she had healed well and we were now confidently able to start her eating and drinking by mouth.

The next challenge for Dolores was the recovery of her speech. The larynx, or voice box, is a very sophisticated and complex noise maker. Depending upon its owner, it is able to generate the high-pitched squeals of childhood, the gorgeous soprano of a Sarah Brightman, the honeyed velvet tones of a Margaret Throsby and the raucously dysphonic musicality of a Rod Stewart or a Joe Cocker — just another uniquely brilliant and vitally important organ. The noise created by the larynx is turned into words by the complicated interplay of tongue, cheeks, lips and teeth.

Researchers discovered many years ago that in the absence of a larynx, a column of air vibrating in the throat can also serve to produce monotone vocal sounds which can in turn be transformed into words. One of the original and most frequently used methods of achieving this end involved the patient swallowing air and then burping it back up in a controlled fashion from the oesophagus into the mouth. To the disgust of their parents and teachers, teenage boys can often perfect this technique without having to go through the inconvenience of having their voice boxes removed.

A number of surgical procedures have been devised over the years to restore laryngectomy patients' voices. None of these procedures ever worked terribly well, but then two Americans invented a little one-way plastic valve that could be inserted across the common wall between the windpipe and the gullet so that air could be pushed from the lungs through the valve and up into the mouth, creating a noise which can be turned into speech.

The great advantage over oesophageal speech is that this form of speech — called tracheo-oesophageal speech — allows the patient to speak in long sentences because he is able to use a lungful of air instead of the staccato voice of the oesophageal speaker, who burps small volumes of air each time. Dolores had a speaking valve inserted on TV and then, I am sure to the amazement of thousands of viewers, clearly spoke the words 'thank you, thank you', about two weeks after the removal of her voice box. Dolores won hearts all over Australia for her fighting spirit and cheerful and gracious stoicism. She underwent six weeks of radiotherapy following her operation, to reduce the likelihood of her cancer growing back in the neck and throat region.

Initially she did very well but in the year or so after the completion of her treatment Dolores found it more difficult to swallow and her voice increasingly became a choked, high-pitched squawk, like Donald Duck. These changes occurred because the new gullet I had fashioned had become constricted and had turned into a narrow, scarred tube. She was otherwise doing well with no sign at all of the cancer returning, so I needed to devise a way of widening the narrowed segment of gullet to allow food to go down and air to be pushed out. This was not straightforward and by agreeing to have the operation filmed to satisfy the interest of the multitude of *RPA* viewers who were impatient to learn what would happen to Dolores next, I felt I was really tempting fate.

I needed to reopen her previous neck wounds, dissect through scar tissue to identify her pharynx (the upper part of her gullet) and open it vertically to break the tight ring of constriction that had caused the problem. This was easily enough achieved but the only way to close the opening that I had made was to insert a patch of new tissue, like a gusset, taken from a part of the body which had not been damaged by radiotherapy and which would have a new and reliable blood supply to ensure that it would heal well to its surrounding tissue and be watertight.

An island of skin with its underlying tissue attachments and blood vessels was lifted from one of Dolores's forearms (the free flap technique devised and perfected by Chinese surgeons in the 1970s) and I sewed it to the sides of her pharynx with the skin facing in to form a new lining.

Thankfully, the operation went without a hitch and Dolores healed beautifully, without any evidence of leakage from this newly fashioned swallowing tube. Dolores left hospital after a couple of weeks and returned home to my great relief and the joy of the enormous number of admirers and followers who had watched her bravely battle the fear and discomfort which must have accompanied every step of her treatment.

Unfortunately, Dolores's heroic optimism was dealt a cruel blow when, six or more months after recovering from her second operation, she was found to have secondary tumour deposits in her liver and then died within a few weeks. Dolores's quiet death was very sad and the nurses who looked after her and who had a genuine fondness and concern for this spirited but gentle woman felt the loss deeply.

CHAPTER 19

Paul's pumpkins and minor celebrity

WHEN DOLORES DIED her husband asked that her ashes be buried in the hospital grounds. This, of course, was an extraordinary request and one can only imagine what the outcome would be if Prince Alfred took on the responsibility of burying in its grounds the remains of patients who had been treated at, or who died in, the hospital. Anyway, in an act of charitable acquiescence that reflected very well on the hospital authorities, they agreed to the request and there is still a small memorial plaque marking the spot where the ashes of Dolores Stephens were buried in a small garden at the back of the hospital near the university. *RPA* viewers were informed of Dolores's passing by way of a simple message at the end of one of the programs read by actor Max Cullen, who provided the informative, dignified and often comforting narration that gave each episode of *RPA* the professionalism, sensitivity and integrity that have contributed to the show's success and popularity over more than a decade.

The readiness and ability of the viewing public to cope with watching some of the most confronting operations and procedures imaginable has surprised both the producers of the program and the staff of the hospital. One of these confronting and complicated cases involved a delightful and cheerfully pragmatic farmer from Ulladulla named Paul Uhbrien, who was famous in regional New South Wales for growing gigantic pumpkins. Paul had won all kinds of trophies and ribbons for his massive vegetables at Sydney's Royal Easter Show and at other country shows. Unfortunately he also grew an unusual and dangerous malignant tumour called a chondrosarcoma in his right orbit (the eye socket). The tumour displaced his eyeball, causing double vision, and invaded the bone of the skull, causing encroachment on the brain. Paul was initially treated by my own neurosurgeon, Michael Besser, who approached the tumour through the skull via an incision around the hairline, and removed as much of it as he could while preserving the eyeball itself.

After a relatively short period of time, regrowth occurred and it was necessary for Paul to have another operation, this time with the aim of completely eradicating the cancer. Besser referred Paul to me to carry out the surgery, which involved approaching the tumour from the front and removing the entire contents of the eye socket, that is, the eyeball and its surrounding fat and muscle, along with parts of the upper and lower eyelids. The decision to recommend to Paul and his wife that he should undergo this operation and sacrifice the sight in his right eye weighed heavily on my mind, so I sought the advice of Besser and my other colleagues in the head and neck team to assure the Uhbriens and myself that the proposed strategy was appropriate and necessary. At the time of the operation the *RPA* crew, with whom I had now worked regularly for several years, were in keen anticipation and readiness. I am not aware that an orbital exenteration (the complete removal of the contents of the eye socket) had ever been filmed and shown to the public on television before.

Before we operated, Paul visited a meticulous and talented prosthetist named Jim Fisher, who worked at the Sydney Dental Hospital and who had manufactured brilliantly realistic prosthetic ears and noses for some of my other patients. Using special silicone material and coloured dyes, Jim would create a prosthesis attached to a pair of glasses that would simulate, to near perfection, Paul's right eye, eyelids and the surrounding skin and soft tissue. A number of visits both before and after the operation were required for this painstaking work. Jim Fisher is outstanding, not only for his brilliant expertise but also for his shy humility, and a lot of talking was needed to convince him to be filmed for the television program.

When the time came for Paul's operation I made a particular point on camera of saying to all those present in the operating theatre, 'Does everyone agree that we are removing the right eye?' There were general comments of agreement from Ian, the anaesthetist and other staff and, following this reassuring confirmation, the operation commenced. Technically, the procedure went along very smoothly and we were able, as far as could be determined with the naked eye, to completely remove Paul's chondrosarcoma.

The gaping cavity of the eye socket needed to be filled, so I removed some muscle from Paul's abdominal wall and literally stuffed it into the hole that had been created by the removal of the tumour, the eyeball and the fat and muscle which normally fills the orbit. The lump of abdominal muscle that I transferred to Paul's orbit was kept alive by slender blood vessels that were harvested with the muscle and then joined to other blood vessels in front of the ear using the operating microscope. With so many complicated steps it may again have seemed that I was risking fate or even inviting failure by allowing this procedure to be filmed, but the opportunity for public education and particularly to demonstrate the wondrous job that Jim Fisher could do in replacing lost tissue was too good to overlook.

Paul came through the operation with flying colours. By next morning, when I visited him at his bedside he was thrilled that everything had gone well, but he was startled at the sight of the swollen blob of muscle protruding from his right orbit when he looked in a mirror. This in fact was perfectly normal because the transplanted tissue swells quite rapidly after the operation and can take a few days to settle down. I reassured him I was very happy with everything and that the muscle looked healthy.

'Jeez, if that's a good result I'd hate to see a bad one!' he quipped.

Muscle that loses its nerve supply wastes away and shrinks quite significantly over a period of weeks, so I knew that the bulging mass in Paul's orbit would not only lose its normal post-operative swelling but that it would shrink to a volume which was just enough to fill the orbital cavity and accommodate the prosthesis which he would subsequently wear.

Because of the risk that the tumour may grow back it was recommended that Paul have radiotherapy to the orbital region after surgery. He went ahead with this and has remained free of cancer for a number of years. The television crew captured a delightful moment at Paul's home with him and his wife dancing happily in their lounge room — an eye lost but a life restored.

Like Dolores, Paul Uhbrien was very popular with *RPA* viewers because of his courageous and good-humoured fatalism. He spoke with infectious enthusiasm of farm life and his oversized produce, and I was surprised to learn that the really enormous pumpkins he grew were only good for animal fodder, which seemed a shame. It was a privilege to have this gentle farmer bring his difficult and life-threatening problem to me and trustingly put his life in my hands.

My involvement with the *RPA* television program added a new and positive dimension to my professional life and seemed to create for me a very minor degree of celebrity. The program was watched all over Australia, to a lesser extent in New Zealand, and apparently has been syndicated to various lifestyle channels in Europe. A friend in the Netherlands told me that he saw an episode of *RPA* on a channel in Amsterdam that also showed soft-core pornography. From time to time, I have been stopped in the street, in a shopping centre or even at an airport and asked 'Are you that doctor on *RPA*?' One particularly droll GP, Greg Wilcox, once sent an old man to see me with a note that read, 'Mr Jones saw you on TV and wanted you to do an operation on him, so I've looked all over him and found a lump on his head. Would you kindly remove it?'

I have found that being recognisable in public because of my association with *RPA* is unusual but it would be disingenuous of me if I claimed that I have found it disagreeable.

Not everything shown on the *RPA* program was a medical extravaganza or tour de force. One of my patients who featured was a cute little fellow aged eight or nine named Matthew, who had a congenital shortening of one of the muscles in his neck that caused his head to be tilted quite sharply to one side, just like a wry neck; a condition called torticollis. Matthew's schoolmates made fun of him and called him cruel but not particularly imaginative names like 'crooked neck'; not surprisingly, this caused distress to both the little boy and his family. Correction of the problem involved a relatively simple operation, although it needed to be carried out with great care in order to guarantee its completeness and also to avoid inadvertent damage to adjacent important nerves. The muscle in question, called the sternocleidomastoid muscle, is attached to the top of the breastbone and the head of the collarbone and extends up to the bony bump behind the ear called the mastoid process. It protects the great vessels of the neck, the carotid artery and internal jugular vein; it is easy to see how, in the course of evolution, primitive men might have enjoyed a survival advantage if they had this muscle to protect these major blood vessels from blows to the neck from their enemies' weapons. The cure for Matthew's problem involved cutting through the tight tendonous bands that connected it to the bones at its upper and lower ends. Access to the muscle is achieved by simple linear incisions a couple of centimetres long, in the skin creases just below the ear and low in the neck above the collarbone.

Matthew recovered well from his operation and on his first visit back to my office afterwards his neck movement was much better, although he still tilted his head a little bit to one side, more from habit than anything else (I hoped). I think there was as much interest and enjoyment for viewers in seeing this small boy's apparently minor problem resolved and his quality of life improved as in seeing a liver or brain transplant or some other horrendoplasty.

CHAPTER 20

Turf battles

THE DISCIPLINE OF HEAD AND NECK surgery has found itself at the epicentre of bitter professional rivalries from time to time. The reasons for this are complex and historical but a contributing factor is that many of the procedures carried out by head and neck surgeons also fall within the scope of activities of other specialties. ENT, plastic, general, and oral and maxillofacial surgeons can all find themselves working in the complex terrain of the head and neck for perfectly valid reasons. Occasionally some of these specialties have claimed head and neck surgery (or big chunks of it) as their own, causing demeaning turf battles. One such long-running argument has involved ENT surgeons wanting to claim the territory and denigrating the rights of other surgeons to undertake head and neck operations. Head and neck surgery does not logically fit as a branch of general surgery and through their training, ENT surgeons do have a much better understanding than other surgeons of head and neck anatomy and the various pathological processes that occur in the region. They also have the necessary skills to properly examine and evaluate the head and neck region, inside and out. As my initial training was in general surgery I was absolutely passionate about being thoroughly trained in every aspect of head and neck oncology, including pathology and reconstruction, so that I could never be criticised for being 'just a general surgeon'. Despite my training, expertise, research output and burgeoning practice, it took a long time for a number of my ENT colleagues to accord me grudging respect. Ironically this was never an issue in the international arena.

Because of the variety of tumours that can affect the head and neck, and because treatment can lead to severe disability and deformity, head and neck oncology is the specialty that — more than any other — demands multidisciplinary input, not only from a range of medical specialists such as surgeons and radiation and medical oncologists, but also from the nursing and allied health staff who help to manage and support patients during their treatment and recovery. The head and neck clinic is the forum that brings together these various individuals, usually in the presence of the patient, so that their experience and expertise can be brought to bear on each patient's clinical problem with the aim of recommending the most appropriate treatment strategy.

While there are many medical societies that allow specialists to meet with their peers and colleagues on issues of mutual interest, both scientific and social, there was no society that catered for the multidisciplinary exchange of information and ideas among those practising in the field of head and neck oncology. To redress this state of affairs, I decided that I would form a head and neck society and spent some months in 1996 deciding how I would do this. I had already gathered together a loose coalition of colleagues in

Sydney who met very occasionally when an overseas visitor was in town and it occurred to me that this group could form the nucleus of the new organisation. A series of meetings was convened and I was pleased by the number and enthusiasm of those who attended.

The principal philosophy behind the creation of a multidisciplinary society, based on mutual respect and goodwill among its members, was to shed the lead weight of professional jealousies and turf battles and to return patient care and the quest for knowledge and better outcomes to a central position of importance. We decided that it was important to try to form a national organisation and to invite our New Zealand colleagues to join with us.

There was, however, resistance from some quarters and individuals, including senior ENT colleagues who felt that this new society would threaten the already established ENT society. This opposition thankfully dissipated after a short time.

In 1999 the Australian and New Zealand Head and Neck Society had its first meeting in Sydney at the Ritz Carlton Hotel in Double Bay. More than 230 people attended and the meeting was opened by Dame Leonie Kramer, then Chancellor of the University of Sydney. We invited two overseas guests: Helmuth Goepfert, a surgeon from Houston and Bill Mendenhall, a radiation oncologist from Florida. The meeting was pronounced an outstanding success scientifically and socially and a modest profit was made.

The society has continued to flourish and, each year, the scientific meeting attracts excellent attendance and submissions of papers of very high quality, with between 200 and 250 participants. More importantly, the society's members and those attending these meetings share the strong conviction that the management of patients who are unfortunate enough to develop tumours and cancers of the head and neck is not the responsibility (or right) of just one craft group or specialty but requires a team approach. When finally I was able to step away from an executive role in the society, and when its survival was no longer dependent upon my continued energy and input because the members themselves had taken ownership of the organisation and it had become theirs, I breathed a great sigh of relief and satisfaction, and I am happy now simply to attend meetings as a member.

Another challenge that needed to be met arose closer to home. The activities of the Department of Head and Neck Surgery at RPA had expanded in a number of directions but needed to be better coordinated. The funded data manager's position had been a feature of our structure for some years now and I had also been able to establish a salary for a fellow, a young but fully trained surgeon wanting to spend a further year or two doing research and learning specialised or advanced operative techniques before taking up a permanent position in a hospital. The department needed to develop a second fellow's position and to begin a basic research program that involved, among other things, the collection of tumour specimens from the operating theatre and keeping these specimens, along with clotted blood, in a tumour bank. When combined with the clinical data of the patients, these biological specimens would become an immensely powerful research tool. There was also an educational gap among general practitioners and students in relation to the diagnosis and management of lumps in the neck and all kinds of other clinical problems in the field of head and neck oncology. Ill-equipped and poorly trained individuals still dabbled in the management of a number of head and neck problems, sometimes with disastrous results and often making the appropriate and definitive treatment more difficult or impossible.

I thought that all of these issues could be addressed if a more formal structure was developed around the RPA head and neck service, so I wrote a proposal to the then NSW Health Minister, Craig Knowles. I had met Craig on a couple of occasions when I was chairman of the hospital medical board and we got on well, so I was confident that he would at least give my suggestions a hearing. I recommended that we should establish a body, which I called the Sydney Head and Neck Cancer Institute (SHNCI), to oversee and coordinate the clinical care of patients, clinical and basic research, education of students, residents, general practitioners and other specialists, and data collection with the aim of facilitating collaborative studies. I attached a budget to the document and sent it off to Knowles. At a follow-up meeting he responded very positively and simply commented that, instead of giving me a one-off grant, he felt that it would be more appropriate and helpful if he funded the institute with a yearly grant and left it to me to raise additional funds if they were needed.

The SHNCI was launched at a grand gala ball at the Regent Hotel (now the Four Seasons) in Sydney, which was attended by Knowles, Frank Sartor (then Lord Mayor of Sydney), Professor Marie Bashir AC, the Governor of NSW — who also accepted my invitation to become patron of the Institute — and her husband, Sir Nicholas Shehadie. The event was a grand success in every way and we raised over $100,000.

The clinical fellowship program in head and neck oncology at RPA is one of the principal initiatives supported by the development of the Sydney Head and Neck Cancer Institute. The program began in 1992 and since that time twenty-three young surgeons have participated in periods of training in the head and neck service. Their specialty backgrounds include ENT, general, plastic and maxillofacial surgery and their countries of origin include England, the Netherlands, Switzerland, Canada, the USA, New Zealand and Belgium. Although one of our early fellows was a young Australian woman trained in general surgery, the intention was never to try to attract young Australians to the position because I believe that there is greater advantage in their spending a year, preferably two, at a very good overseas institution so that the multiple benefits of living in another country, experiencing another culture and obtaining the best training available at an international level, can be gained. Equally we aimed to offer these benefits to young surgeons from overseas.

CHAPTER 21

A diverse mediocrity

IN 1996 A BREAK FROM a long-established tradition was initiated at RPA when a decision was made to group specialties (or clinical departments) into a new structure based on the clinical services they provided rather than their traditional craft group affiliations. For example, my work as a head and neck surgeon meant that I had more in common with a radiation oncologist or medical oncologist than a vascular surgeon, but the traditional practice was to gather all surgical departments together into a division of surgery. Why not do away with this archaic structure and combine the surgical and medical specialties engaged in the treatment of cancer into a large 'cancer service'?

The new clinical groupings brought surgeons and physicians together with the aim of improving communication, efficiency and patient care. I can hear the derisive catcalls of cynics as I write what may seem like administrative propaganda and treacherous doublespeak, but the changes were without question a master stroke.

One of the results was the establishment in 1996 of the Sydney Cancer Centre, the name given to the coalition of clinical departments and research groups that were brought together at Royal Prince Alfred and Concord Hospitals to form the Area Cancer Service.

Although the Sydney Cancer Centre was given a building, Gloucester House (the old private wing of Prince Alfred Hospital), in which it could establish its headquarters and conduct outpatient clinics and some research activity, the physical facilities were inadequate, poorly accessible to patients and did nothing to foster collaboration between clinicians and researchers. In fact we were, and continue to be, more than three decades behind the Americans in the way we organise our cancer infrastructure.

In 1971, the then US President, Richard Nixon, declared war on cancer and established the US National Cancer Institute (NCI). A critical component of the strategy developed by the NCI was the establishment of cancer centres, based on the understanding that creating centres of excellence, where clinical and research expertise were concentrated and integrated, would lead to innovation, research breakthroughs and the very best treatment outcomes possible, especially for uncommon cancers. Some of these cancer centres were given the designation 'comprehensive cancer centre' based on the attainment of rigorous standards across a spectrum of quality indicators including the development of innovative therapies, clinical trial participation, education, outreach and other measurable criteria.

I had already spent time at the University of Alabama Comprehensive Cancer Center in Birmingham and well understood both the concept and the physical elements that were needed to create a cancer centre. The new clinical structure at RPA suited me perfectly and gave me great hope for the future development of cancer services in Australia.

The first director of the Sydney Cancer Centre was Jim Bishop, a phlegmatic haematologist from Melbourne whose leadership had a visionary, big-picture quality that offered the potential to take the Cancer Centre to an international level. Jim's ambitions were given a fortuitous boost when he met Frank Sartor, the then Lord Mayor of Sydney, while Frank was assisting his unfortunate partner to struggle through the treatment of an aggressive tongue cancer and trying to negotiate the obstacles, gaps and vagaries of a disjointed medical system which was anything but seamless, patient-focused and user-friendly. Jim and Frank formed a dynamic alliance and established a foundation to raise $5 million to add a floor to Gloucester House and turn it into an American-style comprehensive cancer centre. Their plans went badly awry when they decided that the upgraded building would become the headquarters of a new organisation called the National Cancer Centre. This plan by RPA to stand across the centre of the field with the widest possible stance and to claim nation-leading status was just too much hubris for some of the medical groups in Sydney, particularly those at Westmead who saw, and continue to see, their own campus as being the geographic centre of Sydney and the site most suited to treating the majority of the state's cancer patients.

The rapid and shrill response, which has since been reprised on several occasions, was that RPA had once again overreached itself and had no right to aspire to world domination or even the national leadership role that the proposed name implied. Jim and Frank were told to pull their heads in quick smart, but this created the opportunity for Jim to conjure up another project, this time aimed at improving the delivery of cancer services across the entire state, not just Prince Alfred: with the establishment of a NSW Cancer Institute.

Jim became CEO of the newly established Cancer Institute NSW, with Sartor overseeing a new Cancer Ministry within the Health Department. I decided to apply for the position vacated by Bishop, directing the activities of the Sydney Cancer Centre and with this job I inherited the $5 million plan to 'Raise the Roof' (as the project was called) of Gloucester House. I really did not think this was a good plan, in fact I thought it would be a waste of money. I suggested to my colleagues and members of the Cancer Centre's foundation that we should instead build an entirely new cancer centre, modern and purpose-built. I knew that this would be a very complex dot-connecting exercise but I advocated vigorously and the plan was soon embraced by hospital and government authorities and a number of wealthy, influential and socially well-connected people.

I had no intention of relinquishing any of my responsibilities or cutting back any of my other activities. The directorship of the Sydney Cancer Centre amounted to a full-time job, although I agreed that I would be paid for two days per week. I continued in my role as director of the Sydney Head and Neck Cancer Institute and carried on with all of my clinical duties, along with supervising and mentoring two clinical fellows, a registrar, an intern and students.

During this period there was also an increasing need for me to travel overseas. These various commitments — in reality over-commitments — meant that I had an extremely busy and compressed schedule.

I had celebrated my fiftieth birthday in 2002 with a party that I entitled 'A Diverse Mediocrity', and to which the guests were invited to wear something gold. My use of the term 'diverse mediocrity' was not an attempt at false humility but really my honest appraisal of what the first fifty years of my life amounted to. I seemed to myself to be adequate, ordinary, average or moderately capable across a spectrum of activities, disciplines and skills without ever excelling at any of them, principally because I rarely committed the time and energy to achieve excellence.

One of these areas of endeavour was guitar playing. I had played the guitar a little when I was in high school but my expertise was confined to strumming a limited range of chords to accompany my very ordinary singing. In the year before I took over the role of director of the Sydney Cancer Centre, I started having guitar lessons to improve my playing, which had not progressed much from the very low standard I had achieved as a teenager.

My teacher was a good-humoured and very talented Latvian named Peter Pik who had a shaved head, earrings and a beard like a toilet brush. Peter had experienced the electrified world of loud rock bands but had focused his creative efforts and work and teaching on solo acoustic guitar using the so-called 'boom chic' finger picking style of Chet Atkins, Gerry Reed and others including Australia's own Tommy Emmanuel, arguably the best and most technically brilliant guitarist in the world. Peter, along with a barrister friend, Paul Hedman, had toured for a time with Tommy and contributed the tablature for a number of Tommy's guitar tunes for a book that Hedman wrote about the Tommy Emmanuel style called *Note by Note*.

Peter would arrive at our house around 9 p.m. on Wednesday evenings and, for the next couple of hours, he would patiently teach me, quite literally note by note, and then we would play together, me in my clumsy and stumbling fashion, while we kept our spirits up with red wine. For a number of years it was the best night of my week and, despite my limitations, I made slow progress. My challenges were threefold: firstly to coax real music, not just a sequence of notes, from the guitar ('try to make it sing', Peter would encourage); secondly to establish a smooth but infectious rhythm that would induce a foot-tapping response from the listener ('that's it, mate, get it to cook!' was another constant admonition); and finally, I had to make time for daily practice.

Unlike James, my youngest son who has all the musical buttons switched on and is an excellent pianist, quick to learn and with an excellent ear, I was a plodder with the guitar and found it difficult to rise above mediocrity because I just could not seem to find (or make) the time to practise enough. I still had difficulty making even technically correct note playing sound musical, but I believe that requires a special gift. A voice singing the correct notes does not necessarily make music and it is the combination of musicality and rhythm that captivates and enthrals.

Peter's guitar lessons brought a window of relief to my busy week but, as additional responsibilities increasingly occupied my time and mental energy, I found it more and more difficult to practise, so I was often ill-prepared for my lessons. My Wednesdays were normally spent consulting in my office for the entire day with back-to-back patients, no time out for lunch and always running an hour or more late and beginning every consultation with an apology, so by the time Wednesday evenings rolled around I was more ready for a rest or a sleep than an activity which required dexterity, concentration and discipline. Peter, to his credit, was always encouraging and gently constructive in his criticism. I was plying him with good wine so perhaps that assisted his positive appraisal of my modest talent.

Being time-poor was a simple fact of my life for which I worked hard to compensate and which I would not let myself use as an excuse for falling down in my responsibilities as a husband and father or any of my responsibilities at work. The answer, as I saw it, was to expend more energy and to work harder at my various tasks.

CHAPTER 22

One world contracts, another expands

My father's initial years as a widower saw him slowly reach a plateau of emotional equanimity and domestic self-assurance, which gave my brother, sister and me confidence that he would not succumb early to a lonely and miserable death.

Because Mum's energy had initiated and stoked the fires of most of their social contacts, Dad inevitably withdrew from their circle of friends in the mountains, but managed to maintain enough contacts to satisfy his need to share conversation and a few drinks with friends or associates from time to time. He was troubled by arthritis in both knees and this painful problem increasingly restricted his mobility, causing him to rely almost exclusively on driving to get himself around. Of itself, this was not problematic but he had previously been a keen and moderately energetic walker. Now he would drive to a club in Lithgow, enjoy an inexpensive meal and then return home to spend the rest of the day reading the newspapers, listening to music and drinking scotch. He was, if anything, well informed because he read all the major daily newspapers from front to back and was able to engage in intelligent discussion on most issues. He mistrusted all levels of government and saw conspiracies everywhere.

Dad particularly loved travelling to Tasmania by boat. What suited him perfectly was the fact that he could drive his car directly onto and off the ship at either end of the journey and enjoy the short voyage in relaxed comfort.

His isolation in Wentworth Falls was balanced by our regular visits to the mountains and his reciprocated trips to Sydney to see Michael and me, and to Wollongong where Carmel and Phil lived. Unfortunately the difficulty he had with walking was greatly intensified when, on a brief visit to Lord Howe Island, he developed a thrombosis in the veins of one of his legs (a problem more often associated with long-haul economy-class air travel). He was consigned to rest in bed and given blood-thinning tablets but he developed swelling and stiffness in the ankles and, almost overnight, virtually gave up walking. A background to these difficulties was his chronic emphysema, which had caused problems for years and required regular use of puffers, with the addition of oral and sometimes intravenous steroids during an acute episode. Both of his sisters had died alone in their homes of acute respiratory failure and I am sure Dad felt his life would end in the same way. His increasing reclusiveness became a constant source of concern and with little difficulty Michael, Carmel and I convinced him that he should sell the house in the mountains and move closer to us in order to be nearer to company and assistance. The house in Wentworth Falls sold quickly and he moved to a small but comfortable unit in a retirement complex not far from our home in Hunters Hill. This sudden contraction of his world and the loss of the leafy garden that had surrounded the house and afforded him the quiet solitude he seemed increasingly to seek, was less of an upheaval than we had anticipated. He settled readily and eagerly into his new home, surrounding himself with favourite items of furniture, pictures, music, books and souvenirs.

The retirement complex was inhabited almost exclusively by elderly widows, although some were younger and dangerously sprightly. There was a married couple among this nest of women, and Dad quickly befriended as a kindred spirit the man of the house, who had served as a glider pilot during the Second World War.

Initially he enjoyed his new surroundings and the polite and mostly unobtrusive fuss made of him by his new neighbours. His mobility further deteriorated but he continued to drive, and he seemed to enjoy the fact that visits from his children had become easier and more frequent and that he could readily reciprocate by eating dinner with us a couple of evenings a week.

Gail, with her heartfelt kindness, was an attentive and tolerant daughter-in-law and met Dad each week to take him for a late morning coffee or lunch. She would sit patiently and listen to his occasional whingeing or ranting about political issues as his mood and outlook swung between choleric and melancholic on an almost daily basis.

There was never the slightest likelihood that my father would find another partner and he said that he missed my mother every day. Loneliness and self-pity combined to severely blunt his initiative and augment his appetite for scotch.

I visited regularly and, more often than not, would find two or three empty whisky bottles in his garbage bin while the cooktop and sink in his tiny kitchenette appeared never to be used. Our attempts to introduce Meals on Wheels to his eating routine met with only modest success, but he sustained himself with a decent meal in the middle of the day and biscuits and tea in the evenings.

By contrast, around this time my own world and its related responsibilities had expanded exponentially and, continuing to take the world two stairs at a time, I found myself busily over-committed on any number of fronts. Invitations to lecture, teach and attend meetings and conferences overseas seemed to double in number each year and, in total contrast to my habit during my early professional life, I was saying 'no thank you' more and more often. Most years I was now travelling to both Europe and the United States, often twice, but I tried wherever I could to take Gail and/or one of the children with me, to make any journey seem more like a holiday.

I had always found travel enjoyable and exciting and so when my popularity as a speaker and visiting professor entered the upward phase of a cycle that inevitably turns downward later in one's career, I was happy to accept invitations and decided that I should just enjoy the ride while it lasted. If I needed to travel while patients were still in hospital recovering, I was always confident that the quality of their care never diminished. The head and neck ward, overseen and superbly managed by one of the hospital's most experienced, able and sensible nurses, Doreen Brine, was known to provide the highest level of care to some of the most complex patients in RPA.

Still, when meetings and travel obligations finally came to pass, I often found the timing inconvenient and wished occasionally that I had not accepted the invitation. I much preferred spending time in Europe than the US because I found the culture much more to my liking, but life in Sydney was so busy that I tended to make all trips as brief as possible. There was inevitably a rush of new patients to see, urgent operations and, increasingly, administrative matters requiring my attention before I left and then a punitive backlog awaiting me when I returned.

In what I now regard in retrospect as a significant error, I rarely gave myself the opportunity to recover fully from these overseas journeys before recommencing work. Invariably I would fly into Sydney early in the morning and return to work either that day or the next, hoping to make some inroads into the phone calls, correspondence and clinical problems which awaited me and to re-establish my normal pattern of sleep.

In 2004, the Seventh International Conference on Head and Neck Cancer, a meeting held every four years in North America, was scheduled to take place in August in Washington DC. I was honoured with an invitation to deliver the most prestigious named lecture in head and neck oncology, the Hayes Martin Lecture. I was the first Australian and only the third non-American to be invited to deliver this lecture in the many years since its establishment.

In an enormous meeting room packed with almost 2000 delegates from around the world I gave my lecture, addressing the issue of aggressive skin cancer, its propensity to spread to the lymph glands of the head and neck, and my experience treating that metastatic disease. I concluded with a recommendation for a change in the international staging system used to describe head and neck skin cancers, based on the outcome of my own experience and research.

Australia has the highest incidence of skin cancer, particularly malignant melanoma, in the world and this is directly attributable to the relationship between sun exposure and skin type. Having underpinned the presentation of my clinical data with a broader cultural and historical introduction, I was able to bring an antipodean perspective to the global skin cancer problem.

My Hayes Martin Lecture was well received. It was a highlight of my professional life which facilitated discussion of a uniquely Australasian health problem in which I had amassed arguably the world's largest personal experience, and which made excellent use of the long-established RPA head and neck database and contributed new understanding to a particular disease and clinical problem.

The following year we returned to the United States in response to another invitation, this time to deliver another named lecture during the meeting of the American Academy of Otolaryngology – Head and Neck Surgery. The Gene Myers Lecture is named after one of the living doyens of head and neck surgery and I was honoured, as an Australian, to be invited to present my work at such an auspicious occasion.

Later in 2005 I was travelling again — this time to Leiden, a small but famous university city close to Amsterdam, in the Netherlands. The ANZ Head and Neck Society held its annual meeting in Sydney that year, and 2005 ended with consulting, operating, teaching and writing all rolling on at a cracking pace, along with the endless responsibilities which accompanied my administrative roles running both the Sydney Cancer Centre and the Area Cancer Service.

On one occasion I flew to New York to give a ten-minute after-dinner speech at a black-tie function at the University Club on Fifth Avenue. The dinner was held in honour of a close friend and valued mentor, Dr Jatin Shah, an elegant and urbane Indian who is the world superstar of head and neck oncology and one of the shining lights at the Memorial Sloan-Kettering Cancer Center in New York. He had been given the rare honour of having a chair of surgery established in his name during his working life. It was an honour for me to be invited and asked to speak and, despite the costs of lost income, airfares and accommodation and the physical wear and tear, I really felt that I could not let my friend down nor, to be honest, miss the opportunity.

I flew back to Sydney the next day, arriving early on a Tuesday morning, and went straight to work, planning not to operate myself but to supervise the fellows and registrar.

The complicated landscape of my professional life was also becoming increasingly dominated by administrative demands. This suited me and, in fact, my decision to apply for the position as the director of the Sydney Cancer Centre had been driven to a very large extent by my desire to find different challenges.

My work as a clinical surgeon had been abundantly rewarding but despite my increasing profile, both locally and overseas, I was growing tired of operating. I felt I had reached a point of what my old mentor Jim May called surgical maturity. I had now carried out literally thousands of operations and the clinical details of each patient, each operation and its outcome, including complications, had been carefully documented for nearly twenty years. I knew that bigger and more aggressive operations were not at all likely to cure more patients. Indeed, the trend in surgery for cancers of all types was for operations to be increasingly conservative and selective, and for non-surgical therapies to play an increasing role.

That said, it is a truism that the single best way to cure a patient with a localised early stage solid tumour is by surgical removal. I knew, however, that factors over which I had no control, like the biological aggressiveness of the cancer and the nutritional state and immune competence of the patient, contributed to the outcome of the treatment as much as, or more than, the quality of my surgery.

I was not particularly yearning to find an administrative job; I was just looking for new intellectual challenges and would have been happy, if I had been independently wealthy, to give up medicine and go back to university to study history and literature.

As director of the Sydney Cancer Centre I was also clinical director of cancer services of the Central Sydney Area Health Service, which included Concord, the inner west and Canterbury.

A reconfiguration of the seventeen health services across the state took place in 2005 following scandalous revelations about the poor quality of clinical care in south-western Sydney, particularly at Camden and Campbelltown Hospitals. Central Sydney was combined with South Western to form Sydney South West Area Health Service and I now found myself clinical director of cancer services for a population of 1.3 million people — approximately twenty per cent of the state — comprising the poorest, the sickest and the most ethnically diverse citizens in New South Wales.

This amalgamation posed immense challenges for everyone, not the least of which were the needs to integrate cultures, raise clinical standards, support and encourage colleagues at Bankstown, Liverpool and Campbelltown and assure them that this was not simply a Prince Alfred takeover, and bring to patients a quality of clinical care which was taken for granted at RPA.

I established a committee structure aimed at including and involving all of those who worked in the area of cancer while trying to encourage and facilitate greater ownership and leadership by senior clinicians. Sometimes my efforts were met with resentment, obstruction or sheer apathy but mostly, my colleagues responded with optimism and positive energy.

CHAPTER 23

Boys sing and a lonely soldier dies

IN MID-2005, WHEN OUR youngest son James was in Year 10, Gail and I had the opportunity to accompany a large group of teachers, parents and boys from St Ignatius' College, Riverview on a music tour. The touring party numbered more than ninety and included about a dozen 'touring parents', eight or so teachers led by Bruce Rixon — the dynamic head of music and instigator and creative heart of the tour — and about seventy boys aged between ten and seventeen, and who constituted a brilliant choir and a number of vocal and instrumental ensembles.

Rixon had arranged for the school choir, called the Ignatian Choir, to participate in the World Choral Festival in Austria and had built the itinerary around two concert performances, one in Vienna and the other in Salzburg. We would also visit the major cities of Austria and Italy, where the boys would be given the opportunity to perform in various combinations on an almost daily basis.

I was invited to act as the tour medical officer. To prepare myself for the role of travelling general practitioner, I undertook a crash course in general practice by consulting a number of colleagues including a friend named Warwick Hutton, who had accompanied a previous tour and who was a goldmine of sensible advice and reassurance. A friendly pharmacist, John Lutman from Strathfield, kitted me out with a plentiful stock of drugs including adrenalin for injection if I had to deal with an acute allergic reaction, and doses of injectable penicillin in the event of someone contracting meningococcal meningitis. I was prepared for everything except an outbreak of plague.

The music tour was one of the most enjoyable, exhausting, chaotic and exciting twenty days we had ever spent.

The ensembles included a concert band, a jazz band, guitarists, strings and wood winds. The Ignatian Choir, coached and trained to an extraordinary level of choral proficiency, had a large repertoire, much of it in four-part harmony; when we reached Vienna and they performed with the Vienna Boys' Choir and choirs from the United States, Japan, England and Ireland, the boys held their place magnificently. It was a rare treat to watch the Vienna Boys' Choir in rehearsals, wearing baggy shorts, T-shirts and baseball caps, and to hear them produce sounds that seemed to descend from heaven with bell-like clarity. The massed choir performance in Vienna's gorgeous Musikverein, reputedly the concert hall with the most perfect acoustics in the world, was a breathtaking event.

In a moment that I hope he remembers for the rest of his life, James led the school choir with a robust and confident solo in an African chant that brought warm applause from the bemused Austrian audience.

During that summer Europe was a hothouse, and our youth hostel accommodation in Salzburg — without air conditioning and with most rooms overcrowded with boys — was disappointing but tolerable. My role as a doctor was non-stop. I had no doubt that the luxury of having a medico available twenty-four hours a day induced in some members of the group the temptation to complain of every ache, sneeze and itch, since I seemed to be endlessly busy, listening to complaints, offering sympathy and advice and distributing medications of one type or another from the small emergency pack I carried with me each day. Fainting, dehydration, sunburn, allergic reactions, tinea, inflamed tendons, sprained wrists, headaches, sore throats and an assortment of out-of-season viral infections had me dispensing my various pills and potions, taking temperatures, feeling pulses and generally being a very busy, if not terribly effective, first-aid man.

The ninety bodies in the travelling group were shuttled across Austria and into Italy in two buses driven by polar opposite drivers. One was a veteran driver named Norbert who spoke no English and not, it seemed, much German either as his conversation was limited to regular exclamations of '*sheizen!*' and '*catastrophe!*' Poor Norbert, who was near retirement, sat hunched over his steering wheel, his brow furrowed in a combination of confusion and concern. He would become lost within minutes of entering any large town or city and must have pushed his younger and more alert and competent colleague, Ziggy, who drove the other bus, to the limits of his patience. What made life particularly difficult was the itinerary and schedule of concerts which necessitated the rapid assembly of equipment including amplifiers, microphones, music stands and a thousand other things, sometimes two or three times a day, followed by the need to dismantle everything, pack it up and then reload it into the two buses. The fathers were transformed into a team of superbly efficient roadies, while the touring mothers collected washing from seventy boys, sought out laundromats from Vienna to Rome and cared for the colourful (and heavy) woollen robes worn by those in the choir. Increasingly the tour became a recurring exercise in logistical efficiency that would have rivalled any military undertaking.

The touring parents were with the boys all day, including supervising bus and walking tours of all the cities we visited. We inevitably finished each day exhausted, hot, flushed and uncomfortable in our sweaty clothes. Sometimes there was no time to shower before the evening performance, so we simply went as we were. At these performances the touring group would be met by so-called 'shadowing parents', who attended the performances and concerts but travelled more comfortably in privately arranged transport and stayed nearby in superior quality accommodation. The shadowing parents would frequently arrive at the evening performance immaculately dressed and sweet smelling and then make noises about how jealous they were of the bedraggled touring parents who, from all appearances, seemed to be having much more fun. There were too many highlights to list but the entire journey was a joyous experience that featured sublime choral and musical performances combined with hilarious mix-ups against a background of civilised and generous camaraderie.

Eventually, after almost three weeks, we boarded an Austrian Airlines jet in Vienna to come home. I was beginning to think that my role as on-call doctor had come to an end when, during the main meal service on our way from Vienna to Singapore, I heard a commotion on the other side of the plane and noticed some passengers crawling over seats to get away from something, followed by cries of 'Where's Chris?', 'Get Chris!'

Gail, who was sitting next to me eating her meal, nudged me and said, 'I think they need you over there.' I looked across and saw a passenger having a seizure. With only socks on my feet, I climbed from armrest to armrest to the aisle and dashed as quickly as I could to the fitting passenger who, thankfully, was sitting in an aisle seat. As I got to him I noticed a vile stench and a disconcerting squelching sensation underfoot.

The cabin crew, including a large and muscular chief steward who may have been called Fritz, gathered to offer their assistance and provided me with their emergency kitbag, which seemed well enough stocked for any eventuality, even an open-heart operation.

'There's a language problem too!' a parent sitting nearby advised me. The passenger of concern was a rough Glaswegian who reeked of alcohol and, when he came to, spoke with an incomprehensible brogue. I searched his gear, found his wallet and was able to talk to him by name. The seizure had stopped but he was in a disoriented state, though with no immediately obvious problem other than revolting faecal incontinence, in the product of which I was standing. Dave, who claimed never to have had a fit in his life before, was a thirty-year-old Scottish labourer travelling to Sydney to visit his girlfriend (lucky girl!). He had spent the two days before takeoff drinking heavily with friends; most likely his seizure represented an alcohol-withdrawal fit. It took some time for Dave to become even partially oriented and coherent and while this was happening he responded to questions and efforts to move him with disbelief, belligerence and attempts to make a run for it. As I sat next to Dave on the armrest of his seat trying to calm and reassure him, the Schwarzenegger-like head steward repeatedly interrupted to proffer his assistance, in particular offering to put Dave in 'ze grip!' and manhandle him to the back of the plane.

I tried, as firmly but politely as I could, to deflect this insistence on intervening with force, and said, 'Look, I think he's okay now. We don't need ze grip!'

My assistant looked sceptical and tried to encourage me to retreat so that he could do his thing. 'Doctor, ze grip!' He insisted again. 'Please, don't do ze grip!' I admonished. 'We don't need ze grip'. If we had needed to restrain our reeking Scot, Fritz Schwarzenegger was the right man for the job but it would have been a messy and smelly, if brief, fight.

Eventually our patient managed to fire up and connect his few limping brain cells and returned to a tolerable state of coherence, although he refused to believe that he and his squelching seat were the source of the horrendous odour that had caused the evacuation of most of the rear cabin of the plane. I was able to lead Dave down the aisle to a spacious rear galley where, still with considerable difficulty, he was coaxed to remove his trousers so that they could be deposited in a plastic garbage bag and go into the toilet to clean himself up. After a few minutes he returned to the galley, near naked except for a T-shirt and quite unabashed. Apart from Fritz the gripmeister, the cabin crew were young women who had remained calm and professional throughout and did not seem at all perturbed by the sight of this hapless creature. They produced a couple of tartan blankets and oversized safety pins with which Dave was able to cover himself to everyone's satisfaction, and so he was taken to a clean seat while valiant attempts were being made to clean, disinfect and deodorise his previous seat and its immediate surroundings.

Eventually order was restored and poor Dave, confused and uncertain about the cause of all the fuss but not at all embarrassed, assumed the demeanour of a sober and continent passenger and gave no further trouble for the remainder of the flight. In fact, he was quite taken with his new regalia, frequently observing that it was just like a big kilt, and had no apparent desire to learn the whereabouts of his trousers.

I managed to jettison my irrevocably soiled socks, wash my feet and get into a clean pair of socks. Later, a uniformed man with a German accent (presumably someone involved with flying the plane) came down the aisle from the cockpit. He leaned across the passenger sitting in the aisle seat and Gail to express his thanks for my assistance and to seek my reassurance that no further problems would occur. I almost felt that I should apologise for the disturbance I had created; I said I couldn't promise anything but all appeared to be quiet at this stage. I was rewarded with a tiny, sample-size bottle of champagne, which was magnanimously but unsmilingly bestowed on me by 'Fritz ze grip'. I left it on the plane when we finally disembarked in Sydney.

We arrived in Sydney mid-afternoon with everyone exhausted, relieved and happy after an immensely successful and exhilarating tour. The group set about identifying and gathering up baggage and equipment, singers helping musicians with bulky instrument cases and the smaller boys rounding up luggage trolleys to facilitate moving all the gear. Suitcases, duffle bags and personal belongings began to appear on the carousel and, as they were hefted to the ground and gathered together, parents, teachers and boys began to say their farewells.

Just then my mobile phone rang. 'Chris? Hello, how are you? It's Mike [my brother]. Where are you?'

'We just arrived back, we're at the baggage carousel at the airport.'

'Dad's dead. I'm at his place now,' came the news.

Gail, James and I bid the rest of our group a hasty farewell and, with a brief explanation, took our leave and caught a taxi home.

Dad's body, dead for a day or more, had been found face down on his lounge-room floor by a kindly neighbour who, not having seen him for a couple of days, sounded the alarm and arranged for the manager to break into his little unit. I met Michael at Dad's unit, which was being examined by police. They had been summoned by the manager and were carrying out a routine and mercifully short inspection of the place to ascertain that there had not been any foul play. Dad's cold, lifeless body lay in the middle of the carpeted living-room floor. He was wearing pyjamas, his arms were under his chest and his face was pushed into the carpet, distorting his nose and mouth to one side.

The cause of my father's death was not immediately apparent from what could be seen but, in the absence of more accurate information, his local doctor attributed his death to a heart attack. The two postcards we had sent while on the music tour were sitting on the top of the china cabinet in the corner of the small living room. All else was neat and tidy, although the refrigerator contained very little food.

Mike and I sat there for an hour after the police had left, talking quietly about the latter years of Dad's life. He survived for ten years after Mum had died, by any measure a remarkably long time given his physical and mental frailty and the fact that he never really recovered from the loss of his life partner. He had only been in the little retirement unit for two years but he had deteriorated slowly in health and outlook during that time.

James Collins, who had baptised James when he was critically ill sixteen years earlier, had become parish priest at Hunters Hill and presided at the requiem Mass. Dad's death was inevitable and perhaps he even wished for it — he was unhappy in the last years of his life.

We buried him in the Wentworth Falls cemetery in a grave next to my mother's after a small but dignified funeral in the Holy Name of Mary Church at Hunters Hill, attended by family, some of his old friends, and other friends of our wider family. Despite the recounting of amusing stories about Dad's life, the funeral was a sad one and I cried hard and without inhibition, particularly when James sang his schoolboy tenor solo of 'Ave Maria' and then the poignant 'Irish Blessing'. As I stood between Gail and Juliette in the front of the church, Juliette squeezed my hand tightly, reassuring me of her love and offering me her strength.

CHAPTER 24

'Machine O'Brien' in high gear

THE YEAR 2006 BEGAN at a fast pace but in fine style with a skiing trip to Japan with James, and a group of friends with whom I had started medicine in 1970 and their families. There are ten or eleven in this group and over our thirty-five years of friendship we have played golf, skied, collected wine, dined out together and watched each other's children grow up. The bond of friendship in this group is both remarkable and heartwarming.

For someone accustomed to the unpredictability and ordinariness of the Australian ski season, skiing at Niseko on the island of Hokkaido is a uniquely exciting experience. Niseko and the surrounding region is the happy recipient of twelve or more metres of light powder snow each year as icy winds from Siberia sweep across the Sea of Japan, pick up enormous quantities of moisture and release it as fluffy snowflakes on Japan's northernmost island.

This little holiday was important since James wanted to board in his final two years of high school, so it would be our last holiday together for some time. Towards the end of the trip I nearly precipitated a major problem when skiing in deep powder outside the roped area. I made a wrong turn and led James and another boy in the group, Nick Boogert, who was on a snowboard, down a steep, densely wooded slope that ended in a gully filled with deep snow. I had expected to find a trail leading down to familiar chairlifts but instead the terrain was unrecognisable and almost impassable. We slogged through waist-deep snow for three or more hours before finally reaching an isolated hut sitting in open space and inhabited by three cheerful Japanese who spoke no English. We gesticulated our way to an understanding and they drove us to a nearby village from which we could ride lifts back up the mountain and then ski home. When we told the story of our adventure to the group that evening I was unanimously banned from leading any further expeditions, but James, Nick and I shared a bond now, having survived a tight predicament, and just laughed.

Later in the year I had planned to travel to Wellington, New Zealand, for the eighth annual meeting of the ANZ Head and Neck Society, and in October to the Cleveland Clinic in the United States to give one of four keynote lectures during a conference to commemorate the centenary of the publication of a scientific paper by an American surgeon, George Crile Snr. It described a beautifully elegant though debilitating and disfiguring operation called radical neck dissection, which was designed to treat secondary cancer involving the lymph nodes of the neck.

Gail and I planned to travel together to the United States in August since I had also been invited to the M.D. Anderson Cancer Center in Houston, recognised as one of the world's leading cancer centres along with the Memorial Sloan-Kettering Cancer Center in New York. My visit to the M.D. Anderson Cancer Center was as a distinguished visitor (their designation, not mine) to give a number of lectures. The Houston visit was especially fun because I was hosted by a close friend, Randy Webber, the chief of the head and neck service. When I was a clinical fellow in Alabama in 1985, Randy held a similar position in Houston and we became close friends. After Houston, Gail and I travelled to Chicago for the annual meeting of the American Head and Neck Society, the leaders of which had previously given me a rare honour (certainly for a non-American) by inviting me to join their council.

The Cleveland trip for the Crile centenary symposium was a wonderful opportunity to enjoy a reunion with many colleagues and friends with whom I shared a close bond through our common interest in head and neck oncology. Those in the specialty have spoken of this often. Perhaps because ours is a relatively small one, it is easy to become well acquainted with most people working in the field internationally. The Cleveland meeting was immensely successful and I returned to Sydney at the end of October with more hurdles to leap over and the hope that the year would end on a high, but with a hope also that the Christmas holiday period would allow me to rest and recuperate.

In early November I oversaw a one-day symposium to celebrate the tenth anniversary of the establishment of the Sydney Cancer Centre. A younger colleague, Jonathon Carter, an outstanding gynaecological oncologist, had volunteered to convene the symposium; the attendance and quality of presentations and discussion were outstanding and gave me both satisfaction and a great sense of pride.

The theme of the day was 'The Future of Cancer Management'. Our celebrations were capped in the evening by a glittering dinner at a Sydney hotel, attended by nearly 300 guests including Australian of the Year Ian Frazer, who was known for his contribution to the development of the Gardasil vaccine aimed at preventing infection by the human papillomavirus (HPV) with the goal of stopping cancer of the cervix. Ian spoke at the symposium and was also our after-dinner speaker. The then NSW Minister for Health, John Hatzistergos, was an almost catatonically shy fish out of water who admitted to those in attendance his discomfort, as a barrister, with discussing medical issues, especially those related to women's health. Early in the evening I introduced the minister to Ian Frazer; despite the widespread publicity and discussion about the practical and ethical implications of Gardasil being made available to young girls and the fact that Frazer had been named Australian of the Year, it was obvious to me that the minister had never heard of him. 'So you're a doctor, are you?' inquired the minister blankly. 'Yes,' responded Frazer, surprised or miffed or perhaps just utterly dumbfounded by the question. I quickly brought Hatzistergos into the picture and explained what Professor Frazer was well known for. Inexplicably they didn't talk much during the evening.

The day's activities, symposium and dinner, were a resounding success and I breathed a great sigh of relieved satisfaction that the wind-down to the year's end could now begin on the back of a string of successful international meetings and successfully dispatched local responsibilities.

For reasons that were not immediately apparent at the time, I had great difficulty recovering fully from the October visit to

Cleveland. I could not shake off what seemed to be lingering jet lag and found myself struggling through the days in a state of unabating fatigue.

Around this time and for no particular reason, I would occasionally become acutely aware of my mortality, not based on a fear of death but more that my entire world and the existence and wellbeing of my family depended totally on my continued good health. This had been an intermittent consideration over a number of years as my responsibilities had increased. These thoughts came and went of their own accord with no element of burden or foreboding, but I tried to use them as a moderating influence as I admonished myself that there were many people who depended on me and that I needed to keep 'machine O'Brien' functioning at optimal levels.

CHAPTER 25

The roof caves in

AND THEN IN NOVEMBER 2006, the roof caved in on my world. The picture I've painted in the prologue of this book says it all: a few days of fatigue and crushing headaches, followed by the diagnosis that I had a cancerous brain tumour and an outlook that was virtually hopeless.

Following my admission to RPA I was transferred to the neurosurgical intensive care ward on my emergency department trolley. When I arrived, the nurses again fussed around, covering their shock with cheerful reassurances. My recollection of that first night is clouded. I was given intravenous steroids and then succumbed quickly to the overwhelming weariness that had dogged me during the preceding days.

I slept soundly and awoke headache free, a little drowsy but comfortable and well oriented. I had a complete memory of the events of the day before and needed no prompting as to my whereabouts.

Gail found herself at the bottom of an abyss of desolation on that first night. When she rang Juliette to explain that I was in hospital and that my admission had been necessitated by a brain tumour, Juliette burst into tears, sobbing repeatedly, 'No, no, no, no, no ...' At the time she was studying journalism and was at work that day in her part-time job with a media monitoring company. She left work immediately to come to RPA.

When Gail and I came to the emergency department, me very unwell but also undiagnosed, James was just leaving home with two or three pretty girls in party frocks to attend an informal function for Year 11 boys at his school. Later that evening when Gail rang to let him know what was happening, James spoke first, asking if he could stay overnight at a friend's place, unaware of my grave diagnosis. 'Mum, can I stay the night please? Lots of the kids are staying here.'

'James, Dad is in hospital. He is really sick and you have to come home.'

'What do you mean he's really sick? What's the matter with him?'

Gail, struggling to maintain her own composure, her head and heart constricted with fear and anguish, replied, 'Jamesie, he has a brain tumour.' She heard James gasp and then begin to cry on the end of the phone.

Adam was at the Police Academy at Goulburn, hoping to graduate the following January. A gentle, guileless introvert, he received Gail's news of my diagnosis with sad bewilderment and made immediate plans to come back to Sydney the next day.

Intravenous steroid therapy is used to reduce inflammation. It can alleviate the worst of asthma attacks by reversing severe spasm in the airways. In my case, the medication acted promptly and with almost miraculous effectiveness to reverse the massive swelling and fluid accumulation in my brain which had caused the headaches, drowsiness and, at the time of admission, near unconsciousness.

By next morning I was alert and felt very much better. The treatment continued for another twenty-four hours and I was released home on Monday, taking the steroid Dexamethasone in tablet form.

In the week before my diagnosis and for several days following my return home we had staying with us close friends from Lausanne, Switzerland: Luc Bron and his wife, Michele, and their baby daughter, Helene. Luc had visited Australia twice before and worked with me, each time for a twelve-month period — first, during his ENT residency and later, after he had finished his training, as a clinical fellow. He was immensely fond of Gail and the children and was like a member of the family.

Luc and Michele deferred their return to Switzerland to stay on an extra week and hold the home front intact: shopping, cooking and running errands, and relieving Gail of what would otherwise have been a burdensome sea anchor of domestic duties. Luc even drove to Goulburn (a 400 kilometre round trip) on the day after my admission to pick up Adam and bring him home.

My response to the steroid therapy was so dramatic that when I returned home after only forty-eight hours in hospital I, along with almost everyone else, found it hard to believe that I had been laid so low. In that first week, plans were made for an MRI (Magnetic Resonance Imaging) scan, a PET (Positron Emission Tomography) scan, an office consultation with Michael Besser and a probable operation. Because oral steroids can cause significant gastric irritation that can lead to stomach ulceration and bleeding, I also took tablets to counteract that.

The only investigation of any significance that I had experienced before was a CT scan of the head a couple of years earlier for chronic nasal obstruction and sinusitis. Now it was my turn to experience what I had put so many of my own patients through. The scans were conducted and overseen by young technicians whose professionalism and kindness, without exception, were exemplary. I found it extraordinarily easy to adopt the passive role of the patient and felt confident and safe as I was led along the pathway of investigations.

For an MRI scan, the patient must lie on a narrow table with his head (or the part of interest) wedged, not uncomfortably, on either side to maintain absolute stillness. An intravenous tube is inserted into an accessible vein in the hand, wrist or forearm to allow the injection of a dye called gadolinium to assist with imaging anatomical abnormalities, a Perspex mask is drawn across the face, then the table automatically slides into a narrow cylinder. People who suffer from claustrophobia can find all this intolerable; in fact, claustrophobia and the presence of irremovable metal in the body — like pacemakers or defibrillators — rule out MRI as an appropriate investigation. Sometimes a general anaesthetic is required for particularly nervous patients.

On the advice of the young technician I put malleable earplugs into my ears, yet I was still astounded by the loudness of the tapping and clicking that accompanied the changes in energy during the scanning process. It was extraordinary to appreciate that this obscenely mechanical cacophony was a unique accompaniment to what is otherwise a very sophisticated imaging process.

The PET scan was performed on the same day, to determine whether or not the anatomical abnormalities identified on the MRI had the biological characteristics of malignancy. At that time RPA had one of the two PET scanners in New South Wales and Michael Fulham, the head of the PET unit, was one of the most experienced practitioners in the world at using this diagnostic test. During a PET scan patients are injected with a radioactive labelled glucose solution that accumulates in cells with a high rate of metabolism, particularly cancer cells.

Throughout these tests I suffered no ill effects and I remained placidly composed. I was comforted by both the caring confidence with which I was treated and the fact that with a diagnosis made — albeit utterly unexpected and potentially fatal — I felt that the process of treatment, recovery and cure was well and truly under way. I am not sure why I accepted these harrowing events so calmly. I felt no shock or disbelief or anger, just quiet acceptance.

On the Wednesday of that week, four days after my initial admission to hospital and two days after my discharge, Gail and I visited Michael Besser in his office to discuss the scan findings and planned treatment. The day before that visit, while I was having one or other of the scans, Gail met Besser on the footpath in front of the hospital and, still filled with desperate sadness and helplessness, talked to him about my situation, almost begging on my behalf for a reprieve. Her heart sank as he reiterated that it was likely that I would die in six to twelve months.

I was upbeat and anything but defeated when Gail and I arrived at Besser's rooms. I had already alarmed an army of friends and colleagues during my short stay in hospital by sending them a text message from my phone which read something like, 'I've been diagnosed with a malignant brain tumour and will have surgery soon. I expect to do well and will keep you informed. Cheers, Chris.' What I thought was simply a polite communication to inform those who would want to know sent a shockwave across Sydney, New South Wales, other parts of Australia and North America. Little did I know that a third or more of the recipients of this message found it too cryptic to comprehend and some just responded, 'Chris who?'

During my discussion with Michael Besser he handed me a couple of photocopied publications detailing treatment outcomes in two or three clinical studies of patients with my particular type of brain cancer. It was glioblastoma multiforme, the most common form of adult brain tumour and one with a frighteningly aggressive, almost inevitably lethal, reputation. Nothing in these papers offered much reason for optimism: few patients survived, irrespective of the treatment.

I had already said to Besser before this meeting, 'Michael, I am not afraid of dying and I don't care if I never work again.' My sentiments had not changed but I did not think that I should repeat that with Gail sitting at my side in his office. Gail asked her sensible quiet questions and I added, 'Michael, I know this tumour has a bad reputation but I want you to do your best to fix me, I want to be cured.'

'Chris, I can operate on you but you won't be cured, not with those satellites there.' He was referring to the presence of two or three additional nodules of tumour adjacent to the main mass, which was about three centimetres in diameter and lying deep in my right temporal lobe (a little above and behind my right ear).

My mind raced and leapt as a hundred thoughts collided. Thinking of James, who was due to turn eighteen and sit his final high school exams in October the following year, I said, like a desperate man trying to cut a deal with the devil, 'I'd really just like to get next year.'

'You will get next year,' he responded, although there was no obvious basis for this assurance. A little later he commented, 'It's not a bad way to go', as if I should be comforted by this additional reassurance too.

He then went on to test my visual fields using a simple technique that demonstrated, to my surprise, that I had a large blind spot in the lower left quadrant of the circle that encompassed what I could see. I had been completely unaware of this deficit although, as I thought about it on the way home in the car with Gail, I recalled that earlier in the week while driving, I had inexplicably run into the gutter on the left side on a couple of occasions. At the time I put it down to inattention and tiredness but now it was clear that I was running into things I just could not see.

I left Besser's office still disappointed at his disinclination even to feign some optimism and hope, but I was satisfied with the information I had been given and I was determined that I would meet the challenges presented by the operation and subsequent treatment fearlessly. I was made apprehensive only by Besser's pessimism and certainty that I would not survive for very long.

Gail sobbed quietly as we negotiated the corridors, lifts and car park and drove home in deep thought, still trying to fathom what was happening to us. It was as though a meteorite from nowhere had suddenly shattered the complex, wonderful, multifaceted and loving construct that was our life together.

CHAPTER 26

The road to recovery and despair

IN THE DAYS LEADING UP to my scheduled operation we were innundated with flowers, fruit baskets, cards, emails and phone calls. A couple of days before, Guillaume Brahimi, the owner and chef of the Bennelong Restaurant at the Opera House (called Guillaume at Bennelong) stopped by to offer his good wishes and leave a magnificent meal for the family — duck, his famous Paris mash, a luscious chocolate tart, and two superb bottles of wine — a 1986 Echézeaux (from Burgundy) and an '82 Château Haut Brion (from Bordeaux). Guillaume had become a devoted friend since joining the board of the Sydney Cancer Centre Foundation a couple of years earlier. He had come to Sydney in his early twenties, having trained in the kitchen of the famous Joel Robuchon in Paris. Passionate about rugby, cooking and his gorgeous family, Guillaume's talent as a chef and his generosity and decency as a human being have led him to acquire innumerable friends and admirers. I was touched by this act of kindness and by the warmth and sincerity of the fond hug and kiss he gave me as he left.

The road to recovery and despair

Gail, Juliette and I left home early on the morning of my operation. Still feeling totally calm, I was soon on a trolley being prepared for the short journey to the operating theatre. I felt confident that the operation would go smoothly and had not the slightest concern about the anaesthetic. I was principally worried about the period of fretful waiting that Gail and Juliette would have to endure. James was at school and Adam back in Goulburn, while friends, family and others too numerous even to consider counting awaited some word of the outcome.

There was little risk that I would die during the operation but it was still unclear how disabled I might be when it was over. Michael Besser had already explained to me that it would not be his intention to remove the entire tumour. One of the satellite nodules in particular was dangerously positioned and Besser explained that its removal would probably lead to a visual disability called a left hemianopia, meaning a loss of sight in the entire left half of my visual field.

'Chris, the most important thing with this disease is quality of life,' he said. 'If I take that satellite and give you a hemianopia you might find life intolerable. You won't be able to read or watch television.'

I knew that he was carrying a heavy burden and I felt sorry for him. 'Mike, just do what you feel is best. I don't care what disability I might have but I'll leave it to your judgement. I trust you.'

It is both a privilege and a challenge when one is asked to look after a colleague or a member of a colleague's family but I'm sure Besser was acutely troubled by his position — believing my condition to be incurable and, in fact, expecting a fatal outcome in the very near future but also wanting desperately, without creating

263

intolerable disability, to give me some benefit and buy a little time. There is no magic formula for dealing with this situation. Once there is an agreed plan, you simply do your best.

In the anaesthetic room, just outside the operating theatre, I was greeted by Roger Traill, a meticulous (some might say annoyingly pedantic) and highly experienced anaesthetist — exactly what I needed.

The only hitch during the operation from Roger's point of view was my slow pulse, a reflection of a sound cardiovascular system rather than a cardiac abnormality and something of which I had always been proud. He later told me that when my heart rate fell to about thirty-five beats per minute his courage was sorely tested, but over the three-hour duration of the operation he resisted the temptation to inject drugs to speed my heart up.

Technically, the entire procedure was carried out without a hitch. After reversal of the anaesthetic I awoke and was oriented and coherent while still lying on the operating table. In the recovery room I lay quietly and happily, my head bandaged and with intravenous tubes infusing fluid and a catheter draining urine quite merrily. Gail and Juliette had endured a long and lonely wait but were elated when Besser rang Gail on her mobile to give her the news that all had gone well.

I was transferred to the neurosurgical intensive care unit, fully alert and with all faculties and limbs working perfectly, and was soon surrounded by Gail, Juliette and James. Although the entire tumour had not been removed my sense of relief was indescribable. I knew that I had not been cured but somehow I felt that the initial big step towards recovery and cure had been taken.

My senses were dominated by an overwhelming thirst, having been dehydrated intentionally for the purposes of the anaesthetic; I craved fluid and downed two cartons of cold chocolate milk. I can't remember ever drinking anything more delicious.

Gail was sitting by my side when my mobile phone rang. She answered it and spoke briefly. Then she said, 'It's Frank [Sartor]. He wants to know how you are.' 'Tell him I'm going to go into politics now I've only got half a brain!' Sartor loved this and dined out on the story for some time afterwards.

Later, Juliette and James bought Thai food in Newtown and we sat together in my room in ICU, eating Asian food and watching television. Ironically, *RPA* was on and it featured the last segment I had filmed for the show. I recalled the patient very well, a young hairdresser from the south coast with an uncommon benign tumour arising from one of the nerves high up in the neck. The experience was quite surreal as I sat there, my head extravagantly bandaged and monitoring leads and venous and arterial lines everywhere, watching with embarrassment as the little story unfolded and my diagnosis of which of the many nerves in the neck was the culprit was shown to be quite wrong. The program ended with Max Cullen quietly announcing to viewers that Professor Chris O'Brien had been diagnosed with a brain tumour and concluding, 'We wish him well in his treatment'. I was later told that the switchboards at the hospital and Channel Nine lit up immediately as literally hundreds of RPA viewers tried to communicate their shock and concern.

It was impossible to sleep in hospital. I was still receiving a high dose of brain-shrinking steroids; besides the potential for gastric bleeding, this therapy often leads to severe insomnia and even mania. Over the ensuing days I dozed a little in the afternoons and evenings but invariably found myself wide awake at one or two o'clock in the morning. Exhibiting early signs of steroid-induced hyperactivity, I occupied myself reading and sending text messages to people scattered around Australia and North America. I fired them off oblivious to the possibility that my cheery missives, reassuring one and all that I had survived the operation, and survived well, were waking people at ungodly times and turning my sleeplessness into a near world-wide epidemic. Many of the responses began with comments like, 'Thanks for the wake up call' and 'So good of you to wake me!' Some of the overseas messages prompted a return phone call and a happy conversation.

My progress in hospital was rapid and positive. By Saturday morning, two days after surgery, Besser — normally conservative in his practice and cautious in his decision making — agreed that I was well enough to leave hospital the next day, with the iron-clad caveat that I should notify him immediately of the slightest untoward development.

I returned home in high spirits, immensely relieved to be (largely) free of my cancer and on the road, I felt, to recovery. I had already decided that I would not go back to work. I expected that I would need to commit every ounce of my mental and physical energy to recovery and, premature as it may seem to have been, I was prepared to completely close the door on my life as a surgeon without any real idea of what I would do in the future. To this day I am still uncertain why it was so easy to make this decision. I can only conclude that deep down in my soul I was ready to move into a new and different phase of my life.

The road to recovery and despair

I continued to take Dexamethasone (steroid) tablets along with a medication called Dilantin to prevent seizures. My appetite was good and my principal concern was my almost total inability to sleep, except for brief naps, which I tried to impose upon my state of energetic wakefulness.

The world came tumbling down on the second night following my arrival home. Gail's initial joy and relief over my survival and rapid recovery from surgery were replaced by a sense of terrified grief. She became convinced that I would soon die and envisaged thirty years or more of lonely widowhood. Not only that, neither of us was clear about whether or not she would cope financially. We knew that my superannuation fund was inadequate to support her and the children without her having to sell the house and possibly return to work as a physiotherapist. These probabilities formed a calamitous aggregate that seized her spirit in its own death grip, causing her to feel smothered in black and hopeless misery. She became convinced that, should I die, there was no way that she could go on, no way that she wanted to go on. In parallel with Gail's living nightmare, my mind — driven by high-dose steroids, which I had now been taking for more than a week, and the effects of sleep deprivation — was in a chaotic whirl, which I failed to recognise and instead interpreted as sharply focused insight.

I tried my best to reassure and calm my broken-hearted wife, who dragged herself forward bravely only to have the small gains she made in restoring calmness, pragmatism and determination to her outlook, washed away in intermittent floods of tears, the product of her recurring and desperate misery. That night we talked for hours about the state of our collapsing world and, in what were the blackest moments we have ever shared, tried to

267

work through all the issues and their complex ramifications, attempting desperately to restore calm and logic to this tempest. I had no confidence at all that I would survive much beyond a year and my mind gyrated in a frenzy of illogical thought which seared through my consciousness like a bushfire. I thought of each of the children in turn and tried to assess whether their lives would play out happily and successfully and whether they would cope with the loss of their father at their different ages and stages. I knew that Gail was too loving and attractive to be alone forever and wondered whom she might remarry and what would become of the house. We sat together for hours combing quietly through our passionately devoted relationship and I shed my own bitterly sad tears in equal proportion to Gail's.

Then, as if we had slowly fought our way to the front of this runaway train, we tried to grasp the controls and at least bring some certainty to our domestic circumstances. With desperation fed by Gail's terror and my irrational mania, we decided that the most sensible course of action was to sell our house as soon as possible and move into a smaller place which would accommodate us adequately if, in fact, I did survive, but which would also provide a comfortable home for Gail in her widowhood, living out a determined pledge that she would never remarry.

Gail and I finally fell into bed at about 4 a.m., exhausted, cried out and empty but comforted by the fact that we had a plan and a way forward. I was satisfied that Gail and the children would be provided for and that she would be comfortable into the future if our plan were enacted.

We knew that there was a small, renovated sandstone house in the district which belonged to friends and which had been for sale for some weeks. By ten o'clock the next morning, after a phone call to our friends asking if we could view the house, Gail and I were walking through the small but attractive rooms calculating where furniture, paintings and personal belongings might fit.

This sudden (but really quite crazy) preoccupation with selling our own comfortable home and moving into a far smaller cottage became a resuscitating diversion that allowed both Gail and me the opportunity to gulp in enough oxygen to feel that, irrespective of the outcome of my illness, a measure of control had been achieved.

I talked in turn with Adam, Juliette and James early in the afternoon. I hugged and held each one and we cried together as they rocked in my arms like little children. I wanted to convince myself that they would live on happily without me and survive unscarred but I felt an overwhelming sadness that I would not see them live out their potential or be at hand to give them help, advice and even money when they might need it most. It was difficult for them, as it was for Gail, not to start grieving prematurely and each of us tried, in our own way, to focus this sadness on the difficult news at hand and not look too far ahead.

This was the first opportunity for the boys to cry and, as I hugged each of them, I thought it was good that the lid came off their emotions. Juliette had stayed devotedly by my side while I was in hospital, quietly resting her head on my shoulder and holding my hand, devastated and desolate but ready at any moment to offer practical assistance. My death was not really imminent so I gave it little thought and remained inwardly calm about the prospect of dying. My own sadness was not for myself but rather generated by my witnessing and feeling the fear and misery of those dearest to me.

During the afternoon I took time, for some reason, to look around me and, as though a veil had been lifted from my eyes, I appreciated fully how comfortable and beautiful our home was and I started to dispel immediately any thoughts that we would sell. No matter what, it was vital that Gail and the children stay together in the house. As the afternoon wore on and emotions lost their turbulent edge and subsided, Gail and I objectively considered for the first time our financial situation and, particularly, whether or not my income protection and life insurance would be sufficient to meet our needs if I survived, or Gail's if I died. It became clear that panic was unnecessary and that there was no immediate need to launch into forced selling and buying. This preoccupation with money may seem odd and inappropriate but it clearly exercised the minds of some close friends too, because in the period immediately before and after my surgery four friends offered completely unsolicited and unexpected financial assistance — one a wealthy former patient who wanted to assist with mortgage payments; another, a close friend from university days who offered to pay James's school fees; the third, a former, and much-favoured, registrar who was now a surgeon himself and who assured me that he had 'a lot of equity in his home and could readily raise cash if we needed it'. Finally, a young surgical registrar from Melbourne who was saving to buy an apartment came to visit me at home and offered Gail all her money if it would help. These touching and heartfelt offers of generosity moved me deeply but I could not even consider accepting these acts of charity. Gail, on the other hand, was less sanguine about the thought of so readily declining assistance and preferred to take comfort in the fact that a safety net of one type or another might be available should she need it.

The road to recovery and despair

As it became clearer that the insurance policies that I held —
the premiums for which I complained about regularly and noisily
— were quite adequate for our immediate and ongoing needs, our
finances ceased to occupy so large a place in our minds. Now my
daily priority was to stay cheerful and positive, to hug Gail, Adam,
Juliette and James as often as I could, and to encourage all around
me not to feel sad or sorry for me.

CHAPTER 27

Learning to say 'never say die'

I STILL HAD NOT STEELED MYSELF, mind and body, to wage a determined battle against my capricious and potentially lethal tumour. Instead, by an extraordinary process of mental contortion I began turning two positives into a massive negative and even started planning my own funeral — who would speak, what music I would like played and by whom, in what ways the children would participate and where those attending might seek refreshments afterwards. Control freak? Moi? Never!

On the one hand I was totally accepting of my situation, still not angry, frightened or in denial. On the other there had begun to wash over me an enormous wave of concern, support and love from family, friends, colleagues and a legion of strangers who knew me only from the *RPA* television show. Literally hundreds of cards and letters began to arrive (many opening with the words 'Dear Professor O'Brien, You don't know me but ...'), along with flowers, fruit baskets, books and other gifts, all expressing shock, sadness and devastation and conveying affectionate sentiments in the most generous terms. Dozens of former students, residents and fellows took the opportunity to thank me for being a positive influence in their lives and I began to realise that what was happening to me was a privilege, the rarest of gifts.

'If I die,' I said to Gail, 'what better life could I have lived?' In fact, I was so buoyed up on this ocean of concern and love, almost adulation, that I was allowing myself, without an iota of resistance, to be carried off to a glorious death.

By the end of my first week at home, still on a high dose of steroids and unable to sleep more than a couple of hours a night, I reached the point of exhaustion and finally submitted to a long, deep and regenerating night of sleep which swept away my disordered thinking and opened the door for two conversations which jolted me from my passive and complicit acceptance of an inevitable death.

The first occurred when George Hruby, the radiation oncologist who accepted the poisoned chalice of overseeing my post-operative radiotherapy, looked me in the eye and with moving determination declared, 'We're going to go after this, Chris.' This was the first time that any of my colleagues or treating doctors had spoken so positively and emphatically about wanting to make me better. Like any other patient, I needed my doctors to bring hope and even optimism to the treatment table, to reinforce the fact that fighting was worthwhile.

The second of these conversations took place when I was visited at home by Brian McCaughan, a lung cancer specialist and irreverent friend who had, in his life, experienced the loss of a number of people close to him, including his mother when he was young, and whose wife had also experienced a life-threatening cancer.

I talked to him about the prognosis as it was initially laid out for me and, after a moment or two of uncharacteristically quiet thought, he declared, 'Well that's all bullshit, and you know it! Patients decide how long they will live, you know that. Doctors don't decide how long patients have. We've both made that mistake. You just have to decide that you are going to fight this and prove them all wrong.' I agreed emphatically; in fact, I had always held that the statistics derived from clinical studies cannot be applied to individual patients, and that trying to predict likely survival times for individuals is a most inexact and ultimately unhelpful endeavour.

Later in the day, when I recalled this conversation, I found it hard to believe that I had allowed myself so readily to adopt a position of passive and even cheerful stoicism when my life was at stake. Brian's enthusiastic pragmatism grounded me and from that point, although I still recognise the reputation and biological potential of my malignant glioma and resist the temptation to look too far down the road, I have remained optimistic, confident and steadfastly committed to enjoying every moment, grasping every opportunity and trying anything which may help me win this fight for my life. This has also helped Gail through occasional episodes of bleakness and fear.

I affirmed to myself that I had 'promises to keep and miles to go before I was ready to sleep'.

Arrangements were made for me to commence radiotherapy within two or three weeks of surgery and the complex planning of this therapy was carried out by George Hruby and Chris Milross, the head of the Department of Radiation Oncology, whom I had stolen from Prince of Wales Hospital. My head would be totally immobilised on the treatment table by a lightweight but rigid fibreglass mask which completely covered my face and was bolted to a frame on the table to allow the great angled gantry of the radiotherapy machine to rotate slowly into different positions around my head so that the radiotherapy beam could be delivered to the correct part of the brain from a number of different angles with pinpoint precision.

Because the latest research indicated that radiotherapy was more effective when it was administered in combination with chemotherapy — specifically a relatively new drug called Temozolamide, which was known to be (relatively) effective against malignant gliomas — I accepted the advice given to me and agreed to have this combined therapy.

My radiotherapy appointments were scheduled to take place early in the morning so that, in theory at least, the treatment might be completed early, leaving the remainder of the day for leisure activities (like vomiting and sleeping). On the morning of my first treatment we were a little rushed but, as instructed, I swallowed the chemotherapy capsules on an empty stomach and we threaded our way through the already intensifying peak-hour traffic. By the time we arrived at RPA early waves of nausea had commenced. As I lay on the treatment table in an otherwise stark room dominated by a giant and brand new Varian linear accelerator (radiotherapy machine), my nausea worsened; when the mask was placed over my face and firmly secured into position, I began to fear that a vomiting attack could have only one outcome — unable to turn my head or open my mouth, I would drown in my own vomit and die like a rockstar. This proposition gave me no comfort so I focused my mind and, recognising the oxymoron, tried very hard to relax. The treatment was utterly painless and took only a few minutes. When my head was released from its temporary prison I thanked the technical staff, who had been kind and reassuring throughout, walked to the nearest toilet and vomited violently.

Over the next months, intermittent nausea and vomiting were almost daily occurrences but my squeamishness eventually settled down as I made good use of effective but constipating anti-nauseants.

I learned so much during this time: most particularly, that nausea can be one of the most debilitating of symptoms, and secondly, that a good vomit invariably gives quick and effective relief. Over the ensuing six weeks the hair on the right side of my head thinned dramatically and fell out and my appetite almost completely disappeared. I continued on a high but decreasing dose of steroids and continued with the anti-epileptic drug Dilantin, but these combined with the anti-nauseants to render my saliva thick and offensive, played havoc with my liver function, and slowed my bowel function to the point that constipation and its management and coping with the effects of this management became a major preoccupation. Among these issues, the loss of my hair was an irrelevance. I had my remaining hair cut very short and enjoyed both the new feel and the new look.

I found it almost impossible to eat a normal meal because anything I put in my desert-dry mouth turned into a gluggy mass that tasted like snot and was impossible to swallow. Rich sweet foods like ice-cream and chocolate also became intolerable, along with red meat and the beefy, fatty smells associated with its preparation. I lived on scrambled egg and ginger beer. A friend's homemade chicken soup was the other tasty and nutritious exception that defied my dietary shutdown. Even tap water tasted offensive. Not surprisingly I lost weight, gaining little relief from the so-called nutritional supplements provided by my dietician and which, to me, amounted to little more than chocolate and banana flavoured puke. Two or three times a week I found myself in such a state of dehydration that I needed to go into the hospital to have a couple of litres of fluid infused intravenously.

My inability to eat developed slowly, allowing me to make it through Christmas Day by restricting myself to a small quantity of baked vegetables and soft drink. By New Year eating, drinking and even the thought of undertaking these activities had become astonishingly difficult for me and I had little choice but to try to force tiny quantities of food into myself in multiple sittings and wait for improvement.

In addition to my nutritional woes, blood tests revealed that my liver function had gone haywire so I stopped both the Dilantin and the chemotherapy in the hope that internal harmony might be restored. In ten days or so it was.

Gail tried desperately to prepare food that would induce me to eat but she had few options. In due course, when I was better able to take food by mouth and to swallow, she energetically and assiduously researched the nutritional literature and set about providing me with fruit and vegetable juices, delicious soups, omelettes and fish meals which sustained me and allowed me to happily avoid red meat, alcohol, coffee and anything sweet. Previously my diet had been healthy and complete but I had a terrible sweet tooth, which would occasionally lead me to eat half a dozen or more chocolate biscuits at a sitting, and I would almost never miss sampling any box of chocolates I found lying around.

Despite my now well-publicised diagnosis and the difficulties I was having with the symptoms of treatment and my inability to eat, Christmas 2006 was a joyous time. On Christmas Eve we were joined at home by my family and a number of friends, including a surprise visit from my great friend and mentor from New York, Jatin Shah, and two other patients who were attending the radiotherapy department on a daily basis and who otherwise would have spent Christmas alone.

By the end of January, during a brief but delightful respite at a magnificent beach house, which belonged to friends, at Palm Beach, my appetite returned and I was on the road to recovery, albeit seven or eight kilograms lighter than when I started treatment.

CHAPTER 28

Yin yang harmonisation and going for broke

TROUBLE STRUCK MORE QUICKLY than I, or any of my treating doctors, had anticipated when MRI and PET scans carried out in April demonstrated progression of the main satellite nodule that had been left behind at the first operation, and other areas nearby which looked suspiciously like recurrent tumour. This was a disappointing, but not catastrophic, eventuality which caught me by surprise because I felt so well and was beginning to build a modest level of confidence about the future.

I was still taking my chemotherapy according to the cyclical schedule mapped out for me, but I had also commenced a novel and unproven form of complementary treatment that was based on acupuncture theory but involved pulsed electrical stimulation, aimed at moderating and aligning the body's natural electrical frequencies in order to create 'better health', whatever that might be. I was introduced to this treatment — which rejoiced in the almost irresistible name of Yin Yang Harmonisation Therapy — by Mark Keighery, a friend who was well known in the fashion industry and who had been battling metastatic kidney cancer for eight years or more. I saw this therapy as a harmless and possibly helpful adjunct to my existing treatment. Although the therapy was quite unproven, I felt comfortable going along with it simply because there did not appear to be a downside.

Mark's cancer had spread to his lungs, which were already restricted by longstanding asthma. He had endured a number of chest operations and travelled to the Memorial Sloan-Kettering Cancer Center in New York several times to seek advice and to have surgery. Finally, more than one cancer expert told him that nothing more could be done and that he should put his affairs in order and prepare to die. Keighery, an irrepressibly positive character, was unwilling to accept the negative advice he was given and industriously sought out alternative and complementary treatments. When all seemed lost, he discovered Leo Fang, a Sydney-based Mongolian Chinese who barely spoke English and who had trained in Chinese herbal medicine, landscape gardening and this novel electrical therapy. In the space of a year of almost daily treatment, Mark found his appetite again, increased his weight by fifteen or more kilos and regained his energy levels and sense of wellbeing. Most importantly, defying the medical opinions and predictions he had received both in Sydney and New York, the cancer deposits in his lungs had diminished in size.

Mark heard of my own illness and, with the infectious enthusiasm of a living-proof beneficiary of this therapy, encouraged me to meet Leo and at least give it a try. I suspended my deeply ingrained scepticism and acceded to Mark's earnest desire to help me. Over a period of two or three months, Mark and I would meet regularly at one or other of Leo's clinics and sit side by side in large firm armchairs which were especially made to facilitate the therapy. We would talk about mutual friends and acquaintances, his experiences in fashion and as a boxing commentator, and our families, particularly the cricketing prowess of one of his sons.

I had no reason, apart from Mark's own astonishing story, to believe that this treatment might work but I liked travelling to the city each day — a walk to the ferry, a relaxing ride to Circular Quay, usually in warm sunshine, and then a bus ride to Bondi Junction or a walk up George Street. In particular, I enjoyed the convenience and relative privacy which public transport afforded me and was happy to sit quietly reading or listening to music through headphones. In my case, the therapeutic benefits of this daily routine probably outweighed the positive effects of Yin Yang Harmonisation, if any existed at all.

I continued with the electrical acupuncture until the disappointing scan result in April but during that period I was increasingly bothered by Leo's escalating claims that his treatment could cure cancer and his persistent requests that I, as a doctor who was well known and respected in the field of cancer, assist him with the promotion of his business.

The scan result signalled to me loud and clear that something radical would need to be done if the glioma was ever going to be eradicated. Importantly, for me, there was no evidence of recurrent disease elsewhere in the brain and this made me feel strongly that the abnormalities only reflected the fact that my first operation had been a conservative and, necessarily, incomplete procedure and that the combination of radiotherapy and chemotherapy had not effectively dealt with the residual malignant cells.

Mark Keighery continued on with Yin Yang Harmonisation for several months, but Leo's business failed and he returned to China. Mark's disease progressed and, to the great sadness of his family and many friends, he lost his courageous battle in July 2008.

I had initially put Michael Boyer, head of medical oncology and acting director (in my absence) of the Sydney Cancer Centre, in a difficult position by asking him to supervise my care, but his special skills lay in the management of lung and prostate cancers. So, with his blessing — in fact on his recommendation (and, I suspect, to his relief) — I sought the advice of another oncologist, Helen Wheeler, who had a reputation for being one of the most knowledgeable neuro-oncologists in the country: responsive, creative and relentless in her approach to the treatment of brain tumours. After much discussion with Gail and both Helen Wheeler and Michael Boyer, it became abundantly clear that it was time to pursue a more aggressive approach.

I decided to seek the help of Charlie Teo, a well-known neurosurgeon at Prince of Wales Hospital, who enjoyed a much-publicised reputation as a brilliant renegade and who was viewed with scepticism, distrust and (one would have to think) jealousy by many of his colleagues. I wanted a surgeon who was radical enough to get the tumour out, irrespective of what the downside might be.

Charlie was about six years younger than I, and was a neurosurgical registrar at Prince Alfred in the early part of my career. At that time he was known to be flamboyant and unconventional but he was also very talented and hard working. At our initial consultation, Charlie bowled in wearing jeans and

T-shirt and carrying a motorcycle helmet. I had not seen him for a number of years but I knew that he was aware of my illness. He gave the scans what seemed to be a cursory glance, holding them up to the window. After a moment or two of consideration, he turned to Gail and me and from his first utterance was sympathetic, not troubled by what he saw and confident he could help. He explained that although the situation was problematic it was not desperate and that he felt he could remove the remaining and recurrent tumour and possibly give me a significant benefit with little downside risk.

This was exactly what I had hoped to hear and Gail and I left Charlie's office feeling that we had been thrown a lifeline. Charlie's manner, his confident optimism and willingness to go all out not only matched my immediate clinical need, it also matched my own approach to clinical problems whenever a patient's survival was on the line.

Since late January 2007 we had been trailed by a *Sixty Minutes* team who, led by the friendly and superbly professional Peter Overton, had joined us briefly during our summer holiday at Palm Beach and a number of family occasions, including Adam's graduation from police training at Goulburn. The *RPA* production team had also filmed me going through the MRI and PET scans in April, so when Gail and I were told the disappointing results, both crews — who remained sensitive to our anxieties and were even apologetic as they quietly did their jobs — were on hand to record the events. I was not at all concerned about the operation being filmed. My illness was being played out in the public arena, and although that was never my intention, I believed that others might benefit or learn from watching my journey.

My second craniotomy was performed at Prince of Wales Private Hospital. By all accounts and from the little I saw on television, it was a very radical procedure that removed much of my right temporal lobe along with the malignant areas, but Charlie elected to leave behind the original large satellite which had caused Michael Besser concern at my first operation. Charlie's reservation was that in order to remove it, he would need to open one of the fluid cavities in the brain; this would further complicate an already aggressive and complex operation by introducing the possibility of spreading malignant cells throughout my central nervous system via the fluid compartments.

Again I woke from the anaesthetic quickly and recovered from the operation with no difficulties — a reflection once more of the immense competence of those looking after me.

I had stopped work completely at the time of my diagnosis and found, since that time, that I had not missed operating or consulting in the slightest. I had relinquished my position as director of the Sydney Cancer Centre and the Area Cancer Service and Michael Boyer, who had been my supremely capable and loyal deputy, was competently carrying on this work.

I resumed oral chemotherapy soon after my second operation, this time taking a combination of drugs — Temozolamide, Procarbazine and Thalidomide, the drug that became notorious for causing birth defects in the 1960s but more recently has been reintroduced as an effective tool in treating cancer. I took this combination of drugs on a cyclical schedule — twenty days on, eight days off — and had my blood count monitored regularly.

Serial scans revealed the original satellite tumour sitting on the right side was persisting and slowly progressing. There was no evidence at all that it was responding to these continued courses of oral chemotherapy. Six weeks after Charlie operated I returned to him and asked him to remove that remaining tumour satellite and to do whatever was necessary to render me free of disease. He warned that the next operation might result in weakness down my left side (a left hemiparesis) and also complete loss of my left visual field (a left hemianopia). Before my first operation I had been told that this visual disability was incredibly difficult to live with but I was ready to accept the risk and do whatever might be required to live with the problem. I felt physically well although my energy levels were depleted, and I was becoming increasingly convinced that my only chance of survival lay with the surgical removal of all identifiable cancer. This is a basic tenet of cancer surgery; whether the remaining microscopic cells could be mopped up by chemotherapy or by my own immune system remained to be seen.

By now my general wellbeing had given Gail and the children a sense of confidence that was only intermittently rattled by my need to have regular scans and what seemed like an occasional craniotomy. Beneath the surface, however, I knew that they were desperately worried that these interventions appeared to have no end; Adam, Juliette and James wondered when, if ever, I might be free of all this. I wondered myself.

Charlie shared my view that for me to have any chance of surviving, we needed to continue with an aggressive treatment policy. He agreed that a third operation was necessary and this was carried out on 1 June. My recovery from the third operation was a little slower than from the two previous procedures. Again,

Charlie needed to be radical with his excision and, for the first time, I awoke from the anaesthetic with detectable neurological disabilities.

The loss of the left half of my visual field made it difficult for me to read; I could not track words along the written line and I needed to hunt for the left-hand side of the page by turning my head, since, at initial glance, it just did not exist. Equally, I began walking into things at home like a door standing ajar that I would fail to see as I walked through the opening ahead of me. In addition, my left hand had become clumsy and my left leg weak and uncoordinated, causing it to swing out wildly as I walked. With the assistance of our physiotherapist friend Jenny McConnell my walking improved rapidly, along with my dexterity. The third disability — which persists even now — was a problem called prosopagnosia (sometimes called face blindness), which describes an inability to recognise faces. I first noticed this while watching television: I commented to the family that I had difficulty telling people apart on the screen. I could tell the men from the women but all the young men looked the same and so did all the young women. Now, in the current crop of TV programs those observations carry a fair deal of veracity anyway but even close friends and colleagues became largely indistinguishable.

A couple of days after I returned home I experienced an emotional meltdown as I lay in bed pondering my situation. I was overwhelmed by a wave of helplessness and hopelessness and a sense of defeat that was entirely new. The likelihood of further tumour recurrence was still high and, with these new disabilities, I found it impossible to look into the future with any sense of hope that I would ever recover. I struggled to get myself up and sat on the side of the bed and cried tears of hopeless defeat. After a few moments Gail came to my side to offer her characteristically gentle and loving sympathy and encouragement.

Slowly my mood of maudlin self-pity dissipated. This was hastened by visits from two friends, Guillaume Brahimi and Dave Pohl, my friend and colleague with whom I shared an office at Kogarah. Separately, about three hours apart, each came to visit and take me for a walk. I clumped along the footpath for a few hundred metres, first with Dave and then Guillaume walking patiently alongside, providing encouragement and physical support. I managed better than I thought I would and admonished myself for not being tougher. By the middle of the day my confidence, optimism and determination to fight on were restored and I have not suffered a similar reversal of outlook since.

CHAPTER 29

Working hard on meditation

I CONTINUED TO FIND chemotherapy debilitating — particularly the Thalidomide, which induced overwhelming fatigue, making it difficult even to get out of bed before eleven in the morning.

About a month before my third operation I was sent a book by a young woman who had assisted me during my private operating days at Strathfield and St George, and to whom I had been an occasional mentor since she had been in one of my tutorial groups in fourth-year medicine. Now married and with a little baby boy, Tanya Pelly was a very tall and bright young doctor who had decided that conventional medical training and practice did not suit her. The book she sent me, called *Quiet*, was written by Paul Wilson, a well-known meditation expert, who now lives in semi-retirement, having worked successfully in advertising and later published a number of little books on love, hope and a range of issues related to peace and happiness.

I had little experience of meditation although, following my diagnosis, my sister Carmel — who had visited teacher and healer

Petrea King's Quest for Life Centre and now meditated daily — had introduced me to her particular method, which involved lying on the floor, listening to Petrea King's CD and quietly visualising a tranquil scene. I found this relaxing but inevitably fell asleep after ten or fifteen minutes.

I rang Paul Wilson to ask if I could meet him and learn about meditation. Middle-aged, with grey hair, dressed in black and exuding quiet serenity, Paul kindly visited me at home two or three times and provided gentle instruction and guidance. I had always been interested in meditation but was sceptical of its benefit as a healing tool. Perhaps now, I thought, the time was right to give it a try. The technique did not come easily to me as I always seemed to have a hundred or more thoughts racing through my mind and my efforts to quieten this noisy consciousness and achieve a thought-free state were quite ineffective.

Wilson also held weekly group meditation sessions at his home and I attended a number of these, sitting with a small number of people in a ragged circle as Paul led the group in an atmosphere of quiet tranquillity overlaid with the smell of sweet incense and music, which filled the room with a faint, hypnotic hum. I enjoyed the group meditation sessions and felt that I was starting to make progress but I found it increasingly difficult to get there. It became a self-defeating exercise as Gail and I left the house in a rush and had to fight our way through traffic to arrive on time. Paul and I spoke at length about meditative experiences and his early advice was that I should free myself of expectation and effort. When I assured him at one time that I was 'working hard on my meditation', it was not what he wanted to hear — I was missing the point.

A couple of months later a journalist named Nikki Barrowclough wrote an article about me for *Good Weekend* magazine. In it, she quoted me commenting that I had tried meditation but I wasn't very good at it. The article was sympathetically and intelligently written and, from all accounts, widely read.

Among those who read the piece was a general practitioner, Tim Carr, who had started medical school with me in 1970 but whom I hardly knew, although I had, from time to time, noticed his Christ-like visage when I flicked through our 1976 graduation year book. Tim had practised transcendental meditation (TM) from his early medical student days and had developed a practice that combined conventional and Ayurvedic (traditional Indian) medicine, including meditation. Quite out of the blue he telephoned and asked if I would mind if he visited and talked to me about TM.

I had just about given up on meditation and had begun to build a wall of resistance to well-intentioned attempts to offer me assistance. It is no exaggeration to say that I had been literally inundated with advice, product information, personal testimonials about particular diets, remedies, magical cures and requests from a multitude of petitioners to meet and exchange stories and experiences. Innumerable people, describing themselves as cancer survivors, cancer sufferers, cancer victims or relatives or carers of the aforementioned contacted me, some even sending lengthy manuscripts which detailed their life story, their cancer journey or the secrets of their cure. Suddenly I was a magnet for every type of alternative or complementary treatment, promoted by a mix of sales representatives and well-meaning individuals who offered their own survival as proof of the efficacy (and potential benefit to me) of a particular compound or product.

Despite all this, I welcomed Tim Carr's call and his subsequent visit. Never really having spoken much at all before, we had an enjoyable and enlightening discussion that lasted a couple of hours, at the end of which I accepted Tim's offer to have him teach me transcendental meditation.

His explanation that the technique is utterly natural and that it should be effortless and easy proved to be correct. Perhaps I was more ready now than I had been previously, but my ability to develop, or immerse myself into, a peaceful meditative state increased quite readily. Tim painted an analogy that was both picturesque and useful, comparing the human consciousness to an ocean with noisy turbulence at its surface and increasing stillness and quiet as one descended more deeply. Thoughts may signal the release of stress and he advised that they should not cause concern or be pursued but, rather, allowed to flow out. He led me through a prayerful initiation to which I took a new clean white handkerchief, six flowers and three pieces of fruit. I observed this traditional rite respectfully and we then meditated together. New practitioners of transcendental meditation are given their own mantra that assists the process and which should not be shared with others. The silent rhythmic repetition of the mantra, allowing it to come and go from the consciousness, is a unique feature of TM and one that really helped me to embrace it successfully.

My reunion with Tim, more than thirty years after our graduation and based on only a loose acquaintance, made me wonder whether chance or fate had caused this old and most flimsy of relationships to gather into a timely focus of positive energy and trace a loop back into my own life's journey. Tim and I agreed that this productive reunion had probably been ordained (although by whom or what I had no idea) and I have since continued to practise transcendental meditation and enjoy the additional peace that seems readily now to pervade my day.

Some months before Tim made contact with me, my friend and neighbour Col Joye — a legendary entertainer since his singing days with the Joye Boys and a former patient — had introduced me to hypnotist Martin St James, who now lives in semi-retirement on the Gold Coast. Col thought that Martin's techniques of hypnosis, which he now uses more to assist people with relaxation, stress control, weight loss and smoking cessation than for entertainment, might be beneficial to me. Martin gave me a number of sessions of instruction and then kindly sent me a relaxation CD, which I added to my iPod play list and used over a number of weeks to aid relaxation. Each afternoon I would lie on a comfortable settee in our lounge room and listen to Martin's quietly encouraging advice, which helped me to release stress and anxiety and lapse into a peaceful sleep for an hour or more.

My spiritual sustenance comes from a number of sources, principally reading but also regular attendance at Mass. I have not lost my scepticism about God and the existence of an afterlife but I enjoy and value the ritual, solemn reverence and spiritual peace that I find at Mass. I don't think I really understand spiritual wholeness or how I can achieve true enlightenment, but as I continue my journey I hope to learn more and I will remain open to all of the influences of nature and God.

About six weeks or so after Charlie Teo removed the last known satellite of cancer from my temporal lobe, a young ENT surgeon, Greg Lvoff, whom I had mentored and taught over a number of years and who was now established with his own practice, arranged a dinner in my honour at one of Sydney's very good restaurants and invited a number of my former registrars and fellows, including a handful who came from overseas. This was not meant to be a grand retirement function but rather a gathering of young disciples who had fond and positive memories of the time they spent working with me. It was an immensely gratifying evening during which we shared stories and recounted experiences. My difficulty in recognising the fifty or so faces I found before me was eased as people introduced and reintroduced themselves to me throughout the evening.

Among those attending the dinner was the director of trauma surgery at Westmead Hospital, Valerie Malka, an attractive young woman who had worked as my intern at RPA sixteen years earlier and whose father, an intelligent and refined Frenchman, was a naturopath and homeopath. At Valerie's encouragement and instigation, I decided to visit George Malka and seek his advice. At the time I was very happy with the care being provided by Helen Wheeler, my oncologist, but I continued to find the prescribed chemotherapy profoundly fatigue-inducing and I knew that it was suppressing my bone marrow, my white blood cell production and, probably, my immunity. It had also taken me a long time to learn how to best deal with debilitating episodes of severe constipation.

George Malka's treatment consisted of an offensive brown liquid made of herbal extracts that I was advised to take twice a day, along with an array of supplements and vitamins (including selenium, fish oil, echinacea, evening primrose oil, flax seed oil, Vitamin C and coenzyme Q10) and tiny homeopathic tablets to be dissolved under the tongue. He had advised avoiding caffeine, as it was believed to negate the beneficial effects of his herbal medicine, and to give up red meat. As it happened, red meat had not been a part of my diet since I underwent chemo-radiotherapy immediately after my first operation, when I found meat repellent and totally unappetising. The problem of course is that there is no evidence from clinical trials that any of this treatment is beneficial. George had numerous anecdotes of 'successes' and even 'cures' but unfortunately nothing like a complete database of patient records.

Although I spent little time pondering my plight and contemplating the cause and meaning of the journey into which I had been thrust, I did wonder from time to time what might have led to the initiation and progression of my malignant brain tumour. I had, for a long time, held the view that stress does not contribute to the development of cancer. I never really regarded myself as having been under stress but there seems little doubt that through much of my working life, I was stretched to the limit. I saw none of my responsibilities or activities as being stressful because I was able to maintain a calm and temperate demeanour and meet deadlines, never losing my temper or displaying the anger, impatience, frustration and contempt that I sometimes felt. I made time for everything and everyone, both at work and at home, and carried on in a state of blissful, sometimes self-satisfied, ignorance, believing that I had my life under control and that I could go on indefinitely with Teflon-coated resilience. I speculate whether my self-control and sense of responsibility sprang from my Catholic upbringing and feelings of guilt and unworthiness with which the dear sisters of St Joseph equipped me when I was in my first years of school.

But everything comes at a cost. I now believe that among the costs that my busy and complicated life accrued was a physiological imbalance or disharmony that somehow diminished the effectiveness of my immune system in providing the surveillance and protection that is its raison d'être.

The possibility that the initiating agent in my case was a high level of mobile phone usage had already been suggested to me by a number of people including Gail, Charlie Teo and another young friend who worked as a neurosurgeon in Canberra, Vini Khurana, who has since gathered together available research linking mobile phone use with the development of brain tumours and concluded that not only is the link irrefutable, but we may be on the cusp of a dramatic increase of brain tumours and cancers. I was a regular (though hardly a heavy) user of a mobile phone, but who can say what the threshold of danger is in someone who is susceptible.

My understanding and appreciation of the initiation and promotion of cancer, along with its prevention and treatment, has undergone a transformation, particularly in relation to my own situation. The interplay of genetic predisposition, the influence of external carcinogens and the immune system (which might be competent in its surveillance duty or compromised by stress, nutrition or other factors) remains the most complex of riddles. Neither genetics nor a definite causative agent could be implicated in my own case.

CHAPTER 30

Into the future

In December 2007 a routine MRI scan, which followed two previous normal scans, demonstrated changes adjacent to the site of my original tumour that were initially interpreted as representing possible tumour regrowth. There was some argument over the significance of these deposits, which appeared on the MRI as multiple white spots, four or five millimetres across, although the largest was about eight millimetres in diameter. Helen Wheeler and Charlie Teo had the view, based on having seen this type of change in many other patients, that they represented a radiotherapy-induced artefact and were not cancerous.

Either way, with a hint that the tumour had returned and feeling sick and tired of the negative effects of continued chemotherapy and with a depleted white blood cell count, I happily accepted Helen Wheeler's advice that we should stop the chemotherapy for a month, repeat the scan and then consider our next move. The decision to stop treatment pleased George Malka, my naturopath, whose nasty brown herbal medicine I had been taking twice a day for some months now, along with an imposing array of supplements.

As an oncologist whose training, decision making and practice are founded on evidence-based medicine, Helen Wheeler did not at all like my taking herbal medicine, not only because it is an entirely unproven therapy but because it may contain compounds or substances that might act as an antidote to my chemotherapy. Equally, George Malka was anxious for his own treatment to have an opportunity to restore my immune competence in an environment not poisoned by cytotoxic drugs. This is a nexus not easily broken but my experience has made me determined to encourage the initiation of clinical trials comparing the efficacy of chemotherapy with herbal medicines in preventing tumour recurrence after removal of the main cancer mass.

Subsequent scans showed no progression of the suspicious changes identified in December and, in fact, there was definite regression and fading of the abnormalities.

Apart from beating my cancer, the other project that has occupied the last year and half, along with daily exercise and much time spent looking for my glasses, has been my continued advocacy for the development of a Comprehensive Cancer Centre at the Royal Prince Alfred–University of Sydney campus.

Soon after my diagnosis in November 2006 I wrote an opinion piece which was published in the *Sydney Morning Herald* and which highlighted the need for change in the way which cancer care is delivered by establishing at least one comprehensive cancer centre in New South Wales. A day or so after my opinion piece was published the *Herald* ran an editorial which emphatically supported the arguments I had made. One of my observations was that we had been very well served in the past by our teaching hospitals but these were based on an English model now almost 300 years old and were essentially limiting in their ability to foster, or even allow, the growth of centres of excellence because different clinical services — dealing with cancer, cardiovascular disease, trauma and all else — were thrown into competition for shrinking resources in physical surroundings which sometimes barely reached Third World standards.

With more than 100,000 Australians diagnosed with cancer each year and 40,000 or more deaths from cancer annually, I concluded that we were anything but well positioned to cope with inexorably increasing cancer numbers and certainly not creating an environment conducive to innovation and discovery. My suggestion was not at all a reversion to the plan that a national cancer centre be constructed at RPA. In fact, while I was director of the Sydney Cancer Centre, I worked vigorously at avoiding the hyperbole and hubris which had previously characterised much of the material emanating from the Centre.

My opinion piece and the subsequent editorial in the *Herald* provoked a galling knee-jerk rebuke from a colleague, slamming my recommendation that an integrated cancer centre should be established at RPA as retrograde, redundant and city centric.

I neither stated nor implied that I expected cancer patients from around the state to make the uncomfortable and inconvenient journey to what was being painted as an ivory tower populated by inward-looking elitists. Rather, my hope was and is that, in what will inevitably be a complicated dot-connecting exercise, we might bring together the critical mass of clinical, academic and research horsepower that will lead to a unity of purpose and concentrated productivity that will facilitate the discoveries and breakthroughs so desperately awaited and needed by cancer patients and their carers and loved ones. The short-sighted and needless professional rivalry that prevents cooperation and collaboration between major hospitals and research institutes in Australia is a blight that must be eliminated so that the welfare of patients is put ahead of inflated but fragile egos.

When I stopped taking chemotherapy in December 2007 I was happy to leave behind the debilitating side-effects of the anti-cancer drugs and to rely solely on the beneficial influence of herbal and homeopathic medicines, along with my vegetarian diet and a range of supplements. As it turned out, my confidence that I could go on indefinitely with this form of treatment was given a sharp reality check in June 2008, a year after my last operation, when a routine MRI scan demonstrated a nodule of recurrent tumour adjacent to the previous resection cavity.

I returned to Charlie Teo to seek his advice and again he expertly and expeditiously removed the tumour. At the time of completing the manuscript for this book it has been a month since this, my fourth, craniotomy and I have recovered well with no additional disability.

My advocacy for the development of a comprehensive cancer centre on the RPA–University of Sydney campus has proved effective on a number of fronts and the project is now proceeding with increasing momentum.

I have met with Prime Minister Kevin Rudd to discuss the project on several occasions, first while he was still opposition leader in late 2007. It was a quietly relaxed meeting, one on one, which covered a number of issues — growing up Catholic, books we liked, our children, and a range of ideas. About a month before the federal election Mr Rudd, still Leader of the Opposition, visited the Cancer Centre with Nicola Roxon and local member Tanya Plibersek to pledge a $50 million federal contribution to the Sydney Cancer Centre development project if Labor was elected to power.

Although Mr Rudd's pledge was generous it would not be enough. The Cancer Centre project had still not been costed but a rough estimate indicated a likely cost of around $200 million. In February 2008, Gail drove me to Canberra and the now Prime Minister and I met again. I explained that we would probably need $100 million from the Commonwealth and, without promising anything, he indicated that it was likely that more funding would be forthcoming.

At a subsequent fundraising lunch the Prime Minister restated his government's full support for the proposed plan. At the lunch, I explained to all present the importance for Australians of the development of cancer centres and pointed out once again that we were more than thirty years behind the United States in the development of infrastructure for the delivery of cancer care. In a prosperous country like Australia which has world-leading facilities for entertainment and sport there remains absolutely no excuse for our having inadequate clinical and research facilities to fight the number one killer in the nation. One of the additional benefits of the new comprehensive cancer centre will be that it will assist us to attract and retain the best and brightest clinicians and researchers in Australia and to attract similarly outstanding talent from overseas. At present there is really no incentive for someone working in a well-funded, well-equipped and staffed department in the United States to come to Australia and work in our public hospital system.

The new cancer centre will be an independent not-for-profit organisation, providing ambulatory and in-patient care to public and private patients outside of the jurisdiction of the Area Health Service, but it will be intimately linked to RPA and therefore gain all the benefits from a seamless association with a world-class medical powerhouse. The new facility will incorporate a Wellness Centre in which complementary and alternative therapies and a range of psychological, social and physical support services will be offered in a scientific environment. Chairman of the Sydney Cancer Centre Foundation, Robin Crawford, and Michael Boyer, the new director of the Centre, have worked tirelessly to complete the business plan with the support and assistance of Mike Wallace, the Area CEO. My illness has necessitated a change in my role to that of figurehead and advisor but there is great confidence that a truly world-class comprehensive cancer centre linked to RPA and Sydney University will be built in the near future and provide our patients with the clinical and research excellence so desperately needed.

I count myself lucky for so much that has happened in the past twenty months. The opportunity to advocate with a fair degree of moral authority for the development of this centre has been a fortuitous gift for which I am truly thankful.

My visual problems have not prevented me from reading and indeed the opportunity to read great literature has been another gift associated with this illness. I have been able to fill in some of the many gaps in my reading and have enjoyed in equal proportion numerous volumes of classic fiction and contemporary non-fiction.

In parallel (though on quite a different level), the invitation to write this book and the experience of completing the task has given me great pleasure and satisfaction.

Over the last year and a half or so I have also had a number of invitations to speak at public gatherings — sometimes at fundraising events for our cancer centre foundation or for the Cancer Council of NSW and other times at schools and meetings of medical students. Sometimes I feel like the owner of a celebrity brain tumour but, on each occasion that I address an audience, I try to bring a light-hearted and positive message that reflects hope and optimism in the belief (and hope) that such positive messages fill an unmet need in the wider community. At the same time I continue to encourage my colleagues working in clinical medicine to give their patients and their patient's families compassionate care and a sense that it is good to be optimistic.

Having lived beyond the twelve to fourteen month median survival period predicted for patients with malignant gliomas, I continue to look to the future with optimism and confidence. Gail has walked every inch of this rocky journey with me, the most devoted, loving and unselfish partner I could have hoped to have in my life. Our understanding and love for each other grows by the day. I will live on just to be with her.

My prognosis remains guarded but, having had one clear scan following my most recent operation, I will continue to set short-term milestones for myself in the hope of putting as much distance between myself and my last operation. I remain careful not to look too far into the future or to make long-range plans, but I am full of hope and I value every day as a gift to be enjoyed and shared.

Into the future

I will continue with a 'never say die' attitude, determined to remain as well as I can for as long as I can. One never knows what new discoveries are around the corner and, in the meantime, I have a lot of living (and learning) to do.

Acknowledgements

THE OPPORTUNITY TO WRITE this book has been one of many positives associated with my cancer diagnosis. What started as a memoir of my cancer journey inevitably became an autobiography as events in my early life demanded inclusion so that the reader might have a more complete picture. At no time did I believe that the Chris O'Brien story was unique or especially important but, like many people, I had wanted to write a book for a long time and so I am grateful to HarperCollins for inviting me to do so. In particular I am indebted to associate publisher Amruta Slee for the patience and encouragement she has extended to me and for agreeing to let me write my own story. It is a rare privilege and the entire experience has been enjoyable and energising, with not the slightest hint of catharsis.

Because my keyboard skills are poor I dictated the manuscript onto tape and I am thankful to Teresa Nicholls from the Sydney Cancer Centre for kindly transcribing some of the earlier sections of the work. Subsequently, Geraldine Kenny, a dedicated volunteer with the NSW Cancer Council to whom I am deeply grateful, took on the challenge of working with me several days each week to continue and complete the task. Without Geraldine's tireless efforts I could not have completed the writing in a timely fashion. Sally Collings has been a wise and effective editor whose advice and skill I have greatly valued. Close friends Di Ross and Ian Davison read early drafts of the manuscript and I thank them for their gentle criticism and advice.

My wife, Gail, was a source of inspiration and encouragement throughout and no words can adequately express the feelings of love and gratitude I have for her.

I also continue to be inspired by my children, Adam, Juliette and James, whose love, resilience and humour sustain me and my sense of hope.

Finally, I am thankful to Harriet Jones, who worked with me loyally as a scrub nurse, for recommending the inclusion of the quotation from Robert Frost at the beginning of the book. I will not launch into a litany of the many names of those who have worked for, worked with, helped and supported me over the last twenty years because it would be too easy to cause hurt feelings by an accidental omission. That said, I am also indebted to Tressa Tuxford, Leslie Honner and Geri Rizzo — three dedicated and selfless scrub nurses who consistently put my needs and those of our patients ahead of their own. I have named those who have provided me with wonderful clinical care but must acknowledge senior nurse practitioner Keith Cox who has done so much to smooth my path. Everyone else; yes, I'm eternally grateful. I love you all.